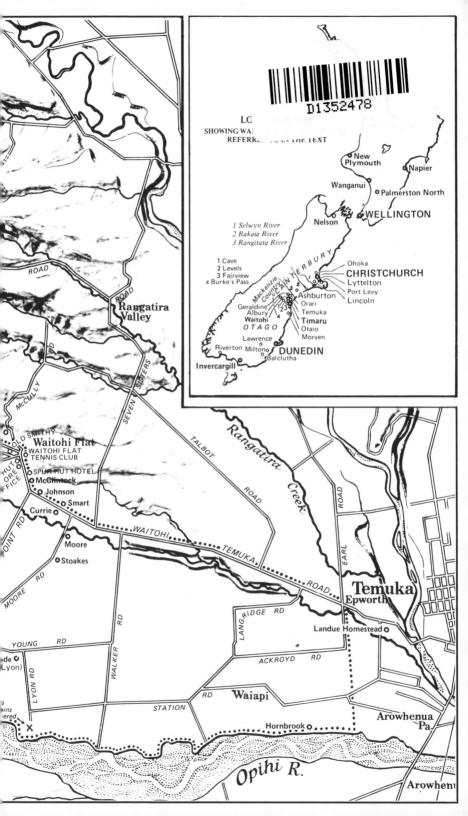

LOCATION MAP
SHOWING WAT... ...
REFERR... ...IN THE TEXT

New Plymouth
Napier
Wanganui
Palmerston North
WELLINGTON
Nelson

1 Selwyn River
2 Rakaia River
3 Rangitata River

1 Cave
2 Levels
3 Fairview
4 Burke's Pass

CANTERBURY

Ohoka
CHRISTCHURCH
Lyttelton
Port Levy
Lincoln

Mackenzie County

Ashburton
Orari
Temuka
Timaru

Geraldine
Albury
Waitohi
OTAGO
Otaio
Morven

Lawrence
Riverton Miltono
Balclutha
DUNEDIN

Invercargill

Rangatira Valley

ROAD
ROAD

McCULLY RD
SEVEN SISTERS

OLD SMITHY
Waitohi Flat
WAITOHI FLAT TENNIS CLUB
...HUT
...ORE
...FFICE
SPUR HUT HOTEL
McClintock
Johnson
Smart
Currie
Moore
Stoakes

POINT RD
MOORE RD
YOUNG RD
LYON RD
WALKER RD

...de O
(Lyon)

...ins
...ered

TALBOT ROAD

Rangatira Creek

WAITOHI
TEMUKA
ROAD

EARL ROAD

Temuka
Epworth

LANGRIDGE RD

Landue Homestead

ACKROYD RD

STATION RD
Waiapi

Hornbrook

Arowhenua Pa

Opihi R.

Arowhenu

The Riddle of Richard Pearse

Gordon Ogilvie, one of New Zealand's most widely published non-fiction writers, is a graduate of Canterbury and Victoria universities and spent much of his career as head of English at his old school, St Andrew's College, Christchurch. The author of 16 works of history and biography, he has also contributed a number of entries (including that of Richard Pearse) to the *New Zealand Dictionary of Biography,* and has been a freelance feature writer for nearly 50 years on topics ranging from literature and history to travel, cooking and music. He has won the J.M. Sherrard Award for regional history and two of his biographies, *The Riddle of Richard Pearse* and *Denis Glover: His Life*, were Book of the Year finalists. A regular speaker at literary occasions and an enthusiastic tour guide — with a particular interest in Canterbury and Banks Peninsula history — Gordon Ogilvie was in 2000 awarded an Honorary Litt.D. by the University of Canterbury. He is presently working on the sesquicentennial history of one of New Zealand's most famous department stores, J. Ballantyne & Co. Ltd. of Christchurch, to be published in 2004. His interest in writing is shared by his wife, Elisabeth, herself a published author. They have three lively daughters and a geriatric cat.

By the same author:

St Mary's Church, Heathcote (1960)

Moonshine Country: The Story of Waitohi (1971)

The Port Hills of Christchurch (1978)

Introducing Denis Glover (1983)

Historic Buildings of New Zealand (contributor) (1983)

Banks Peninsula: Cradle of Canterbury (1990)

High Flies the Cross: The 75th Jubilee of St Andrew's College, 1917–1992 (1992)

Picturing the Peninsula (1992)

Little Feet in a Big Room: Frances Ogilvie of China (1994)

Pioneers of the Plains: The Deans of Canterbury (1996)

From Gigs to Rigs: Steel Brothers and 120 Years of Road Transport in New Zealand (1997)

Denis Glover: His Life (1999)

Enjoying the Port Hills (2000)

Picts and Porridge: An Ogilvie Family History (2002)

The Christchurch Writers' Trail (2002)

The
Riddle of
Richard Pearse

The Story of New Zealand's
Pioneer Aviator and Inventor

Gordon Ogilvie

REED

For Libby, Anne, Margaret and Susan

Established in 1907, Reed Publishing (NZ) Ltd
is New Zealand's largest book publisher, with over 300 titles in print.

For details on all these books visit our website:
www.reed.co.nz

First published 1973
Second edition 1974
Third edition (revised) 1994
Fourth edition (revised) 2003

Published by Reed Books, a division of Reed Publishing (NZ) Ltd,
39 Rawene Road, Birkenhead, Auckland, New Zealand.
Associated companies, branches and representative throughout the world.

1973, 1974 Gordon Ogilvie

ISBN 0 7900 0329 5

Cover design by Rachel Kirkland

Printed in Singapore

Contents

Illustrations

Pearse's powercycle.
(Whites Aviation)
Pearse's first Christchurch house.
(E.B. McGregor)
Pearse's third Christchurch house.
(Author)
The Utility Plane in its shed, circa 1947.
(J. Collins)
Pearse's Utility Plane as delivered to Auckland Airport.
(Fremar Print)
Utility Plane being checked on receipt.
(*New Zealand Herald*)
Howard Galt, Ruth Gilpin and Florence Higgins.
(Press Photo Service)
Sunnywide Hospital, Christchurch.
(Dr Ian Lockhead)
Relics recovered by the author, 1970–72.
(E.B. McGregor)

Diagrams

Acknowledgements
to the first edition

No one can undertake a study of Richard Pearse at any level without acknowledging a heavy debt to the late George Bolt. It was Bolt who rescued Pearse from oblivion and the documents and letters in the 'Bolt File' reflect the vigour with which he pursued every trail then discernible. I am grateful to Captain J.H. Malcolm who, on behalf of the trustees of George Bolt's papers, allowed me to study this file which is now housed in the Walsh Memorial Aviation Library, Auckland. Captain Malcolm, chairman of the management committee of Auckland's Museum of Transport and Technology, and Mr R.J. Richardson, its executive director, have also given me every opportunity to examine the Pearse exhibits in the museum. I have, in addition, made use of research done by the late Mr H. Cederman, who assisted George Bolt.

The following have also helped me, in their official capacities, with my research: Mr C.W. Wadham, Commissioner of Patents at the Patent Office in Wellington; the Commissioner of Patents, Canberra; Henry Hughes Ltd, patent attorneys of Wellington, and P.L. Berry & Associates, patent attorneys of Christchurch; Mr N.G. Ockwell of the Public Trust Office in Christchurch; Mr R.A. Barber, the New Zealand Ministry of Defence Librarian; reference librarians at the Alexander Turnbull Library in Wellington, the Hocken Library in Dunedin, and the Auckland and Wellington public libraries; the medical superintendents of the Christchurch Public Hospital and Sunnyside hospital; the Registrar of Births, Deaths and Marriages in Christchurch; the Registrar-General of the Department of Justice in Wellington; Mr R.C. Lamb and Mr E.B. Jackson of the Canterbury Public Library; Mr J.C. Wilson, archivist of the Canterbury Museum; Mr J.B. Hamilton of the South Canterbury Historical Society; Mr N.G. Robertson, Assistant Director (Climatology) of the New Zealand Meteorological Service; Mr L.N. Larsen, Meteorologist in Charge, Auckland; the City Engineer of the Christchurch City Council; the New Zealand Returned Servicemen's Association; the Milton Borough Council; the Temuka and Geraldine County Councils; the editors of Christchurch's *Press* and *Star*, and of the *Bruce Herald*.

I thank Longman Paul Ltd and Mr Lloyd Wilson for their permission to quote from *Moonshine*, by Helen Wilson, published by Paul's Book Arcade.

A large number of people throughout New Zealand, most of them referred to in the text, have helped me with their recollections of Pearse and his activities. I thank them for their readiness to do so. I am particularly indebted to: Mr J.D. Coll of Tauranga, formerly of Waitohi, who has tracked down several important witnesses from Pearse's home area who had eluded George Bolt; to Mr D. Connell and Mr F.R. Cartwright, who gave me additional help with the Waitohi background; to Mr A.J. Currie and Mr M.T.D. Bryce of Milton, who rounded up many useful contacts for me in Otago; and to Mrs A. Birchall and Mrs E.M. Turner, who put me in touch with a number of people who knew Pearse in Christchurch. Several researchers with a particular interest in Richard Pearse have generously let me see and use material in their possession. A range of these private files and unpublished studies is listed in the bibliography.

I an grateful to the NZBC [now TVNZ] for permission to use some of the material gathered together by Mrs Maria Hill in researching a television documentary on Pearse. And I have been given particular help by Mr C.G. Rodliffe of Auckland, a licensed aircraft engineer formerly with the De Havilland design staff, who assisted the NZBC team. For some years Mr Rodliffe has investigated Pearse with incomparable gusto, paying particular attention to the construction of Pearse's two planes and the dating of the first flight attempts. I owe him much for his enthusiasm and willingness to share his knowledge with me. Mr Rodliffe has been aided, on the technical side, by the work of two fellow Aucklanders with Air New Zealand, Mr E.R. Gibson and Mr R. McMillan.

Several Christchurch members of the Aviation Historical Society of New Zealand have also helped me considerably. A most thorough study of Pearse's several patents done on my behalf by Mr D.N. Peters, a patent attorney and society committee-man, has been of tremendous benefit to me in my examination of the bicycle and aeroplanes. I thank Mr Peters for his judgement, scholarship and generous assistance with the text as a whole.

I am grateful, too, to Mr J.W. Johnston, an NAC engineer and vice-president of the AHSNZ, for his careful analysis of Pearse's aero engines and for checking technical details generally. Both Mr D.P. Woodhall, the AHSNZ's secretary and journal editor, and Mr W.S. Dini, the society's president, have carefully perused the manuscript and offered me useful advice. I also thank the New Zealand Division of the Royal Aeronautical Society for its interest; two instructors from the Canterbury Aero Club,

Mr J.J. Goddard and Mr C.J.C. Collings, for explaining and demonstrating some of the more baffling aspects of flight control; and Mr D.T. Kemp of Auckland, an Air New Zealand engineer, for valued help and advice on problem areas relating to Pearse's convertiplane.

Mr Charles H. Gibbs-Smith, Keeper Emeritus of the Victoria and Albert Museum in London, and an Honorary Companion of the Royal Aeronautical Society, has given me substantial aid. I have benefited much from reading his aviation histories, and he has also given me direct assistance. Mr Gibbs-Smith's insistence of caution, accuracy, and the strictest possible surveillance of eyewitness testimony is a model for all to follow. I thank him for checking those parts of the typescript which relate to Pearse's aircraft and the flight testimony, and for helping me put Pearse into historical perspective.

Members of the Pearse family have been most generous with their reminiscences, family papers and photographs. Mrs Florence Higgins and Mrs Ruth Gilpin of Auckland, Richard Pearse's surviving sisters, have carefully checked the manuscript. So too have Mr R.W. Pearse and Mrs D.B. Gardiner of Waitohi, a nephew and niece of the aviator. Mr H.C.C. Galt of Wellington and Mr A.S. Pearse of Christchurch, two other nephews, have assisted me as well.

Finally, I would like to express my indebtedness to the editor of the New Zealand quarterly *Islands*, Mr Robin Dudding of Christchurch, who has encouraged my from the outset in this project and who helped edit the manuscript; to Mr Peters and Mr Gibson for their excellent drawings of Pearse's planes; to Mrs Blanche Ladanyi for heroic work with the typewriter; to Mr E.B. McGregor for his artistry in processing and refurbishing the photographs; and to my wife and daughters for their patience, often in the face of extreme provocation, during the several years that I have been absorbed by the writing of this book. My wife has also helped me greatly by her encouragement and sure touch with the red pencil.

G.B.O.

Preface to the first edition

On or about 31 March 1903 Richard William Pearse of Waitohi, New Zealand, became airborne in a high-wing monoplane he designed and built himself. This aircraft, of prophetic design, was powered by an ingenious petrol engine which he also designed and constructed. It was not until 17 December 1903 that the Wright brothers' *Flier I* took to the air at the Kill Devil Hills in North Carolina.

Though Pearse himself later conceded that the Americans deserved the honour of being the first to make a controlled and sustained flight, it is almost certain that he got into the air under power before they did. There is no indication of a 'race' as neither party seems to have been then aware of the other's work.

In this biography I have assembled all the available evidence and arguments which relate to the 'flight' claims. Further testimony may yet come to light. However, at this point I am satisfied that Richard Pearse not only achieved a powered takeoff in March 1903, but probably several others during the course of that same year. This makes him, by a substantial margin, the first British aviator to leave the ground in a powered heavier-than-air machine, and the fifth person in the world to succeed in doing so. Moreover, Pearse's aircraft appears to be the first full-sized conventionally shaped monoplane in history.

Naturally, this aspect of Pearse's achievement will earn him most posthumous fame. But there are other examples of his vision and ingenuity to be seen in a range of further inventions. These culminated in his extraordinary 'convertiplane', patented during the Second World War and now housed in Auckland's Museum of Transport and Technology.

Readers of this book, after examining for themselves the evidence of Pearse's resourcefulness, should not find it difficult to conclude that Richard William Pearse was an uncommonly gifted man of whom New Zealand may be justly proud.

Gordon Ogilvie
Christchurch, 1973

Preface to the third edition

This is a year of anniversaries for Richard Pearse. For me, as well. It is 90 years since Pearse's first flight attempt in his first aircraft. It is 50 years since Pearse began negotiating the patent for his visionary Utility Plane, and 40 years since his death at Sunnyside Hospital.

It is also 30 years since I began a four-year teaching stint at Pleasant Point in South Canterbury where I encountered, for the first time, fragments of the Pearse story, and it is 20 years since my biography of the elusive inventor first appeared.

With the passing of the decades one would expect that the earlier controversy over what Richard Pearse did or did not achieve might have been resolved. But the dust refuses to settle and much of the riddle remains. Pearse is the Flannan Isle, the *Mary Celeste*, the Bermuda Triangle of New Zealand's otherwise conclusively documented aviation history. He is even more a figure of controversy now, I suspect, than he was before *The Riddle of Richard Pearse* was first published in 1973.

Much has been said and done during these last two decades and this seems an appropriate time to update the Richard Pearse story. There is still a marked lack of agreement among the pundits as to precisely what Pearse did, how well he did it and when. Richard Pearse, despite such scholarly dissent, emerges undiminished; a reserved, solitary, decent, gentle, cultivated, dignified figure who did not ask to be the centre of contention and would probably be mortified to discover that he is. Regrettably it was another aspect of his character — his publicity-shy, secretive working habits — that created most of the subsequent trouble for researchers. Apart from his exchanges with the patent office and two press letters, he left us no personal records at all: no photographs, no journal or diary.

Fortunately, there is enough other evidence for it to be clear that in Richard Pearse New Zealand produced an inventor of rare vision and ingenuity, worthy of the international attention he is now beginning to receive.

I would like to thank Reed Books for its continuing interest in Richard Pearse. I am particularly grateful for the encouragement and help given to me by the editor of the biography's first edition, Arnold Wall; as well as by Ian Watt and Deidre Parr, who have seen this third, revised edition safely into print.

Gordon Ogilvie
Christchurch, 1993

Preface to the fourth edition

This revised edition of *The Riddle of Richard Pearse* could hardly be more timely. On 31 March 2003 occurs the centenary of the date on which, most evidence suggests, Pearse made the first publicly witnessed powered takeoff in his Waitohi monoplane. The year 2003 also marks the fiftieth anniversary of the inventor's lonely death at Sunnyside Hospital, Christchurch; and it will be 40 years since I first began investigating his life and achievement.

Nearly nine years have passed since, in the 1994 third edition, I described developments in the Pearse story since the biography first appeared in 1973. One of many responses to the new edition came from a fresh witness, John Dick of Wakefield, who as a lad had seen Richard experimenting with his plane. Some wrote confirming evidence I already possessed. Others just wanted to argue! In 1994 a heritage trail was mooted for Waitohi to publicise Richard Pearse and other inventors, writers and historical events connected with the district. In October 1995 a cleverly subversive television 'documentary', *Forgotten Silver*, produced by Peter Jackson, made adroit use of some of Peter Muxlow's *Richard Pearse* footage from 1975 and pictures from *The Riddle of Richard Pearse* to give the impression that Pearse definitely flew in 1903. My phone was running hot for days.

In December 1995, Earl Scott of America's *Virginia-Pilot* newspaper published an excellent feature on Pearse entitled 'Wrong Place at the Wrights' Time'. September 1996 saw a new play on Pearse, *Too High the Son*, by writer/actor Stephen Bain, workshopped at the City Gallery in Wellington, then produced by Balcony Theatre Productions. In 1997 the South Canterbury Museum in Timaru augmented its Pearse exhibit; and the Cornwall Aircraft Park at Culdrose Manor, Helston, realising Pearse's father was Cornish, mounted a display featuring his achievement. In the same year the indefatigable Pearse investigator Geoff Rodliffe published *Flight Over Waitohi* privately and lent archival assistance to Helene Moore, who was writing a novel on Pearse, published two years later as *Oh, for the Wings of a Moth*. A television programme on Pearse, part of the 'Invention Series', was rather scrappily put together for the Discovery Channel.

A 1999 issue of *New Zealand Geographic* published a well-researched account of Pearse, 'The Birdman of Upper Waitohi', by Vaughan Yarwood (Yarwood later included Pearse in his book *The History Makers: Adventures in New Zealand Biography*), and a replica of the Pearse monoplane was put on display at Wellington's new airport. A Pearse postage stamp had already appeared in the 'New Zealand Achievers' series in 1990 and the Millennium Series of 1999 also featured the Pearse monoplane on its

80-cent offering — a fastpost denomination, aptly enough. Sherry Ede produced *The Pain and the Passion*, based on the Pearse story, for an Auckland theatre. *Time* magazine listed Pearse in its 'The Most Influential People of the South Pacific' issue. Evan Gardiner, Pearse's great-nephew, inaugurated an 'Ultralight Fly-In' each Easter at Waitohi to mark the aviator's achievement.

In July 2002 the South Canterbury Aviation Heritage Centre was opened at the Richard Pearse Airport, Timaru, with the inventor's nephew, Richard Warne Pearse, as the centre's patron. The driving force behind the project is centre president Jack Mehlhopt. One of his committee members is Hamish Cameron, the son of Maurice Cameron, who helped both George Bolt and me to locate Pearse aircraft parts from a riverside farm dump at Lower Waitohi. Auckland's MOTAT has donated a replica of the Pearse monoplane for the centre's permanent display. Not far away at Temuka 285 pupils at the local primary school performed, on 9–10 December 2002, a musical adaptation by the the staff of Steven Roberts's poem, 'The Ballad of Richard Pearse'.

A major centennial commemoration of Pearse's first historic flight attempt, 'The Richard Pearse Centenary of Flight Air Pageant and Celebration', will take place in South Canterbury over the weekend 29–31 March 2003. On the first two days, events will centre on a pageant held at the Richard Pearse Airport nine km north of Timaru. On 31 March the focus will be on Pearse's home district of Waitohi, where a working replica of Pearse's first monoplane will re-enact his first public flight attempt. Another of the aviator's great-nephews, Jeffrey Pearse, is a leading organiser of the Waitohi event. Richard Pearse deserves all this attention and I am pleased that the launching of this edition will form part of the celebration.

Working on a larger scale still, the Celebration of Life Trust, a concept of Stuart Eyes, planned a Festival of Flight to celebrate all aspects of New Zealand aviation, but with a special emphasis on Canterbury's contribution. The festival kicked off with a public lecture on various aspects of Pearse's life and achievement, presented at Christchurch's Repertory Theatre by Geoff Rodliffe, Wing Commander Don Fleming and myself, on 3 December 2002. Part of this festival is a production at the Repertory Theatre of *The Pain and the Passion*, the play's South Island premiere. On the fiftieth anniversary of Pearse's death, 29 July 2003, the trust plans to mark each of Pearse's Christchurch homes with an historic plaque.

All this Pearse activity over the last few years has been accompanied by a massive increase of information and (regrettably) misinformation on the Internet. I have been regularly involved with radio, press and television enquiries, answering correspondents and leading tour groups to

Waitohi. Towards the end of 2002 a spirited and sometimes acrimonious correspondence broke out in several national dailies on the merits of various claims made for Pearse. Naturally I got involved. The *Press*, realising that Pearse was a Canterbury man who had spent his last 32 years in Christchurch, let the correspondence run for many weeks. At the centre of the debate were arguments over how to define 'aviator', 'flying machine', 'true flight', 'powered take-off' and (with reference to Rodliffe's aircraft reconstructions) 'replica'. All were useful themes to discuss, though time consuming.

But I have been rewarded with unexpected breakthroughs. In 1994 two Pearse sleuths sent me letters — not hitherto located — that Pearse had published in 1909: one on scientific knowledge for the *Temuka Leader* and another on his 'improved spark plug' for the *Scientific American*. After their lecture at the Repertory Theatre, Geoff Rodliffe and Don Fleming went off to view the three houses Pearse built in Christchurch and discovered, at his Dampier Street address, a downpipe made of the same 10-cm diameter steel irrigation tubing from which Pearse constructed his first two-cylinder 'oil engine'. This authentic material will be invaluable in any further attempts to build a replica engine. Most remarkably, a previously unknown photograph of Pearse was sent to me in 1996 showing a slightly perplexed and dishevelled Richard at a Waitohi picnic about 1907.

This activity gives me continued cause to hope that vital information may yet be uncovered which will help to solve, once and for all, the riddle of Richard Pearse.

Gordon Ogilvie
Christchurch, 2003

Prologue

On the last day of June 1951 an elderly gentleman was taken from his home in Woolston, Christchurch, to Sunnyside Hospital on the outskirts of the city. He gave his name as Richard William Pearse. Clearly in a weakened and agitated condition, Pearse was positive that someone was trying to steal his inventions. He also believed that attempts were being made on his life.

The policeman who accompanied Pearse to the hospital and filed the necessary report believed his charge to be a retired farmer, possibly single, a native of Ireland and with no known relatives in New Zealand.

At 2.30 pm on the day he was admitted, Richard Pearse was examined by a doctor at Sunnyside who noted: 'This elderly man is rather confused and disorientated in time and place . . . He knows his age and year of birth but does not know what year or month it is at the present time. He knows that today is Friday because he heard someone else say so — in fact it is Saturday. His spontaneous conversation is jumbled and largely incomprehensible. He jumps from speculations about planetary collisions and vague ramblings about astronomy to fragmentary accounts of his everyday affairs. His speech is articulate, but he is inclined to ramble and become incoherent.'

Though Sunnyside is a psychiatric hospital, Pearse was not insane. He was merely old, mixed up, and incapable any longer of caring for himself adequately. His mental condition was diagnosed as arteriosclerotic psychosis, a state frequently associated with old age.

On his admission to Sunnyside, Richard Pearse was aged 73, 177 cm tall, 67 kg in weight, slim but erect in figure, slightly deaf, with long curly white hair and a straggly moustache. His physical state was described as feeble, but he ate well, slept well and gradually built up his strength. Though moderately well orientated he still had worries on his mind. One doctor recorded that he 'has delusions of a persecutory nature and becomes quite agitated while recounting these'. People, apparently, were still after his inventions.

After a month or so he was well enough to be moved to a general ward. His conduct was good, he was observed to be clean in habits and dress, and he was given work to do about the place. He also busied himself with occupational therapy — basketmaking and similar activities. At no stage did he seem concerned about being in hospital.

As Pearse was no longer capable of managing his own affairs, and as no relative had at this stage been located, the Public Trust Office was asked to take over. Acting with commendable briskness the Trust located a brother of the patient — Warne Pearse of Timaru — arranged for a weekly comfort allowance of five shillings to be paid to the patient, and began an enquiry into his assets generally.

Almost immediately it received a complaint from the tenants, Mr and Mrs John Collins, with whom Pearse had shared most of his Woolston home in Wildberry Street. Pearse had confined himself in recent years to a front bedroom, just over three metres square, with the use of the bathroom and half the entrance hall. In this bedroom he lived, slept, cooked and ate. Collins protested that his landlord 'must have left foodstuffs in there which are going bad, as there is an exceedingly unpleasant smell coming from the room'.

A property inspector who was detailed to put the matter right searched Pearse's home for items of any value and made an inventory of everything in the room he had occupied. He listed the contents of the bedroom from gas range to cycle lamp but found nothing interesting except an old cello. He then moved out to a garage-workshop which, he was told, Richard Pearse used for storage and invariably kept locked.

To his surprise the asssessor discovered in this building, along with numerous tools, farm implements and a homemade powercycle, what he eventually listed as 'wings and parts of improvised autogiro'. Clearly this was no ordinary estate.

Further investigations by the Public Trust revealed that Pearse, far from being impoverished as his circumstances suggested, was receiving rent from three houses, all of which he had built himself; and these houses together with his savings gave him assets worth close on £5000.

Shortly afterwards Pearse approached his hospital superintendent, Dr J.D. Hunter, to say that he would like an extension of his Australasian patent rights. He described how the Wright brothers had infringed one of his patents in 1906 and how some of the helicopter manufacturers in America had infringed a later patent. This was all news to Dr Hunter, who had no inkling of the remarkable background of the man he was caring for. Henry Hughes Ltd, patent attorneys in Wellington, were able to assure Pearse that both his Australian and New Zealand patents on the 'autogiro' were paid up to November 1959.

Pearse fell in with the routine of institutional life reasonably well — dormitory duties, medical checks, strolls in the garden, occupational therapy, communal meals and occasional visits from his brother Warne. But his physical condition gradually deteriorated as the months passed and in his last weeks he became completely bedridden. On 29 July 1953, after a heart attack, he died.

So ended the final melancholy chapter in the life of one of New Zealand's most remarkable sons; a pioneer aviator of historic importance and an inventor of ingenuity. But by one of those wretched ironies that sometimes bedevil the lonely and the brilliant, Richard Pearse's death was the beginning rather than the end. Up to his death he had received neither publicity nor recognition, in New Zealand or abroad. His courageous attempts to fly, near the turn of the century, had created little interest at all outside his home district in South Canterbury.

Yet Pearse's earliest aeronautical experiments almost certainly predate the Wright brothers' first flights at the Kill Devil Hills and may have been the most successful powered flight attempts made anywhere in the world up to that time. He was certainly the first person in the British Empire to make a powered takeoff in a heavier-than-air machine. And that is not to mention the farsighted features of his first aircraft's design; nor the ingenuity of his last plane, a convertible aeroplane-helicopter; nor his other assorted inventions.

It was not until five years after Richard William Pearse's death that the investigation of his achievement got under way. This operation and the startling revelations which have resulted are the substance of what follows.

1. The rescue

Richard Pearse died unmarried. But there were still two brothers living (Tom and Warne), and three sisters (Annie, Florence and Ruth), so the Public Trustee contacted these five as well as two nephews and a niece. All were asked about the disposal of Pearse's estate. As some interest was shown in the aeronautical patents Richard was known to have held, his patent attorneys in Wellington were asked to give an opinion on their worth. A representative of Henry Hughes Ltd replied that the helicopter invention was 'of extremely doubtful value' and if the patent was kept alive it would 'remain a liability on the estate, not an asset'.

The Public Trust Office informed all Pearse's close relations of this verdict. It also asked Warne, who was nearest at hand and would most ably represent the views of the Pearse family, what his directions were regarding the disposal of Richard Pearse's effects still stored at his Christchurch address. 'The biggest item of course is the aeroplane constructed by our late brother, and there are some very old sticks of furniture, mattresses etc which are not saleable and would have to be dumped.' Warne was told that the garage would cost £7 to clear and it was 'problematical whether the saleable items would realise sufficient to cover this cost'. It was also suggested to him that the plane seemed to be of little use to anyone.

Warne Pearse's answer was to let the patent rights lapse, put the properties and any saleable articles up for auction and have the remaining items, including the aeroplane, dumped. He saw no need to inspect his brother's effects and understood the Trust's difficulty in arranging for their disposal. As his brother Tom (a doctor in Australia) had died within a few weeks of Richard, Warne was now the only surviving brother and was quite certain that no other members of the family would wish to take over any of the Woolston items. Largely for sentimental reasons Warne asked that he himself might have possession of the cello and Richard's watch chain. Nothing else was claimed.

A Christchurch auction firm, George Anderson & Son Ltd, had

already been asked to value Richard Pearse's shed-full and advised that 'it was a physical impossibility, but from their outward observations the lot was of no value'. The Public Trust nevertheless asked the firm to remove the goods from the shed and sell them off by public auction and, if need be, dump 'the aeroplane contraption'.

If this insruction had been carried out one can be fairly sure that Richard Pearse would not have been heard of again. What saved the plane was a sudden thought of auctioneer George Anderson. Why not ask the local aero club if it was interested? This would certainly be a less expensive method of clearing the shed than having the firm do it.

So Anderson rang up John Neave, manager and chief flying instructor for the Canterbury Aero Club. He told Neave that he had a funny-looking flying machine 'more like a windmill than an aeroplane' in a shed full of junk down at Woolston, and would the club be interested in taking it away? John Neave and the club engineer, Laurie Counsell, took a look at the plane but did not think it would be of any use to the club. Neave contacted Harry Walker, the club captain, and took him to Wildberry Street for a second opinion. Walker was at once keen to buy the plane himself to save it from the scrapyard. The date was 29 June 1954, exactly eleven months after the inventor's death.

'It was quite a job taking it away,' recalls Neave. 'There were bits in all directions, and we gathered them together. The machine was very flimsy-looking. It wouldn't stay in one piece so we wired it up with fencing wire. Harry paid £5 for it and we took it away on a trailer behind his car. We put it in the back of the club's hangar at Harewood, and there it stayed for about two years. Nobody took any notice of it at all. It obviously couldn't fly — it was too frail. And it was far beyond anyone locally to fix it up or make it work. I've flown quite a few home-made aeroplanes myself but I certainly wouldn't have set foot in that one.'

Only two journalists saw anything of interest in these proceedings: R.T. Brittenden, sports editor of the *Press*, Christchurch, and J.S. Drew of the *Weekly News*. Brittenden interviewed Warne Pearse — then 72 years old — about this brother's activities, and a detailed report appeared in the *Press* of 5 July 1954. This contribution was the first attempt made by any writer to describe and evaluate Richard Pearse's achievement. Drew's item, much smaller, mentioned two days later how the 'plane from the past' had been rescued from the Woolston shed and described something of its construction. Another *Press* reporter wrote a brief follow-up article on some of the more interesting aspects of Pearse's specifications for his last plane. The matter was then dropped.

The plane's new owner, Harry Walker, a Christchurch electrical engineer, rescued more than the aeroplane. Accompanied by an officer of the Public Trust he 'made a thorough search for any records relating to the machine but found that the house had been cleaned out. However he [the officer] remembered at the last minute that there were some papers on the rubbish heap. After quite a few hours' work I found myself in possession of about 200 to 300 sheets and scraps of paper recovered from the rubbish heap and windblown around the yard. Every one of these was examined carefully and everything that appeared to relate in any way to the aircraft was sorted out. I gave particular attention to dates but found nothing apart from an envelope cover from the Australian Patent Office dated some time in 1920. The correspondence was missing. After a lot of sorting I managed to assemble a complete set of patent specifications covering the aircraft and engine.' These papers, with several of Pearse's rough sketches and some of his specifications in their manuscript form, were sent by Harry Walker in February 1956 to George Bolt in Auckland, along with an account, reproduced in part above, of how he acquired them. He left a typewritten transcript of one of the helicopter's provisional patent specifications with an instructor of the Aero Club.

Thrown in with Walker's purchase was a decrepit-looking power-cycle, obviously homemade. After storing it for a few weeks behind his Tuam Street repair shop, Walker got tired of seeing it lying around and gave the machine away. The new owner was Harry Williamson of Tai Tapu, a vintage-car enthusiast, with at that time a special interest in old motorcycles. Williamson collected the power-cycle from Christchurch, about twenty kilometres away, and stored it in a shed at Tai Tapu with his other old vehicles and machines. The salvage operation was now well under way.

However, the future of the strange aeroplane was still far from assured. After lying in the Aero Club's hangar for some time it again came close to being condemned as junk. Then occurred the luckiest thing that ever happened to Richard Pearse, posthumously or otherwise. George Bolt turned up.

Bolt, himself a pioneer pilot and a former chief engineer of Tasman Empire Airways (TEAL) called in at the Aero Club one day in mid-March 1956. While talking casually to Harry Walker and Stan Dodwell, one of the club instructors, his eye fell on the strange contraption at the back of the hangar. They approached it for a closer look.

'Where on earth did you get that from?' asked Bolt, trying hard to control his excitement.

'Oh, from a deceased estate over at Woolston,' answered Walker. 'An old man died there a couple of years ago and this machine was found in his back shed with a lot of other stuff. They let me have it for £5. It's been lying here ever since.'

'I could find some use for it,' said Bolt quietly.

'You can have it then,' said Walker. 'We're not getting anywhere with it here.'

Stan Dodwell handed over to Bolt the typed papers on the 'antique aeroplane' (as Dodwell referred to it) and its engine, and the Aucklander returned north well satisfied.

George Bolt had for some time been interested in aviation history and was collecting bits and pieces wherever he could find them so that he could start up an aviation museum in Auckland.

It was not entirely by chance that Bolt had located the plane. He had been tipped off by Captain J.H. Malcolm of National Airways, a member of the Royal Aeronautical Society and one of the founders of the Western Springs Museum of Transport and Technology. It was thus that MOTAT acquired one of its star attractions.

The crew of a US Navy Deep Freeze Globemaster agreed to transport the plane to Auckland, where it arrived on 25 November 1956 and, according to Bolt, Tasman Airways engineers offered to move the aircraft out of the Globemaster and take it to the TEAL hangar. However, the Americans preferred to do it themselves, and they wheeled the old plane along the tarmac in front of the large crowd, making numerous witty remarks about the delivery of a new aircraft for TEAL.

'Pearse's helicopter' remained in the hangar for several months, creating a great deal of interest. During this time many crews of American aircraft calling at Auckland went to see the plane and some attempted to obtain it for United States museums. George Bolt resisted all offers. The machine was beyond price and was not to leave the country. Not even Auckland. Christchurch citizens now began to grind their teeth at the thought of what they had lost. A correspondent to the *Press* asked why 'this historic flying fretwork' had not been made 'as much a monument to flying development, at least in this country, as Smith's *Southern Cross* has for the Australians'.

A photograph of the plane appeared in an Auckland paper early in 1958 and this brought forward Richard Pearse's two surviving sisters, Mrs Florence Higgins and Mrs Ruth Gilpin, both then living in

Remuera, an Auckland suburb. The sisters gave George Bolt enough of the inventor's history to get him thoroughly interested in learning more. They also put him in touch with their brother Warne down in Timaru.

So, five years after his death and more than half a century after he first tried to fly, Pearse began to attract the attention his achievement deserved.

George Bolt, moreover, was just the man to initiate the rescue operation. An ex-flyer himself, he had established five long-distance flight records in New Zealand between 1919 and 1921; and his experience stretched from hot air balloons and Lilienthal-type gliders to TEAL Electras. Along with a sound understanding of the mechanics of flying he was a painstaking investigator. With as much publicity as he could raise and with the sponsorship of the New Zealand Division of the Royal Aeronautical Society, George Bolt set about uncovering what information he could on Richard Pearse.

The first important facts that Bolt learned from Pearse's sisters were that the aviator came from Waitohi in South Canterbury, not from Christchurch, and that the plane at Auckland was not his first plane but his last one. Before Pearse retired to Christchurch he had farmed at both Waitohi and Milton in South Otago. While Richard Pearse was at Waitohi, Bolt was told, he had flown a homebuilt monoplane several times, at about the same period that the Wright brothers had been doing their pioneer work in the USA in 1903.

Nothing could stop George Bolt now. With the assistance of T.T.N. Coleridge, secretary of the New Zealand Division of the Royal Aeronautical Society, and Harold Cederman of Timaru who was an old friend and airline associate of Bolt's, the Auckland engineer began a careful investigation of a number of the witnesses to Pearse's early 'flights' who still survived in the South Canterbury area. He also attempted to track down the plane in which Pearse was alleged to have first flown.

Information reached him to the effect that Gilbert Lyon of Waitohi might have the plane stored in a shed somewhere. There was some truth in this. Gilbert Lyon had been raised on a farm in Lower Waitohi about four kilometres from the Pearse family property. Young Gilbert had always been keen to fly. He was taking lessons in 1932 when only fourteen years old, and had qualified for his licence at sixteen. In 1936 he got a job working for New Zealand Airways, an air-taxi firm based at Saltwater Creek just south of Timaru. His father and Warne Pearse were, in addition to being neighbours, both directors of the Temuka Milling Company and used to see a lot of each other.

One day Warne had mentioned to Lyon that he knew of a barn with the remains of an old aeroplane in it that his brother had left behind when he went south to farm at Milton before the First World War. The remnants had been left in Richard's workshop for some time, and had then been transferred to an old hayshed on Jack Pearse's property when the workshop had to be demolished. This farmer had later taken the iron off the shed to cover his grain and the plane parts were left exposed to the weather. Visitors to the farm used to souvenir bits from time to time, but Warne thought that Gilbert might be interested in looking at what was left.

'Would you lend the thing to us?' asked Tom Lyon, Gilbert's father.

'Come up and help yourselves. It's completely yours,' said Warne.

So next day Tom Lyon and two sons, Gilbert and Les, took a car and trailer to the hayshed — situated well back in a paddock opposite where the Centennial Hall now stands in Lower Waitohi. There they loaded aboard the trailer an assortment of Richard Pearse's aeronautical left-overs.

'It was a real scrapheap job,' recalled Gilbert. 'Everything was in pieces. There was nothing complete. There was a four-cylinder engine, horizontally opposed like a Volkswagen's. Three or four single cylinders were lying around in a rusted or seized-up condition. There was a lot of blackened bamboo strewn around, some of it in the form of wing struts with steel clipped joints. Lots of piano wire too . . . good quality. No wing fabric though. I collected a forge-welded propeller, broken in the middle, with what looked like windmill blades. There was also some of the undercarriage . . . large bike wheels with metal slats across the rims, probably to prevent the plane sinking into soft ground. That was all.'

Leaving the wire and bamboo where it was, Gilbert took the rest back to his father's farm. The Lyons had a disused chicken incubator shed behind the house. Gilbert cleared this out and turned it into a 'museum' where he stored all the Pearse oddments as well as his own model aeroplanes. They seemed safe enough.

In 1938 Gilbert Lyon went north to Christchurch, joined the Royal New Zealand Air Force (RNZAF) in 1941 and after a year's training went overseas. He returned to Christchurch in 1945, took a job with the International Harvester Company and thought no more of his Pearse museum. One day late in 1958 he received a message from Richard Pearse (nephew of the aviator and a son of Warne) asking on

George Bolt's behalf if there was anything of the plane or its engine left.

Gilbert rang up his brother Les, who had taken over the family farm, and learned to his dismay that the Pearse relics had been cleared out during the war and now lay in one of the farm's rubbish tips somewhere along the Opihi riverbed. Les said he would do something about locating them for George Bolt. Maurice Cameron of Temuka, whose sister was married to Les Lyon and was working on the farm until his Rehabilitation Loan came through, offered to hunt up the remnants. Gilbert badly wanted something to be found — 'even if it were only a bolt'.

Les Lyon could not remember which dump, among several along his farm's river boundary, was the vital one. So Cameron searched two or three without success, then started on another one. He vividly recalled what happened next:

'I started to root around. The first thing I saw was a piece of bike wheel sticking out of the junk. It was poking half out of a mass of farm waste — rusty wire, broken glass, old tins and so on. I pulled it out, and looked further. I now saw a long stem or shaft. Then a propeller. Fancy a man expecting to fly with that, I thought. Then I spotted the engine. It was over to the side of the tip, half silted up. I felt terrifically excited. Hell's teeth, this would have been the first piece of metal to actually fly! I carried the motor up out of the dump and across the paddocks to the farm buildings. There I propped it up against a wall. Gilbert came down to pick up the bits, took them up to Christchurch, and RNZAF transport eventually got them up to Auckland.'

George Bolt heard in April 1959 from Harry Walker that a powercycle existed also, and the two of them went out to Williamson's farm at Tai Tapu to view the machine. When Harry Williamson heard that the powercycle would be greatly valued by an Auckland museum which already had Pearse's last aeroplane, he willingly agreed to part with it. Bolt asked TEAL's Christchurch manager to arrange transport: 'Tell the boys who go out to take some string and tie any odd pieces securely on the bike that may be loose, such as the battery box . . . The bike is in a dreadful mess.' The machine was air freighted safely to Auckland and Walker also forwarded to George Bolt the Pearse documents in his possession.

So Bolt not only had Pearse's last aircraft: he had a powercycle and key portions of what appeared to be the first plane as well, plus some of the inventor's own papers. These remains he now set about analysing. He also assembled all the testimony on the Waitohi flight attempts that he and Harold Cederman — who was in turn aided by Pat McArthur

— had been able to gather from some twenty-five located witnesses. Bolt's researches gained good coverage in the national press, as did some of Warne Pearse's reminiscences on his brother's aviation experiments. Unfortunately, some of Warne's claims were a shade unguarded and sooner or later there had to be trouble.

The bubble burst on 16 October 1959 when a letter from Charles H. Gibbs-Smith, Britain's foremost aviation historian, was published in *Flight*, the aviation journal. Gibbs-Smith had spent years of his life investigating dubious and phony flight claims. One of the most recent had been a claim by a brother of Preston Watson, a Scot, that the latter had made a powered flight of between forty-five and ninety metres in 1903 — before the Wright brothers, naturally. It took from 1953 to 1955 to disprove this proposition, the discovery being made at the finish that Watson's 1903 machine did not even have an engine. It seemed that the news he received about Pearse was no more promising.

'Here we go again!' wrote Gibbs-Smith. 'I always dread this season for it is the season of claims — amongst other things — to have flown before whoever it was that made the previous claim. Now we are back on the merry-go-round, and again it is a loyal brother who comes forward!' He then proceeded to take Warne's testimony asunder, especially his dating methods for the flight attempts and the assertion that Richard Pearse had patented 'wing and tail controls' ahead of the Wright brothers.

Two months later Gibbs-Smith wrote direct to George Bolt, knowing that he was investigating the Pearse claims. While encouraging Bolt in his researches he cautioned him to be 'extra-extra careful' with his evidence. 'The eye witness who tells you what he saw fifty or more years after is, as often as not, completely unreliable . . . People simply do not remember without prejudice . . . So, I pray of you, beware of eye witnesses.' He suggested that Bolt check what age the witnesses were in 1903 and send him any relevant photographs, plans, diary entries, and newspaper accounts. Writing to W.H. Shaw of QANTAS shortly afterwards, Gibbs-Smith showed further concern: 'About Pearse O dear, O dear, O dear. Tell Mr Bolt to be very careful. On present showing it smells to high heaven!'

George Bolt sent the English historian a copy of Pearse's complete patent specification for his first plane. Gibbs-Smith replied on 3 September 1960 explaining how thoroughly documented the Wright brothers' experiments had been and giving his opinion of the Pearse patent: 'The Pearse specification of 1906 shows a great talent in some respects, but it certainly does not read as if its author had ever had any practical experience in aviation. If he had really flown in 1903, a number of his items would, I feel, have been differently arranged and described. Surely, too, he would have kept records, and there would have been a patent applied for sooner.'

By return mail Bolt sent Gibbs-Smith a copy of the drawings which accompanied Pearse's complete patent specification. The historian pronounced these 'very interesting' and sent Bolt, on request, details of the Wrights' engines. He asked for information on Pearse's books and papers, if any, and suggested that the aviator might have read something of Lawrence Hargrave, the Australian aeronautical pioneer. Gibbs-Smith followed this up in November 1960 with a further letter, somewhat brisk, urging Bolt to stop Warne Pearse from saying any more about his brother until the facts were sorted out, and casting doubt once more on any 1903 dating.

Despite all these vicissitudes, George Bolt had just about concluded that his evidence pointed to 1903 flight attempts on Pearse's part when two newspaper cuttings were found in a Pearse family album. These cuttings were of letters published by Richard Pearse in two different papers. They seemed to state quite plainly that the inventor did not start his flight experiments until February or March 1904. Obviously disappointed, Bolt conceded in a letter to Gibbs-Smith of 29 November 1960 that though most of his witnesses remained fairly firm on 1903, 'I do not think we can go past Pearse's own statement.'

A summary of George Bolt's findings, amounting to eighteen cyclostyled foolscap pages, was circulated privately in 1961. Bolt intended to publish something more substantial but did not live to complete the task. Though his investigation of Pearse was never completed and some of his data now needs revision, George Bolt nevertheless retrieved Richard Pearse and his accomplishment from outer darkness. He initiated the rescue, he did the preliminary spadework, and those who have followed on since must not fail to be grateful for this.

No one will now dispute Bolt's verdict that 'Pearse was a very remarkable man' both as an aviator and an inventor. But to many, the most astonishing aspect of the whole Pearse story is that he should have achieved anything in the first place. He was a back-country farmer for most of his working life, with no workshop facilities to speak of and no technical training whatsoever. Nothing in Richard Pearse's upbringing, education or environment was of any special advantage to him as an inventor. For insight we must look elsewhere.

2. Origins

Many families have albums and scrapbooks. However, only a few — and the Pearses are among them — can boast a collection of family letters and documents dating back to the early eighteenth century. Most of the Pearse family record was gathered together in the 1930s by Florence and Ruth Pearse, with the help of an English cousin, Dr J. Steele Pearse, who made a hobby of family genealogy.

The Pearse name has long been a familiar one in England's West Country. The name is derived from Pierre, French for Peter, and has been common in parts of England since the Conquest. Pierce, Pearce, Pears, Peers, Perse and Pearson are all variants. A Guhelm Piers, 'farmer of the King's taxes' in the reign of William the Conqueror, is mentioned in the Domesday book. 'Piers the Plowman' was immortalised by Langland's long allegorical poem in the fourteenth century. Tom Pearse of Widecombe Fair needs no introduction. The family scrapbook records with cheerful impartiality the talents and foibles of a whole host of Pearse connections. They range from ecclesiastics, physicians and military men to farmers and wool merchants. The early documents display a great deal of piety and brotherly concern: 'Elizabeth Pearse desires to return humble and hearty thanks to Almighty God for safe deliverance in child birth,' runs a jotting from 1820.

A long letter from 1852 hints at a more dastardly development. Here is an excerpt:

My Dear Brother,
As a parent it is your duty to avoid the sin of which Eli was guilty and thereby brought down on himself and his children the displeasure of God by which his sons were taken from this world in their sins and doomed to everlasting misery . . . Tell Thomas plainly and most certainly that you will give him till Michaelmas and no longer utterly to renounce his present associates and practices . . . If he does not in that time become engaged to a

respectable woman for his wife, you declare to him positively that you will sell his horse and carriages . . . May God give you courage to act firmly.

The scrapbook includes a number of press cuttings mostly gleaned from British newspapers between the wars. They touch on a wide range of events affecting the family and its connections: marriages, funerals, christenings, honours, anniversaries, accidents and misdemeanours.

What impresses at once is the wide variety of interests and accomplishments represented. G.V. Pearse is shown playing cricket for Oxford University at the Oval. Dr R. Pearse is quoted in a fiery speech made against trade unionism: 'The so-called middle classes have a greater right to be called workers than those workers of the Labour Party who will not work themselves and prevent other people from working.' William Pearse is responsible for selling to the Prince of Wales a farm on which to breed South Devon cattle. Councillor J.E. Pearse of Plymouth is elected mayor of Northampton. Harry Pearse is the on-the-spot correspondent of the *Daily News* throughout the siege of Lady-smith. A son of his, William, was the original 'Tommy Atkins' of the *Penny Illustrated Paper*. Mrs Woodhouse Pearse is taken to court by Methuens the publishers for trying to fob off a forged manuscript in the name of Oscar Wilde. Francis Pearse, the first man in Plymouth to own a motorcar, takes off from the spire of a Plymouth church in a balloon. Thomas Ernest Pearse gains distinction as a surgical-instrument maker. The Rev. Mark Guy Pearse establishes a reputation in both Britain and the USA as preacher, lecturer, quick-sketch artist and author of more than thirty books on theology and Cornish folklore. His son is appointed Dean of Winchester Cathedral. A Pearse dentist wages a campaign against quackery in his profession. Another qualifies as an architect.

F.W. Pearse registers a silent protest against the increased tax on cars in 1921 by taking the engine out of his motor vehicle and pedalling the car around Plymouth like a bicycle. Wilfred Pearse becomes medical officer of health at Hong Kong. A Pearse serving with the Middlesex Regiment is dismissed from the service by a general court martial in 1915, while another relation in an Australian regiment, Samuel George Pearse, is posthumously awarded the VC for heroism in North Russia in August 1916.

Any coverage of Richard Pearse's family background would be incomplete without a study of Captain Alfred Pearse. Though Richard's

English connections display a superb diversity of skills, none seems to have possessed much inventive or artistic talent except Captain Alfred Pearse, a cousin of Richard's.

Alfred Pearse was born in London in 1854, 23 years before his Waitohi cousin. Though Alfred came to New Zealand with the Duke and Duchess of York, and though Richard went to Britain during the First World War, there is no evidence that the two ever met. This is a pity, for they had a certain amount in common, even if diametrically opposite in temperament. They were both non-smokers and teetotallers, both were musical and keen chess players, both were accident-prone and both became increasingly eccentric as they got older — though in different ways. Alfred turned mystic and Richard turned recluse.

Captain Pearse's list of achievements is considerable. But he was principally an artist, and a versatile one at that. During his lifetime he won 25 major prizes for drawing and painting including the first prize for figure subjects in black-and-white at the International Exhibition in 1884. All told, more than seven thousand of his drawings were published. In fact, art was almost a family business for Pearse. His father, grandfather and great-grandfather had been painters, and Alfred himself was married to a niece of Sir John Tenniel, the famous *Punch* cartoonist and illustrator of *Alice in Wonderland*.

He was special artist for *Pictorial World* and the *Strand Magazine*, did illustrations for *Wild World* and *Boy's Own Paper*; sketched for the *Sphere* on the Royal Colonial Tours 1901–3; was specially commissioned to draw the coronation of King George V in Westminster Abbey; painted a portrait of Queen Mary; designed royal costumes for investitures and ceremonies; was seconded as official war artist to the New Zealand Expeditionary Force; sketched eighteen battle scenes, several of them by the light of exploding shells; and was the first to paint a tank in action. After the war he did the offical portraits of 160 Victoria Cross winners, and painted the miniatures still to be seen in the Royal Doll's House. He also travelled extensively and wrote four books on his experiences.

But the most fascinating material on Captain Pearse has nothing to do with his artistry, literary skill or inventiveness. A file of old newspaper cuttings records Alfred Pearse's other escapades while he was making a more orthodox reputation with brush and pen. He must certainly have been a boon to Fleet Street. One reporter labelled him 'surely one of the most astonishing men in the whole City of London'.

In the first place Alfred Pearse was a firm believer in reincarnation. He maintained he was living out his fourth time on earth. In one life he had dwelt at Chios, more than two thousand years ago. At the time he was governor of the island, and fell in love with 'a girl of surpassing beauty', but unfortunately she had been earmarked by the priests for sacrifice. Pearse (in his pre-incarnated form) secured the maiden in a rock chamber and prepared to defend her from attack; the priests eventually rushed the two lovers and a javelin, aimed at the governor, struck and killed the girl instead.

Whereupon, Pearse later confided in the *Daily Mail*, 'I put forth the last ounce of my strength, hurled my sword in the face of the leading priest and, siezing my lady's body in my arms, leaped through the great window of the chamber into the sea below.' So they perished both.

The sequel to this dramatic episode took place shortly before the First World War when Alfred Pearse was walking down the Strand one day. He suddenly saw a woman whose face stirred romantic and heroic memories and, heedless of other pedestrians, he rushed up to the lady with out-stretched arms and cried:

'Vaelissa! My wife of two thousand years ago!'

Nothing is known of this unfortunate woman's response.

It seems that Captain Pearse's second life was as a slave in the mystic African city of Zimbabwe. He later claimed to be in contact with spirits from these former states of existence, and in the last few years of his life derived much companionship from those across the Great Divide.

Alfred Pearse also believed he had strange healing powers caused by the exceptional amount of electricity in his system. He assured others that he had only to touch a paralysed limb and it became mobile once more. Explain them how you will, but there are authenticated cases to support his claims. Sir Herbert Barker, the famous bone specialist, became afflicted by neuritis of the spine and his doctors declared they could do nothing for him. Captain Pearse merely stroked the man's back and by degrees the neuritis vanished.

Policemen who knew of the Captain's powers called him down to the Strand on numerous occasions to assist people having fits. All Pearse had to do was touch the victim and he or she fell asleep. He even applied this technique to a pair of horses one day when they panicked at the sound of a steamroller. He put them to sleep right where they were, between the shafts.

Alfred Pearse led an incredibly charmed life and his narrow escapes from injury or death became legend. He had, altogether, more than thirty serious accidents. He all but drowned as an infant when he was inadvertently dropped over the side of a Channel steamer. At the age of seven, during a critical illness, he was actually certified as dead by a doctor. Later on he was nearly killed by an infuriated bull in Chilham Park. As a young man he was one day seized by a madman who held him suspended over the well of a deep staircase. On another occasion, when climbing at St Moritz, he went careering down a slope towards a 150-metre drop, and managed to pull up only a matter of centimetres from the edge.

When he accompanied the Duke and Duchess of York on the Royal Colonial Tour 1901–3 Pearse was critically poisoned by the bite of a red spider. Another time, when caught in a storm in the Australian Bight, he was informed as he lay in his bunk that there was no hope for the vessel, which was in a sinking condition. Pearse decided to stay where he was and the next day, the ship having survived the tempest, he was the only uninjured first-class passenger aboard.

He was wounded by shrapnel at de Rougemont while sketching by the light of the gun blasts, and also survived a serious bout of trench fever. Later he was held up at pistol point in a dark alley off Fleet Street by a destitute American soldier.

In total Pearse was nearly drowned three times, had concussion five times, was thrown from the top of omnibuses four times, shot once, fell down Beachy Head once, was drugged once, certified as dead twice, fell between train and platform once, was injured by a runaway horse once, rundown by a motorcar once, blinded for two days, had his shoulder out of joint, his legs and right arm paralysed and his left eye forced out of its socket.

Despite all these misadventures, he was still able at the age of 70 to run 45 metres in 6 seconds. He kept up his outdoor pastimes and other interests such as music and photography till his death on 29 April 1933 at the age of 79.

A reporter visiting him in 1925 described Alfred Pearse as 'sitting all day in the quaintest of offices strewn with antiques and knicknacks such as one seldom sees in the usual run of artists' offices; and all day his companions, he says, are people from the spirit world.' Some of these knicknacks may well have been the inventions Alfred Pearse is credited with. It is a pity we know no more about them. As it stands the principal evidence for Alfred Pearse being an inventor is family tradition plus an entry in the British *Who Was Who*, 1929–40. The New Zealand *Gazette* for 1908 records a patent lodged with the Wellington Patent

Office for an 'advertising device' invented by A. Pearse of Hampstead Heath. This is very likely Alfred at work, but no other details survive.

Surprisingly enough, Alfred Pearse died peacefully in his bed. The London *Times* obituary described him as 'a lovable character, generous and kind to all' and regretted that readers would no longer have the benefit of 'A.P's virile drawings'.

Richard Pearse's father, Digory Sargent Pearse, was born on 5 June 1844 at South Petherwin, a small Cornish village five kilometres from Launceston. His father, William Pearse, was a well-to-do farmer with four properties attractively named Trewarlet, Tregellan, Trebullet and Landue. His mother was a Sargent, of the same family as the conductor, Sir Malcolm. This relationship, plus a kinship to John Curwen who devised the tonic sol-fa system for sight-reading music, does a little to explain the pronounced musical talent which the Pearses reveal from time to time.

Digory was brought up at Trewarlet along with two sisters and two brothers. One sister was clever at languages, the other was artistic, but neither married. The three sons, after a grammar school education, worked for their father to gain experience. Digory then set sail for the colonies in 1864, and his brother William followed him six years later. Richard, the third brother, stayed on at Trewarlet and farmed the property. He did not marry and when his parents died he employed a housekeeper, Miss Husband, who stayed with him till his death. After this brother died and the Pearse association with Trewarlet ended, several valuable family heirlooms were sent out to Digory in New Zealand — a valuable violin, a 200-year-old clarinet, a flute, a piccolo, and some china and silver.

William Sargent Pearse, possibly at Digory's invitation, joined his brother in South Canterbury and stayed with Digory until he bought his own property at Waitohi. Later William married a daughter of the Rev. George Foster, the first Anglican minister at Timaru. The couple had two children, Thomas and Laura. William did well with the sale of his Waitohi farm and in 1905 went for a trip back to Cornwall, where he died unexpectedly. His wife, son and daughter returned to New Zealand, where Tom took on a run of his own and ended up a wealthy bachelor. Laura married Dr Edgar Babst.

Apart from two children of Laura's, the only Pearses left, immediately related to Digory, are his own descendants in New Zealand; and it is to Digory himself that we must now turn.

3. Trewarlet

At the age of twenty years and one month Digory Sargent Pearse left Cornwall for the Antipodes. Though he lacked years he was certainly not short of confidence or natural talent. A sound academic education and some useful farming experience further fitted him for pioneering life in Australasia. He also had £1000 from his father to fall back on if necessary.

Digory Pearse left Plymouth aboard the ship *Murray* in July 1864. His destination was Port Adelaide in South Australia. The *Murray*, under the command of Captain Smart, was the last word in ship construction at the time, and carried 30 passengers.

According to Digory in later years, one of the passengers, a large burly Irishman, used to become demented when the sea got rough. During one such crisis he felled the cook's mate with a tremendous punch, because of some small slight or other, and remarked to the postrate body, 'Now, that's only a caution!'

There were no ports of call, and land was not sighted at any stage during the three months' voyage until Port Adelaide was reached. At Adelaide Digory stayed with his uncle Amos Sargent, a retired brewer, who had purchased an extensive area of land and was then general-farming near Kapuda, about thirty kilometres from Adelaide. The weather at the time was scorching hot, and the thermometer registered 49°C in the shade for days on end. Coming direct from England Pearse was disconcerted to meet a drought so severe that even the weeds were dying.

Nevertheless, in order to acquire some colonial experience Digory stayed with his uncle for seven months, learning as much as he needed to know about managing four-furrow ploughs and eight-horse teams. He then set off for New Zealand, via Melbourne. His uncle made the trip also, in order to see a sister, Mrs Parrish, who lived just out of Christchurch, on Lincoln Road.

In order to gain practical knowledge of New Zealand conditions

Digory took a job as ploughman with John Brook at Halswell for seven months. At the end of 1865 Digory went down to South Canterbury and purchased a farm of 60 hectares at Waitohi, about ten kilometres inland from Temuka. After paying for the land he rejoined the Parrishes at Christchurch for a month before taking on harvesting work with Frederick Murray and William Callum, two farmers in partnership who owned two big farms, in the Selwyn and Lincoln districts.

When he finished harvesting the 280 hectares of wheat, barley and oats involved in his contract, Digory Pearse took to horsedealing. In this business his knowledge and sound judgment enabled him to get together a useful sum of money within twelve months. He now had enough finance, with what remained of his father's money, to set up his own farm at Waitohi.

As soon as he reached Waitohi, Pearse engaged a man named Scott to build a single-room sod hut with thatched roof. Here he began homesteading and continued to live for a couple of years, during which time he broke in his property. His first job was to mark off the boundary. This he did with a sod fence three turfs high on which he planted gorse seeds, at that time quite an expensive item. The channel from which the turfs were cut acted as a drainage ditch round the perimeter of his farm. His aviator son, Richard, would have cause to remember gorse hedges such as these in later years.

Though Digory was by now himself an experienced ploughman he hired a man for 25 shillings a week, plus keep, to do the cultivation. This ploughman, called Stephen, operated a single-furrow plough pulled by two horses. One of these horses, Billy, was a fairly independent thinker and used to get it into his head that it was 5 o'clock when it was only 4.45. On these occasions it used to be necessary for Steve to show Billy his watch before he would resume work. Stephen was a determined fellow and eventually earned enough by ploughing for Pearse and others in the district to return to England and marry.

Life was getting lonely for Digory Pearse too. For some little time he had had his mind on a young lady named Sarah Browne who hailed from County Derry and was then living with her sister, Mrs K.F. Gray, in Temuka. Digory, after a short but determined courtship, put the question and received a favourable answer. As a press item on Digory Pearse much later expressed it, 'Sarah Browne was so captivated with the manliness and charm of her stalwart young suitor that she gently and graciously acquiesced in the proposal of a bond of indissoluble union for life.'

It was intended that the Rev. George Foster of St Mary's, Timaru, should marry the couple, but owing to some miscalculation the young couple exceeded the time limit and could not be married by him on the day arranged. Anglican clergy conducted wedding services only up to twelve noon at that time, marriage after that hour of the day being regarded as illegal. To get over this difficulty, the ardent pair interviewed Timaru's Presbyterian minister, the Rev. George Barclay, on 16 January 1871. Digory was 26, Sarah 21.

Digory and Sarah began their married life in a four-roomed sod dwelling they called Trewarlet, built to replace the one-roomed habitation that Pearse had started with. They lived in this house for twenty years and it was the first home for seven of their nine children. Helen Wilson, who would have known this cottage in the last year or two before it was replaced, described the Waitohi of pioneering days most graphically in her novel *Moonshine*. Here is the hero's first glimpse:

The outlook was simple, a level extent of farm lands, rectangular fields of wheat, oats or barley, intersected by high straggling ill-kept gorse hedges. Clumps of tall bluegums and macrocarpa marked the homesteads. Through these you could catch a curl of smoke, a peep of thatched roof or a haystack.

The scene was pleasing enough but the houses near enough to be examined led one to expect very little. They were of sods — more rarely of cob. The sods were cut into squares and laid one on the other to form low walls which supported a shapeless thatched roof. The architecture was always a variation of the same style. One middle room with a crazy front door opening outwards and standing perpetually open by day, a small window on either side of the door deeply embedded in the earth walls, smaller rooms with even smaller windows flanking the main apartment, sometimes all in a row, sometimes stuck on at right angles. The number of rooms might vary from two to five, but always there was a huge misshapen cob chimney on one end of the livingroom, buttressed at its weaker points by bluegum saplings, bits of wire, iron or flax. This was the most prominent feature of the structure. It was quite as large as some of the rooms and its special shape seemed to give a character, and individuality, to each dwelling.

One or two small detached huts, windowless and with rough thatching, served as outbuildings. A cowshed, a dairy, a barn, some hens, pigs, cows, well-chewed trees and a few haystacks complete the picture. Such was the district setting in which Digory and Sarah Pearse established their household.

Only a few crumbling fragments of their cob house now remain. It burned to the ground in the 1890s and only a bell-topper hat and a pair of boxing gloves were saved.

The present Trewarlet homestead was built about 1888 of Kakahu limestone quarried from the property of a neighbour further up the Opihi, Henry Collett, who accepted £1 in payment. An early photograph of the home shows it to be solid, square and plain — perhaps more appropriate to a windswept Cornish headland than a pioneer colonial settlement. Its roof was of galvanised iron, a front door led to a long central hallway with three rooms running off to each side and a kitchen at the back. There was not much attempt at a garden, nor were any paths laid down. A white picket-and-lattice gate gave access to the front of the house, and a post-and-wire fence lined with straggly shrubs marked off the front lawn.

At the new Trewarlet Digory and Sarah Pearse's children grew to adulthood, their last two daughters being born there after the move. This household produced among others an inventive genius, a tennis and chess champion, a doctor, and two renowned craftswomen. It was a happy, alert and unconventional ensemble. Talent abounded. Its members could all sing, recite and play chess. Handicrafts and reading were encouraged. There was a family orchestra of nine players. Parents and children were crack tennis players and could field a full tennis team any day of the week. Even the pets had a style of their own: peacocks and pheasants strutted about the garden, a parrot used to call out each morning, 'Time to get up and get the breakfast', and a pet monkey swung about with a hat on his head and a pipe in his mouth. There were also guineafowls, goats, guineapigs, ferrets, rabbits, and numerous breeds of dog.

The Trewarlet property expanded as briskly as did its owner's family and pet collection. Digory Pearse kept adding to his 60 hectares by the purchase of additional land round about — ranging in price from £20 to £74 a hectare — until his holding reached a total of 322 hectares freehold.

He needed a property of this size to support adequately a family of nine children, five of whom were sons and might wish to go on the land themselves one day. The first child was Thomas Sargent, born in 1871.

Tom was sent to Edinburgh University by his father to qualify in medicine, spent some years as a ship's doctor and subsequently practised at Brisbane. Charlotte Anne ('Annie') was born in 1873, married William Smart, a local man, and moved to a farm at Otaio, south of Timaru. John Brown ('Jack'), born two years after Annie, farmed in Waitohi on some of his father's land. Richard William came next, in 1877. Margaret May Mary ('Maggie') who arrived two years later, married a Christchurch draper, Charles Galt, in 1906. Digory Warne was born in 1881 and eventually took over most of his father's farm. Reginald was the last son, and after farming for a while on a block of his father's land moved to North Canterbury, where he took on a property at Ohoka. The youngest two children were Florence Sarah, born in 1888 and Ruth Beatrice, born in 1894. As Mrs Florence Higgins and Mrs Ruth Gilpin, both widowed, they later lived together in Auckland.

Today Trewarlet, reduced in size, is a deer farm run by Jeffrey Pearse, grandson of Warne and great-grandson of Digory. The property is immaculate. Situated about midway along the southern flank of the thirteen kilometre-long Waitohi Flat, it comprises 190 hectares of fertile and well-drained land neatly fenced and accessible. Looking north and west there are superb views across the rolling Waitohi downlands to Four Peaks and the Two Thumb Range. Eastwards, well-tended farmlands stretch to the sea some sixteen kilometres away. Southwards, there is a sharp drop to the Opihi riverbed, then an uninterrupted panorama of the downs country behind Pleasant Point and Cave with the Hunters Hills forming a memorable backdrop.

Digory Pearse's homestead has been extensively modernised and enlarged. Backed by large pines and gums, fronted by an attractive flower garden and approached from Pearse Road by a birch-lined drive, Trewarlet has completely outgrown that severe, remote look of a century ago.

4. Waitohi

When Richard William Pearse was born on 3 December 1877 his father had owned Trewarlet for twelve years, and Waitohi was still being settled and broken in. Waitohi Flat (or Lower Waitohi) was further ahead than Upper Waitohi. The Flat had by 1877 its own school, smithy, Wesleyan church, library, post office and store. It was shortly to have its own pub, the Spur Hut Hotel. The school was being used, out of hours, as a meetingplace for temperance, debating and singing groups, the drama and tennis clubs, and a Masonic lodge. Regular concerts, dances, tennis parties and district picnics enlivened the leisure hours and there was a strong community spirit in the area. Upper Waitohi, as soon as its own school was built in 1885, developed an identity of its own and a vigorous social centre was made of the school and its adjoining tennis court.

As early as 1879, when Richard Pearse was two, the *Temuka Leader* could describe Waitohi's 78 square kilometres as 'teeming with life' with 'well cultivated farms, beautiful homesteads, well-formed roads, concrete bridges and culverts'. Even allowing for a certain amount of local pride, and the fact that a lot of the Upper Waitohi downland was still being rescued from its native wildness, this is an agreeable picture. Temper it a little with a second glance at Helen Wilson's account and the focus will be about right.

Waitohi had altered a great deal since Maori times. Its limestone overhangs then provided convenient overnight resting places for Maori hunting parties from the island pa at Wai-a-te-ruati (near the mouth of the Opihi) or from Temuka and Arowhenua. These used to follow the Opihi River inland to the Mackenzie country in quest of wekas and eels. Waitohi had changed a lot even since 1851, when Major Alfred Hornbrook and his brother William became the first European owners of the territory. In that year the Hornbrooks established Arowhenua station, the second earliest run (after George Rhodes's at the Levels) to be set up in South Canterbury. Its area of 12,140 hectares was bounded by the Hae Hae Te Moana River to the north, the Arowhenua Maori Reserve to the east, the Opihi River to the south and 'the back range of hills' inland. Waitohi's downlands were the hills in question and they soon came into use as the only elevated country available on a run that was predominantly flat. Early documents refer to Waitohi as the 'Arowhenua sheepwalk' and a musterers' hut plus sheepyards were erected in about 1854 at the foot of what is now Spur Hut Road. Spur Hut corner, where the war memorial now stands, later became the focal point for Waitohi Flat village.

A large proportion of the fifty or so settlers were Irish and such names as Baxter, Gibson, Connell, Friel, Coll, Casey, McCabe, and McAteer are later to appear as witnesses to Pearse's early flight experiments. Among the property owners were such disparate characters as Leonard Harper, the son of a bishop and discoverer of the pass through the Southern Alps which bears his name; Robert Heaton Rhodes, one of New Zealand's leading land magnates in his day; J.J. Melhuish, later to establish one of the country's best known sauce factories; Thomas Hall, who in 1886 featured in one of Canterbury's most sensational murder trials and was eventually found guilty of poisoning with antimony both his wife and father-in-law; and Patrick Hamilton, who lived to the advanced age of 115 years and was for some time the oldest European citizen in the British Empire.

Digory Pearse, then, was one of Waitohi's 'originals'. Naturally, most of the land he bought up was also in an original condition. Waitohi's terrace land was covered in native tussock, speargrass and matagouri, with clumps of flax, niggerhead and toi-toi in damper parts. Streams intersected the flat, fed from valleys and gullies which led down from the rolling hills behind. These downs are still notable for their limestone outcrops, large clusters of cabbage trees, and stands of scrubby bush in sheltered places.

Waitohi was not only rugged but isolated. The Provincial Government had considered the area so remote that it did not even provide for a road in its first survey of the district. Daniel Hally, who took up his Waitohi farm in 1867, recalled that it was once possible to ride in a straight course to Timaru (32 km away), without encountering a single fence. Swampland and the Hae Hae Te Moana River lay between Waitohi and Temuka some nine kilometres east; hills, swamp and rivers separated Waitohi from Geraldine nineteen kilometres northwards; the tricky Opihi lay between Waitohi and Pleasant Point six kilometres due south; and inland, the Waitohi downs cut the district off from Kakahu,

Hanging Rock and Raincliff. The first shingle roads laid down in Wai-tohi were notoriously rough, and none of the rivers was bridged. The end result of all these disabilities was that pioneer life in Waitohi meant enforced isolation and, for many, a fairly primitive existence.

Mixed farming was the line most adopted and it included some cropping — wheat, oats and barley — along with sheep, pigs and cows. With uncertain markets, and, during the depression of the 1880s, very uncertain prices, many housewives eked out the budget by selling eggs and butter to a grocer, Kernohan, who came out weekly from Timaru. Large families (anywhere between eight and fifteen children) seemed to be the pattern of the times, and offspring were almost as numerous in some backyards as chickens or piglets.

You made your own fun. Concerts, dances and tennis parties have been mentioned. There were also cribbage evenings, tin-kettlings, sports meetings, cycling trips, picnics down by the river or up at Gully Bush, fishing expeditions, eel hunts, hare drives, harvest-homes, and rare trips to Timaru.

The Pearses formed a sociable and lively family and Richard must have had as happy a childhood as any. He was a good-looking boy. A Waitohi Flat School photograph shows him as a ten-year-old seated in the front row of the senior classes' line-up. Tom, Annie and Jack are in the same photograph while Warne and Maggie are shown in the junior classes' photo. Richard, known at school as Willie, is of average and even build, with short wavy brown hair well clear of his eyes and slender, capable-looking hands. He is wearing a white shirt with bow tie, a striped frock coat buttoned all the way up, matching trousers a great deal too short for him, long dark socks and sturdy boots. He eyes the camera with interest but mistrust.

Though Richard was quiet and reserved even as a child, he enjoyed himself as much as the next lad. There was later some friction between him and his father, but so far no causes of disagreement were evident. Richard got on particulary well with his younger brother Warne, whom he later confided in when working on his inventions. Jack, in contrast to Richard, was impulsive and perverse, and used to bait his brother a great deal. Richard, fairly even-tempered, usually came off best when there were arguments. Reg remained neutral. Tom left home so soon that his youngest brothers and sisters hardly knew him.

There was no suggestion of the hermit in Richard at this stage but his distant and contemplative manner perhaps marked him out as different from the average boisterous schoolboy. He was in no way self-ish or self-centred but just preferred to mind his own business. This independence did not detract from a gentle and considerate nature, and it is unlikely that Richard Pearse deliberately gave offence to anyone in his life.

His solitary rambles should not have lacked variety. Even if Richard kept only to his father's property he had a wide range of terrain at his disposal: riverbed, riverflat, terrace, downland, gully, cliff and limestone outcrop. There was a swampy paddock below the terrrace where wild-duck eggs could be found in abundance. Digory also had several holdings up in the hills and on two of these, rock drawings in the limestone over-hang showed evidence of Maori occupation over four centuries earlier.

At his first school, Waitohi Flat, Richard Pearse appears to have made no impact at all. He was so quiet that hardly anyone remembers him. He started there in 1883 under Mr Campbell and stayed on under Mr Joseph Watson, Campbell's successor, who fell out of favour with the school committee in 1889. Watson had received a whole series of adverse reports from the inspector and eventually he resigned, just beat-ing his committee to the punch. Waitohi, both Upper and Lower, was something of a disaster area for the South Canterbury Education Board in these days. Since the school had first opened at the Flat in 1875, three out of four of its teachers had resigned after disagreements with the school committee, which had absolute right to hire and fire. The next three teachers after Mr Watson went the same way, one of them after an accusation of immoral behaviour had been recorded in its minute book by the comittee: ' . . . it having been reported that certain females are in the habit of stopping in the house with the teacher at night'.

Two of Richard Pearse's companions at Waitohi Flat school, Sam and Tom Thornley, later achieved reputations of quite a different sort. Tom was a good all-round athlete, but Sam became a remarkable one. At the age of seventeen he made his debut on the games circuit, trying everything: throwing the hammer, putting the shot, tossing the caber, sprinting, jumping, wrestling and dancing. Indeed he persisted with Highland dancing until he reached a weight of 120 kg. In 1890, when only nineteen years old, Sam Thornley won the New Zealand wrestling title from Billy Uru. Thereafter, for the next seventeen years, Sam was the most formidable figure on the southern sporting circuit — a giant of a man, 193 cm in his socks and weighing 139 kg. In 1907 Thornley moved to farming and contracting work in North Canterbury where his weight increased to 177 kg. His feats of strength are still spoken of with awe.

During Richard Pearse's time at Waitohi Flat School there were two sensations worth mentioning. The first of these was the evening in August 1885 when the Spur Hut Hotel burned down. This hotel had been in business since only 1880 and was over the road from Melhuish's store, which had in earlier years supplemented its income by the sale of sly-grog. The fire broke out about 7 pm while James Woods the licensee, with splendid irony, was attending a temperance meeting at the nearby Flat school. A large number of local residents and regular bar patrons were there with him listening to a lecture on the evils of the demon alcohol. The licensee's wife, who had been left at home with the family, suddenly smelled smoke, rushed her three children down from their bedrooms before the staircase burst into flames, and called to the nearby blacksmith for help. Alex McClintock summoned the Blue Ribbon Army from the school round the corner and all personnel arrived at the double, but too late to save anything except the stable. The hotel was never rebuilt, and the stable eventually became the new smithy. The old blacksmith's shop, Spur Hut itself, had leaked so badly that customers used to prefer standing outside under the gum trees when it rained.

The other sensation was the whisky trial of 1887. Put Scots or Irishmen of this vintage into a hilly setting with water laid on and you are bound to get a still or two. With the local store doing only legitimate business now and the public house burnt to the ground, the temptation to do-it-yourself was too hard to resist. The 1880s were a hard decade. There was an agricultural slump and, in a farming community like Waitohi, not much money about. Illicit whisky was cheap to produce and could make a handy profit for its manufacturers — if they got away with it. Between the years 1886–7, when the Waitohi distillers were doing their best business, court actions numbered 38. Several cases were heard in the Timaru Magistrate's Court.

Helen Wilson's *Moonshine* gives a lively account, only thinly tricked out as fiction, of Waitohi's experience with the poteen. Whisky stills operated in several gullies running west from the Spur, notably Monkey Gully and Gully Bush. Here there was isolation, good cover, running water, firewood, and a clear view of approaching intruders. There were good reasons why the police did not enter into the spirit of things and a £50 reward was offered to any persons who could furnish evidence leading to the conviction of lawbreakers.

The casualty rate was high, especially among Upper Waitohi settlers. In 1886 James Hamilton was both fined and jailed for having an illicit still in his possession. William Paul was prosecuted and wrote a poem about it all. In 1887 James Matthews was fined £100 plus costs for having distillation apparatus on his property. There must have been considerable excitement in Digory's household over this last episode, as the site of this particular still was nearby on William Pearse's land.

William Pearse, Digory's brother, had acquired land in Upper Waitohi in 1870. Though he had choice pasture up on the downs where his cottage was, there was also some riverbed property, greatly overgrown and suitable for concealing whisky operations. At Matthews' trial, held in Timaru, several of his neighbours were asked to give evidence and William Pearse was one of them. The evidence in all cases was singularly unhelpful to the prosecution, but the police won their case nevertheless.

Digory Pearse, whose farm was conveniently situated between the Lower and Upper Waitohi schools, moved all his children across to the latter in 1891. Mr Vilant Graham, Watson's successor, was having a sticky time with both inspector and committee, so Digory — in common with other parents — took his business elsewhere. Upper Waitohi School, by the time Mr Charles Goldstone took over in 1891, had been the Waterloo of every teacher doing service there since the place opened in 1885. Mrs Minnie Worthington, Miss Nellie Ostler, Mr George McAlpine and Mr Thomas Kelly all resigned after unhappy exchanges with the committee. In most cases the committee objected to spending the householders' money on staff they considered to be inexperienced or incompetent.

Nellie Ostler, herself just out of school, had a particularly difficult time with the committee, who eventually ousted her for being uncertificated. The committee of seven was made up of a majority of Irishmen and Miss Ostler never really forgave the Hibernians, nor Waitohi, for her discomfiture. Many years later, as Helen Wilson, she wrote *Moonshine*, a very entertaining novel on the whisky days at Waitohi. In this book most of the ne'er-do-wells are portrayed as 'bog' Irish and the district is described as being a great deal more backward than it probably was. *My First Eighty Years*, Helen Wilson's autobiography, likewise gives Waitohi a poor press. She had been rather ungraciously treated, and was entitled to harbour some resentment, but many in Waitohi were dismayed in 1944 and 1951 when the two books appeared, and believed a serious injustice had been done to the settlement.

Richard Pearse stayed on at school, as was the custom, till he was sixteen. Under Mr McAlpine the school prospered and the roll rose to 57 pupils, the largest ever. A photograph of the senior classes at Upper Waitohi in 1893 shows Richard standing alongside his teacher in the back row of boys. He is now a tall and well-built lad, plumper in the face than before. He is wearing an unbuttoned white shirt, a jersey, a dark jacket fastened near the neck — and a serious expression. Also in the photograph are Warne and Maggie. Reg is in with the junior classes; Florence and Ruth were too young to be there at all. Others of interest in the photos are Jack and Dick Connell, later to make their names as champion cyclists.

Richard was just an average pupil. He was amenable and a keen reader, but his attention often used to wander. Michael Friel of Waimate, a former schoolmate, recalled that Pearse would sometimes sit in class dreaming. One day an inspector arrived to examine the pupils and during the course of the day he shot a question in Richard's direction. Richard rose to answer but his thoughts had been miles away and he was wordless. 'Yes, the poor fellow stood there as white as a sheet. The schoolmaster knew the young chap was going to faint if he carried on long like that and took him out.'

While he was still at school, Richard made his first knicknack. It was a needle-threader for his mother, but no details of its construction have survived. It was also at Upper Waitohi School that Richard Pearse gave his first indication of aeronautical cunning.

5. Preliminaries

'One day,' Peter Friel recollected, 'Dick Pearse arrived at school with some bits and pieces — a cotton reel with spikes on it, a peg, the lid of a herring tin cut and twisted to form a propeller, and a length of string. Putting it all together he wound the string round the reel, gave a quick tug and the thing was airborne.'

By coincidence or design, Richard had constructed a mechanical toy whose pedigree may be traced back to about the twelfth century. The string-pull helicopter, which came on the scene soon after the introduction of the tower windmill in Europe, is the earliest form of active airscrew known, and the ancestor of every helicopter flying today.

A small beginning, but perhaps Richard Pearse sensed where his future lay. After he left school in 1893 the sixteen-year-old Richard worked on the family farm. He took no interest in the land: in fact he seems to have actively disliked farming and followed this career only because there appeared to be no other course possible. There was no other work at Waitohi and his education had not been advanced far enough to gain him better employment in Temuka or Timaru.

Not that his education was of a slight nature. The syllabus at both Waitohi schools covered drawing, geography, history, science, object lessons, repetition and recitation, reading, composition, and arithmetic. But without futher schooling he could not hope for anything more attractive than labouring work. And Richard Pearse was not the stuff of which navvies are made.

What Richard really wanted was to be an engineer. Anything mechanical fascinated him. He spent hours reading scientific magazines and fiddling about with wire, scrap metal, screws, nuts and bolts. He took clocks apart, watched the way steam engines worked, examined the movements of gears and pulleys and studied the flight of birds.

One day, possibly in 1895, Richard approached his father and asked if he might be allowed to attend the engineering course at Canterbury University College in Christchurch. Digory refused permission. 'If you want to know anything about engineering, go and see the blacksmith at Pleasant Point,' was his rejoinder.

All that Digory could afford to spend on higher education was being invested in his eldest son's medical degree. Tom, after training at Edinburgh, went on to become a capable doctor; but what Richard might have done with the aid of a university training and a little financial backing is anybody's guess. This is one of the more tantalising 'ifs' in the story of aerial technology. Considering his isolation, modest education and humble resoures, it is incredible that he achieved as much as he did.

If he had gone to Canterbury College he might have fallen under the spell of Professor A. W. Bickerton, the university's first professor of chemistry, who was also a brilliant improvisor and prolific theorist. Bickerton's advanced views of marriage, his brown-paper houses, 'partial impact' spatial theory, and Wainoni Park Pleasure Gardens were for many years to enliven the Christchurch scene. But more important to the scores of students who passed through his hands were those remarkable lectures, full of explosions, pongs, wisecracks, digressions, and ingenious demonstrations. Ernest Rutherford, the pioneer atomic scientist, was his pupil from 1891–4. Who knows what Bickerton might have triggered off in Richard Pearse?

Neither 'Bicky' nor Pearse gained the chance of fruitful contact. Richard plugged away at the farm routines instead, though they never earned much of his attention. 'He was absolutely wasted on a farm,' one sister remarked. His younger brother, Warne, remembered him in these days. 'It was quite usual to find Richard driving his team of horses in the plough with the reins around his neck, while he walked behind and read some book on engineering.'

There were other distractions also. Notably tennis. From the early 1890s when clay courts were chipped out near the Spur Hut intersection and at the Flat school, Waitohi had been dedicated tennis country. Hugh McIntyre, who succeeded Charles Goldstone as Upper Waitohi's head teacher in 1894, was a keen sportsman and encouraged his senior boys to chip out a court next to the school. Geoffrey Feilden, a local farmer and a former champion fives player, helped coach the pupils. Upper Waitohi residents with old-style rackets and smooth rubber balls spent happy hours in the evening playing on this court till in 1898 James Orr had two courts shaped, tarred and sanded. These courts were on Orr's property but were opened to the public as the Waitohi Terrace Tennis Club. The Orrs were most hospitable people and frequently held garden parties at their home to raise funds for local causes. One such gathering was held on 24 March 1898 in aid of the Wesleyan Church. Over fifty residents attended and the new courts received a lively baptism. The *Temuka Leader* reported the occasion:

> Lawn tennis, foot races, bicycle riding, shooting, an electric battery, and a tent with curiosities managed by Mr Southby, helped the visitors to pass a pleasant afternoon. Not the least interesting of the sights were the many inventions of the Messrs Orr junior for saving labour: a waterwheel providing power for an electric motor and a tree-spraying apparatus being amongst them. One of these young men took several photographs of the garden party.

This young man was Tommy Orr junior and mercifully his photographs have survived the hazards of time. In addition to several shots of tennis games in progress, Orr took two group photos or, rather, Tommy took one and Jimmy Orr took the other. The ladies may be seen sporting boaters, pin-tucked blouses with leg-of-mutton sleeves, long dark skirts and sensible brogues. The men wore boaters or cloth caps, suits with waistcoats, white shirts with long collars, and sturdy shoes. Several small girls squat in front wearing boaters, dark blouses and pinafore frocks. In one of the group photographs afternoon tea is being handed round and it is obvious from the looks on the faces that photography is still a novelty.

No one in either of these photographs is studying the lens with greater interest than Richard Pearse, now twenty years old. Wearing a white shirt buttoned to the neck, high lapelled jacket, dark trousers, muddy shoes and what looks oddly like a school cap, he appears to be at the function in the role of spectator rather than player. In one group he is with Annie, Jack and a mischievous-looking Warne.

Richard's tennis playing seems to have been a more spasmodic affair in these Waitohi days than it was later on at Milton. His name appears in Waitohi team lists, on and off, from 1889 until he left the district in 1911. Sometimes he played for the Terrace Club at the Orrs', where his brothers and sisters played, but his name also appears with others in the Upper Waitohi team, whose base was the school. Richard also played table tennis in these days, competing once more in the Upper Waitohi team. The fact that he played in a different club from that patronised by his family is an early instance of the independent line he later took with them.

All the Pearse family played tennis. Digory himself was very keen on the game and did not give up match tennis until he was 73. In later days when cars chugged round on one or two cylinders and were frowned on by farmers for frightening the stock, the Pearse buggy would often be seen on the South Canterbury roads, carrying a tennis team to play some other club or district. And the team would be made up mostly of Pearses. Whenever a tournament cropped up, Warne, in particular, would just drop everything and go. Sometimes, even in harvest time when the rest of the district was labouring into the twilight, the Pearses would knock off at four to play a game or two. None of the Pearses of that generation was a very dedicated agriculturalist. 'Gentlemen farmers' the neighbours called them. As Ray McAteer recalls, 'They did not bother to cut their fences as other farmers did, and the Pearse fences were always the highest in the district. If they were trimmed then it was with Bell's safety matches. That was their gorse-cutter!'

Warne Pearse developed into an outstanding tennis player with a national reputation. His playing career spanned 50 years and for about thirty of these, 1898–1927, he was playing competitive tennis. The only break in his playing came with the First World War when he went overseas, rose to the rank of lieutenant and fought at the Somme, where he was wounded in the knee by machine-gun splinters.

For 23 years he entered in the national singles championship and for most years he competed in at least four or five other championship meetings as well. Altogether Warne Pearse won the South Canterbury singles title twelve times and on various occasions took the singles championship at Hawke's Bay, Wairarapa, Rotorua and Otago. On one celebrated occasion he competed at Nelson, cycling both ways, adding up to a ride of more than 1100 kilometres. It was a pity that the top national honour always just eluded him. Anthony Wilding and Geoff Ollivier usually headed him off. Warne played some particularly fine games against Anthony Wilding, who was Wimbledon singles champion from 1910 to 1914 and is still regarded as New Zealand's most illustrious tennis player.

Warne Pearse was also the first president of the Temuka Returned Servicemen's Association, a layreader and vestryman for 30 years at St Peter's Anglican church in Temuka; a capable violinist and vocalist; a much admired after-dinner speaker and raconteur; and an inaugural member of the Temuka Chess Association. When he died in 1968, aged 87, he left behind him a considerable reputation in a number of fields.

Richard Pearse turned 21 at the end of 1898. Digory, no doubt hoping to buttress his son's faltering interest in agriculture, let him have the use of 40 hectares up the road from Trewarlet. It seems to have been Digory's practice to set up each of his sons at the age of 21 with a property for which the son paid a modest rental. He also presented each one with some sheep, a horse or two, a violin and a watch.

The property Richard Pearse took over is now owned by Richard Lyon, and was taken up originally by Peter Friel in 1877. Friel had come out to New Zealand from County Donegal, spending six months en route in Australia. He was twelve years in Otago before working for three more years on the Levels estate. His twenty years at Waitohi were spent in cropping, contracting, and allowing his gorse fences to get out of control. By the time Digory Pearse took the land over in 1896 it needed a lot of close attention and, unfortunately, Richard was not the man for that task.

The next few years were critical. The condition of Richard Pearse's property deteriorated swiftly as he put more and more time into his hobbies. The young Orr brothers, Jimmy and Tommy, were mechanically inclined and had a well-equipped workshop where Pearse spent a lot of his spare time.

Pearse was a near neighbour of the Orrs and is remembered signalling to them at night with a morse lamp. The Orr boys too were of an inventive frame of mind and seem to have given Richard the encouragement he needed to proceed with his own ideas.

So Richard continued to live at home and converted the old three-roomed sod-walled thatched cottage the Friels had lived in into a workshop of his own. He travelled to and from his farm by bicycle.

He preferred to work alone, though in his early years he did not object to visitors unless they interrupted his work or meddled with his gear. Sometimes his mother felt sorry for him and sent a hot mid-day meal over with the girls. As his experimentation became more advanced he grew increasingly touchy about casual callers until most locals learned to leave him alone. 'Look out! He might butcher you,' Tom Wade was warned by his brothers, when he suggested a visit to the workshop. An exception was Mrs Charles Inwood from the farm next door. She used to cross the paddocks to the workshop, pushing a pram with her baby in it, to talk to Richard or just watch him at work. Mrs Laura Granger (her daughter) writes:

Mrs Inwood provided a meal and he often did mechanical repairs for her. Although almost a recluse, Richard Pearse never minded her going over and talking with him as he worked because she never picked up or handled things lying about in his workshop. Although most people regarded him as a 'crank', Mrs Inwood, an educated and intelligent woman, considered him a very intelligent and unusual man.

She was one of the few who recognised Pearse's talents. In later years she told her daughters that Richard was a 'reserved, quiet man, a brilliantly clever one'.

From 1900 his life's pattern was established and whether in Waitohi, Milton or Christchurch, his workshop was all that really mattered to him. His neglect of his farm in favour of non-pastoral sidelines created more than a little awkwardness at Trewarlet and was the cause of much tut-tutting among the neighbours. Indeed his mediocrity as a farmer, in both South Canterbury and Otago, is almost as much of a legend as his engineering talent.

There was a cycling club in Waitohi and the Connell and Orr brothers were keen competitive cyclists. So, fittingly enough, the first machine Pearse tried to patent was a new type of bicycle. This machine is still spoken of by oldtimers, but the best contemporary account of it is a report published in the *Temuka Leader* of 21 May 1903:

A bicycle ridden by Mr R.W. Pearse of Waitohi attracted considerable attention at Temuka on Thursday last (Sale Day) by reason of its novel driving gear, a device patented some fourteen months ago by Mr Pearse.

In place of the sprocket wheel the machine is fitted with cranks about half as long again as those of the ordinary bicycle, and these go up and down in arcs instead of revolving in cycles. Attached to the cranks at right angles are a couple of arms, thus making what is technically known as bell cranks. For the rear sprocket wheel there are two grooved covered-in pullies [sic] fitted on a principle akin to that used in the construction of the free wheel. The grooves in the pullies are for the reception of the two driving bands or wires which are attached to the upwards arms of the cranks.

It is claimed for the invention that it makes riding easier as there is no waste of energy, the rider being able to keep a steady strain on the machine the whole time. The gear can be instantly changed to suit the class of road that is being traversed, and on the bicycle which Mr Pearse was riding on Thursday, the gear could be made anything from 56 up to 84. All that is necessary to effect a change is to adjust a moveable pin. It is said that the idea is shortly to be placed on the market.

Until recently it had not been clear whether Pearse succeeded in patenting his bicycle, but in September 1972 David Peters, a Christchurch patent attorney, uncovered a reference to the patent in the New Zealand *Official Gazette* of 1902. Subsequently the patent specifications were located in the Wellington Patent Office. Pearse's application for the patent, accompanied by a provisional specification, was filed in the Patent Office by the then Christchurch branch of Henry Hughes Ltd, patent agents, on 8 February 1902. The specification was entitled 'Improvements in and connected with Bicycles', and it was given the official number 14507. The complete specification was filed nine months later and its acceptance was advertised in the *Official Gazette* of 27 November 1902.

The most unusual feature of the bicycle is its vertical or reciprocating pedal operation. The specifications make clear what the *Temuka Leader* report does not, that the pedal action is dependent on a ratchet-and-pawl system working on the back wheel. There are two rotatable ratchet wheels, one on either side of a disc mounted rigidly on the axle and offset to one side of the wheel. The teeth of the ratchets engage pawls attached to the disc. The front and back bellcranks constituting the pedals are each connected by metal driving bands to the top of one of the ratchet wheels and to the base of the other, so that each ratchet wheel has two connections and the four bands cross over one another. When one pedal is depressed, the ratchet wheel to which it is connected at the top is rotated forwards, picking up the pawls of the central disc as it goes, so driving the rear wheel. Simultaneously the second ratchet wheel is rotated backwards to raise the other pedal so that the operation can be repeated. Owing to the arrangement of the ratchet teeth and the fact that the pawls are capable of one-way movement, the bicycle can be freewheeled or reversed.

In the *Temuka Leader* report the bicycle's second most distinctive feature seems to be its gear system. The specifications describe how the system is to work. It amounts quite simply to adjusting the driving bands to different positions along the arms of the bellcrank pedal levers to which they are connected. The band connections may be locked by means of pins in any of about eight notches in slots provided in the arms. Thus the more distant the pin attachment is from each bellcrank's point of pivot the further the metal bands travel and the greater the rotation of the ratchet wheels; and the further the ratchet wheels are turned the further the bicycle wheel turns for each depression of the pedal. Low gear works on the reverse principle, the driving bands being then pinned into the closest position to the pivoting points of the bell-cranks. As described here, and as the *Temuka Leader* reporter observes, the gear position has to be preset. But in Pearse's provisional specification, reference is made to a rod-and-rack device which would permit the rider to change gear while cycling.

Two other features of Pearse's bicycle are accounted for in the specifications but not in the press report. The first of these is a back-wheel rim brake operated by depressing either pedal further than normally necessary. The second consists of integral tyre pumps.

These tyre pumps were to be fitted to both front and rear wheels and would allow the cyclist to pump up his tyres while still riding his bicycle. The provisional specification describes their operation most succinctly:

I further provide discs eccentrically mounted upon both wheel axles from each of which is driven a specially devised air pump. The eccentric disc is furnished with a projection or knob that engages with a stop that is actuated by the rider. By these means the eccentric is caused to remain stationary, and the pump is thereby actuated through suitable connections as it evolves with the wheel around the eccentric disc. When desired by the operator the eccentric may be released and it will then revolve with the wheel and the pump cease working.

At the end of the complete specification eight claims are listed. One is a general claim and the remainder concern the abovementioned features. All are stated to be in combination with the drive mechanism. The drawings which accompanied the complete specification illustrate two side elevations and a plan view of the rear lower portion of the bicycle in which the novel features are concentrated.

The text and probably the drawings seem to have been prepared on Pearse's behalf by P.M. Newton, from Henry Hughes' Christchurch agency at 83 Hereford Street. Newton had come from Tasmania with machine shop, mining and patent experience. After serving as Henry Hughes' Christchurch manager for a few years he returned to Australia.

The patent firm of Callinan and Newton in Melbourne still perpetuates his name.

The patented bicycle, Pearse's first serious invention, shows one interesting similarity to the inventions described in his later patents.

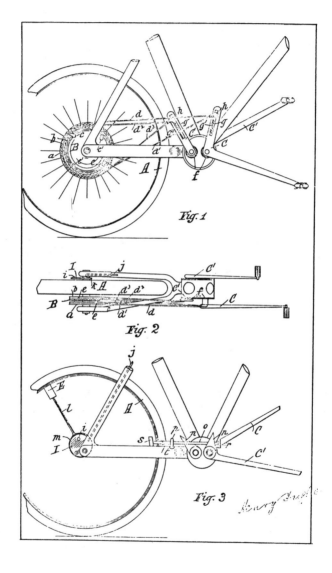

The drawing filed with Pearse's bicycle specification No 14507, dated November 1902, in the Patent Office, Wellington.

That is, his habit of inventing a vehicle with several original features which are not necessarily related. He apparently liked to combine in one invention as many novel ideas as he could think of.

The ideas incorporated in his bicycle are not only intelligently executed but original. To put his machine into perspective, the 'penny-farthing' had been out of fashion only since John Starley's chaindriven Rover safety bicycle went into production in 1886. Pneumatic tyres were not invented by Dunlop until 1888. The free wheel did not arrive until the 1890s. Variable-speed transmission had been in use since 1881 but Sturmey-Archer hub gears were not patented until 1901. External brakes of various sorts had been experimented with since the velocipede of the 1860s, and backpedal brakes since the 'safety' bicycle; but there seems to have been nothing on the market resembling Pearse's rim brake. His pedal action and gearing system were also quite novel. But most ingenious of all were the self-acting tyre pumps.In the early days of tyre manufacture with tubes of inferior quality, this idea might have had a great deal of merit. All things considered, this bicycle invention is highly typical of Pearse's individual approach; and typical also of his resourcefulness with simple, even commonplace components.

The cycle frame was apparently made of bamboo, a material other cycles were being made of at the time. It was also a material which he made frequent use of elsewhere, hence one of his nicknames, 'Bamboo Dick'.

His belief that the ordinary crank action lost too much leverage near the top and bottom of the stroke is probably a valid one. At any rate, with the gears to help him, he managed to sail up quite steep hills with little effort. Yet the idea did not catch on. Pearse let the patent lapse and no attempt seems to have been made to manufacture the machine. His own prototype of the bicycle has vanished.

But flying, not cycling, was his dream. There is some evidence that he was working on ideas for an aircraft before the turn of the century. At this stage no one anywhere in the world had yet made a sustained and controlled flight in a powered aeroplane. There had, however, been four documented takeoffs. Du Temple, a French sailor, had at Brest in about 1874 piloted a steam-powered tractor monoplane down a ramp from which it had flown for a few metres. In 1884 a Russian, Mozhaiski, had run his plane (powered by a British steam engine) down a ramp and into the air for twenty or thirty metres. Another Frenchman, Clement Ader, was airborne for about fifty metres at Armainvilliers in 1890 to become the first person in a powered plane to take off from level ground. And Sir Hiram Maxim, the wealthy American inventor of the machine-gun, had sustained flight for a second or two in his steam-driven biplane tested on a railed course in the County of Kent, England, in 1894.

The only others so far credited with achieving a powered takeoff before Orville and Wilbur Wright flew on 17 December 1903, were Samuel Pierpont Langley on the Potomac River in October and December 1903; and Karl Jatho of Germany, who in August and November 1903 made hops of 18 and 60 metres in his petrol-driven semi-biplane. The Germans coined the term *flugsprung* (leap into the air) to describe Jatho's efforts.

In New Zealand the field was wide open. Although by 1899 there had been several balloonists in the news, there had been no attempts at winged flight by glider or powered plane. Not that one can overlook the heroic and hazardous escapades of these balloon men. 'Professor' Baldwin at Dunedin in 1889 was the first person to ascend into the New Zealand skies, suspended beneath a gas-filled balloon. In 1890 'Professor' Jackson attempted to lift off from Lancaster Park in Christchurch. 'Captain Lorraine' (Mahoney) ascended from near the Christchurch gasworks in 1899, crossed the Port Hills and drowned in the sea off Port Levy. Other aerial exhibitionists with assorted motives and capabilities followed.

Pearse's aeronautical experiments predate those of better-known New Zealand aviators such as Bertram Ogilvie (no relation) of Napier who built three machines between 1907–10, Arthur Schaef of Wellington who constructed a plane in 1909, Leo and Vivian Walsh of Papakura who did their pioneer work in 1910–11, H.J. Pither who flew at Riverton in 1910, and George Bolt who was gliding from the Christchurch Port Hills in 1911.

It must, therefore, be clear that Pearse's pioneer work from perhaps as early as 1899, but in the years 1903 to 1906 particularly, not only makes him the father of powered flight in New Zealand but entitles him as well to a place in the history of international aeronautics. The fact that he never won this honour in his lifetime and that his influence on the course of aviation both in New Zealand and abroad was absolutely nil should not be allowed to detract from the impressiveness of his achievement.

6. The planemaker

Though Pearse worked in isolation and obscurity, he knew something of what the rest of the world was up to. It is evident from the two newspaper letters he later wrote, outlining some of his work, that he was aware of the experiments being made elsewhere by Maxim, Langley, the Wright brothers, and the French aviators, for whom he seemed to have a special respect. And he later kept up to date with advances made by Santos Dumont, Glenn Curtiss, and others. He is known to have subscribed to the *Scientific American*, which kept him abreast of technology generally. Warne later recounted how it was this periodical which brought to his brother's notice a £10,000 prize being offered to the first person who made a manned flight in a powered aeroplane.

However, the *Scientific American* did not offer any aviation prizes until 1908 and 1909, both being won by Glenn Curtiss. The Wrights did not win any prizes until 1908, and when they did it had nothing to do with the *Scientific American*. Therefore, Warne's memory that his brother was 'disappointed at the Wright brothers beating him to the prize money' cannot be used as a method of dating Richard's early flight attempts.

The *Scientific American* around the turn of the century contained references to some types of internal-combustion engines being developed for the automobile. It also recorded a number of aeronautical experiments being carried out in various parts of the world, particularly in the fields of ballooning and gliding.

Pearse would have been interested by an article appearing in the issue of 22 February 1902 which described the Wright brothers' first gliding experiments of 1899–1901. The article summarised Wilbur Wright's paper, read before the Western Society of Engineers, entitled 'Some Aeronautical Experiments'. It described the brothers' indebtedness to Lilienthal, Pilcher and Chanute, and went on to give a certain amount of technical data on the Wrights' innovations in glider construction. Five photographs of a Wright glider were reproduced with the article, showing the glider both on the ground and in flight.

Even if Richard Pearse saw this article — and there is no certainty about when he began subscribing to the journal — he does not seem to have adopted any of the Wright brothers' ideas. Indeed, he apparently did no preliminary work with gliders, nor did he follow the Wrights in their biplane wing configuration or use a front elevator and tailfins as they did. Nor would he have learnt anything about the Americans' use of wing-warping to achieve lateral control. For though Octave Chanute revealed the technique at a lecture in Paris in 1903, little was made of it and the Wrights did not disclose the details themselves until January 1906.

Anyway, by the time the *Scientific American* gave publicity to the Wrights' gliding experiments, Pearse may have started on his own plane. It is possible, even, that he had already attempted to fly.

Before he was ready to begin work on his plane, he spent night after night poring over books and journals pertaining to flight, mechanics and engineering. Apart from the *Scientific American* it is thought that he subscribed to other magazines of the *Popular Mechanics* variety which were mailed to him direct from the USA.

The Lower Waitohi Library, which was operating from 1877, had by the turn of the century a stock of about four hundred volumes and a membership of 40. Surprisingly enough the remnants of this pioneer library survived until the mid-1980s in the old concrete-block building next to the now derelict Waitohi Flat School. Reference books in stock when Pearse was a member of the library and which could have helped him, include the following: *Popular Scientifc Recreation* (no author or date); *A History of the Growth of the Steam Engine* (R.H. Thurston, 1887); *Lives of the Engineers* (Samuel Smiles, 1878); *Tomlinson's Cyclopaedia of Useful Arts and Manufactures* (3 volumes, no date): *Popular Electric Lighting* (Captain Ironside Bax, 1892); *Cassell's Cyclopaedia of Mechanics* (Paul Hasluck, 1902); plus a handbook on engineering tools and a biography of famous inventors.

None of these volumes touches on aviation, not even ballooning, but there is a great deal of other useful advice on mechanics and engineering. For a person like Richard Pearse who was setting up a workshop of his own from scratch, these books contained all the information he needed. Pearse read like one possessed. Bert Smart, visiting Warne Pearse at Trewarlet for violin lessons, often used to see Richard lying under one tree or other, absorbed by his books. You could get no conversation out of him at all beyond passing the time of day. He would take his books with him even when off to do routine farm work like gorse grubbing. 'Sensitive and withdrawn,' writes Shirley Holdsworth, an Auckland journalist, 'his mind was filled with exciting ideas that could not be shared with the extrovert farming community in which he lived.'

One of Pearse's sisters recalls what people thought of him at the time: 'They all thought he was a bit gone in the upper storey. They said anything that could fly, heavier than air, was an absolute impossibility, and he used to keep very quiet about it because I think he knew what the general opinion was. He never talked about it at the table or anything like that. We knew he was doing it but never discussed it, except Warne. We wondered what on earth was going to happen.' Robert Gibson remembers how locals thought the inventor was 'an absolute crank. He was Mad Pearse'.

According to Warne, Harry Brosnahan, Jean Currie and others, Richard started at the turn of the century working on designs for a plane and successfuly testing a model. Pearse himself wrote later that he designed the plane 'before anyone had made a flight'. At some stage or other, Ethel Bourne and Nellie McAteer remembered, Richard Pearse tried flying a model plane — probably hand thrown — inside his workshop. When satisfied that his plane could work he set about building it to full scale.

'Dick's first job was to make himself a lathe', recalled Warne Pearse in his interview with the *Press* in July 1954. This lathe he painstakingly assembled from mechanical castoffs rescued from rubbish tips. *Cassell's Technical Educator* may have supplied the advice he needed. The lathe was foot operated. 'He had then to make his own forge and bellows and he erected a sketchy sort of [canvas] shelter to house the machine while it was under construction.'

It is possible that this work began as early as 1899. Jean Currie of Timaru, in her twenties at the time, writes: 'I remember one Sunday when my father Tom Currie and his brother-in-law Alex McClintock [the Waitohi blacksmith] walked up to Richard Pearse's workshop to visit him and when they returned I remember my father saying "If he gets that contraption up into the air he'll fall out of it and kill himself." My father said it was all "hoop iron and wire". My family left Waitohi and went to live at Morven in 1899 and my father's visit to Pearse took place quite some time before we left Waitohi.'

Department of Lands and Survey records confirm that Thomas Currie's application for Section 7 Block VI in the Waitaki Survey

District was successful as from 30 March 1899. Morven is some 80 kilometres south of Waitohi. Though others speak of Pearse working on his plane at the turn of the century or during the Boer War, Miss Currie's is the only date that can be authenticated.

The simplest description of the plane he eventually built — his first aeroplane — comes from Richard Pearse himself and may be found in his Christchurch *Star* letter of 1928: 'This machine was a monoplane mounted on three air-tyred wheels for starting and landing, with a horizontal rudder behind for balancing fore and aft, a vertical rudder for steering, and also two small horizontal rudders at the wing tips to prevent side tipping. The propeller was in front and was mounted directly on the engine crank-shaft, thereby rendering clutches and gearing unnecessary.'

It all looks simple enough on paper. But consider for a moment the magnitude of the task facing the inventor at the outset. Waitohi was still an isolated horse-and-gig community. There were not even motor-cars in the district till 1908–9. Pearse had no technical training, no facilities except those which he built himself, no financial backing, and little encouragement. Yet he was trying to do what overseas inventors with government grants and factory workshops at their disposal had so far failed to achieve: to build a heavier-than-air machine and fly it successfully. Only a man of exceptional vision and optimism would have given the proposition any chance at all. The district remained sceptical.

Maurice Cameron of Temuka remembered Tom Lyon recounting the times he used to see 'Aeroplane Pearse' biking to Temuka for supplies. He would return loaded up like a mule with bamboo and coils of wire for his plane.

'What are you doing, Dick?' Tom Lyon once asked.

'I'm going to fly,' replied Pearse.

Tom just shrugged his shoulders, smiled to himself, and got back to the job in hand. 'Poor old Dick' was his reaction, and also that of most others in the neighbourhood. 'Cranky Dick,' said the less charitable.

'God,' cried an indignant Mrs Gibson as she spanked a son for watching Pearse at work on his plane, 'didn't mean men to fly.'

Pearse's achievement is all the more startling when it is realised that he made most of the machine out of bamboo, wire and bits of scrap metal. Even the studs and bolts were homemade.

The most formidable problem was of course the motor. How was he to construct an engine sufficiently small and light to make powered flight practicable? No such engine could be bought, and car engines were far too heavy, so Pearse set about making his own lightweight motor. It is possible that he was experimenting with such an engine as early as 1899 when, according to Jean Currie, some of the strange sounds issuing forth from Pearse's farm, behind those monumental gorse hedges, were already puzzling his neighbours. Towards the end of his life, when in 1951 Pearse was being examined before his committal to Sunnyside Hospital, he told Dr J.R. Gilmour that he had made an engine away back 'during the Boer War'. This could mean any time between 1899 and 1902, but in any event it indicates an early start. And it is not likely that the engine would have related to anything else but his aeroplane, for Pearse never tried to build a car and he did not attempt to motorise his bicycle and farm implements until he went to Milton.

The only engines he would have seen much of up until this time were steam engines. There were several threshing mill contractors nearby — William Walker and Sam Thornley in Lower Waitohi, Lachlan McCormick in Upper Waitohi and the Orr brothers who lived on the next property but one to Trewarlet. All these contractors used steam for power. The Lower Waitohi Library had several reference books which described in detail the workings of steam engines. Warne Pearse had borrowed in 1896, according to the library issue book, *Thurston's History of the Growth of the Steam Engine*. His older brother would certainly have seen it. The first volume of *Cassell's Technical Education* is particularly helpful on the mechanics of steam power. Its pages on cylinder construction — if thumbprints are any guide — show more signs of dedicated use than any other article.

The internal combustion engine had been invented as early as 1860 by Lenoir, and petrol-driven motors as developed by Otto, Daimler and Benz were by the late 1880s rated as efficient power units for bicycles and cars. Oddly enough most aviators were still persevering with steam as a source of power right up to the turn of the century. The first to take the petrol engine seriously as a means to achieving powered flight was Samuel Pierpont Langley of the USA.

Langley, a distinguished astronomer and mathematician who later became secretary of the Smithsonian Institution, had been investigating flight since 1887. By the end of 1896 two of his model aeroplanes, steam-powered, had flown distances of about a kilometre. In 1898 the US War Department granted him a subsidy of $50,000 to build a man-carrying aeroplane, and in the same year Langley commissioned Stephen Balzer of New York to build a suitable petrol engine. Balzer produced an engine within the prescribed weight of 100 lbs (45 kg) but it delivered only about 8 hp, which was not enough. Langley's assistant, Charles Manly, redesigned the engine and it was successfully tested at the beginning of 1902. A quarter-sized model aeroplane powered by a small 3.2-hp petrol engine was tested several times and finally flew in August 1903. This is credited by aviation historians with being the first flight by an aeroplane powered by a petrol engine. Langley's full-sized plane, the Aerodrome, was powered by a Manly-Balzer engine when Manly twice failed to fly it off the top of a houseboat on the Potomac River on 7 October and 8 December 1903. Karl Jatho's small plane was powered by a 9-hp petrol engine; and in the last quarter of 1903 the Wright brothers designed and built the 12-hp petrol motor which was to take them into the air on 17 December.

Pearse may have read in scientific periodicals of Langley's attempt to have a lightweight internal combustion engine constructed, but no news of Jatho or the Wright brothers would have been available to him then. Though he could have read about 'oil' or petrol engines in scientific magazines the only experienced help available to Pearse at the turn of the century was from Cecil Wood, an engineer in Timaru. Cecil Wood was, in 1895, the first person in New Zealand to construct an internal combustion engine. He was also the first New Zealander to build a motorcycle (1895) or automobile (1901). Wood later told Cederman that Pearse visited him several times in 1901 and 1902, and was shown how to make sparkplugs with the central electrode insulated by mica. Wood also helped him with the design of surface carburettors.

Working largely by hit-or-miss methods, Pearse set about making a motor to power his plane. From the outset he seems to have rejected steam as a possibility though he introduced into his 'oil engine' some characteristics of the steam engine such as the double-acting principle, a cross-head and stuffingboxes. In the early stages, he tried to cope with the mechanical problems largely on his own. Robert Gibson maintains that he got no help from anyone except the Pleasant Point blacksmith, Billy Hayes, who probably made Pearse's first crankshaft. Jack Connell thinks that the Orr brothers assisted occasionally as well. One source of cheap metal for Pearse was Mark Saunders' scrap dump at Pleasant Point. Gibson, who later worked for Saunders, thinks that Pearse got a lot of his material from that dump. Saunders used to cut up boilers and other machinery and dispose of what he could. He was also something of an engineer in his own right, and built a small electric power generator on the Opihi River at about this time.

It is difficult to identify and date the engines which Pearse subsequently built. The only firm evidence is that he had developed a two-cylinder double-acting horizontally opposed engine by 1906 when he filed his first patent application; that he had a four-cylinder single-acting horizontally opposed engine in 1909, when a reporter described it in a *Temuka Leader* feature; that he progressed to a sixteen-cylinder horizontally opposed engine in his last years at Waitohi and took it south to Milton with him in 1911; and that after he moved up to Christchurch in 1921 he constructed a four-stroke double-acting two-cylinder motor which could be converted into a two-stroke if desired. The problem is complicated by the fact that Pearse in his letters refers only to the second and third of these engines. (He had not constructed the fourth engine at that stage.) George Bolt refers only to the second and fourth engines. He suspected the existence of the first engine but had no definite information about it; and though he was told by a Temuka witness, James Parmenter, of a 'sixteen-cylinder rotary engine', he apparently dismissed the evidence as too shaky, for he made no mention of it in his final report on Pearse. It is also suspected that Pearse pottered about with a single-cylindered motor before developing his first two-cylindered model.

The four-cylinder engine recovered from the dump by Maurice Cameron in 1958 and passed on to George Bolt has hitherto been thought of as the first engine with which Pearse tried to fly. Two developments in 1971 caused this notion to be set aside. The first of them was when Geoff Rodliffe of Auckland located in the Patent Office Pearse's provisional specification for the 1906 patent which differed in a number of vital respects from the wording of the complete specification. The provisional specification quite plainly recommends a two-cylinder horizontally opposed double-acting 'oil engine'. Pearse's first flight attempts certainly predated his 1906 patent so it is reasonable to assume he would mention the most successful engine he had used up to that time.

However, it was generally believed that any two-cylinder engine he may have had was lost or destroyed. The writer, having learned from Gilbert Lyon that there was probably more in his aviation museum than was ever recovered from the dump, organised a second excavation on 15 May 1971. Maurice Cameron agreed to lead the way and Tom Bradley of the *Timaru Herald*, who had been investigating the Pearse territory for several years on behalf of Geoff Rodliffe, was also invited to participate. After a great deal of slashing and probing in tangled riverbed undergrowth just across the stopbank from the end of Lyon Road, the dump was relocated.

A few minutes' digging exposed a wide range of farmyard jetsam — kerosene tins, lengths of wire, plough harness, paint pots, broken glass, old piping — and finally a rusty and silt-clogged object which looked splendidly like a cylinder. Excitement mounted as the digging continued. By the time the morning was up, five cylinders, a piston and several small metal clips used to secure the bamboo wing framework had been unearthed.

Next day Dudley Gardiner (married to Margaret Pearse, a niece of the aviator) joined the dig. The whole dump, about five metres square, was closely forked over a second time. Nothing new resulted except another metal clip, but a week later Dudley Gardiner and Kevin Piper from Timaru made a final check and discovered just beyond the edge of the forked area a further piston with con rod still attached.

These historic artifacts, plus a few other oddments which might have been part of Pearse's plane, were taken to Christchurch and shown to Gilbert Lyon. Lyon was able to say with certainty that the cylinders, pistons and metal clips had been in his Pearse collection but that the other bits and pieces had not.

The engine parts were now more closely inspected. Three of the cylinders were of cast iron with a length of 8 1/8 inches (20.6 cm) and a 4-inch (10 cm) bore. In each was a seized-up or rusted-up steel piston with gudgeon-pin boss showing but no con rod. Of the two pistons, one was of cast iron with con rod attached and the other was of thin steel (no con rod) and similar to the pistons in the three cylinders already described. Like the cylinders, these pistons seemed to be factory-made but showed clear signs that Pearse had lathed them to suit his own needs. These cylinders and pistons all appeared to relate to the second engine, his 25-hp four-cylinder model. Presumably, all these components had experienced mishaps of some sort and been rejected by Pearse in the course of developing and operating his four-cylinder engine.

The two remaining cylinders were by far the most exciting outcome of the excavation. They were obviously homemade, and the crudity of their construction indicated that they predated anything else of Pearse's so far discovered. The author passed them over to J. Wilton Johnston, a National Airways Corporation (NAC) engineer and vice-president of the Aviation Historical Society of New Zealand, for closer analysis.

NAC technicians carefully removed the silt and corrosion from the two cylinders and Wilton Johnston gave them close study. They were seen to be fabricated from 30.5 cm lengths of 10-cm diameter steel irrigation tubing, of a sort readily at hand on farms in Waitohi from the 1890s. It is similar also to piping used by goldminers a generation earlier in Central Otago and on the West Coast. An end was fitted to each cylinder consisting of a disc of steel plate retained by steel right-angle lugs riveted to the cylinder wall and endplate. Brazing had been applied around the edges to provide a gas-tight joint. The outer end of each cylinder had two valve apertures and provision for a sparkplug, and one was fitted also with a small petcock, apparently for cylinder priming. The inner ends were missing and must have been screwed on to enable the pistons to be fitted or removed. There was no brazing at these ends.

Apart from their amateur but ingenious construction there were three aspects of these cylinders which gave them a unique value. Firstly, there was a corroded hand-lathed piston in one of them which showed no sign of possessing a gudgeon-pin boss, but featured instead the remains of a rod projecting from the underside of the crown. Secondly, each cylinder showed clear signs of having once had a cover at its opposite end. There was a strong likelihood, too, that each had been double-acting.

The conclusion drawn from this analysis was that these were the cylinders from the engine Pearse describes in his July 1906 provisional patent specification, the engine which every Pearse researcher, George Bolt included, had presumed to be lost.

'The engine has two cylinders which are opposed to each other,' it was written in Pearse's specification, 'and I construct four end pieces in which are fitted the valves and sparkplugs, and the end pieces are fitted into the ends of the cylinders. The pistons are fitted one on each end of a single piston rod, and the piston rod is passed through the two end pieces of the cylinders. The cylinder ends are provided with stuffingboxes, which prevent any leakage, similar to those of a steam engine. The two cylinders take in and explode mixture at both their ends, and as the cylinders are double-acting, there will be two explosions to each revolution of the crank, and by these means, idle strokes will be avoided.'

At a conservative estimate, this engine could have produced 15 hp. This is quite enough power to get a plane off the ground. The Wright brothers, after all, managed their 1903 flights on 12 hp.

7. Aloft

Pearse was very proud of his first completed engine. As he wrote later in his letter to the Christchurch *Star*, the bulk of his time had been spent in developing a light motor and an airscrew:

> The Wrights and myself were the first to produce motors sufficiently light to make flight possible, and we both designed and built our own motors as they could not be bought at the time, while the French aeroplane men, like Santos Dumont and Blériot, who came in the field later, were able to buy their motors. An ordinary motor-car or motor-bicycle motor weighs about 20 lb per hp, and my first aeroplane motor of 25 hp weighs 5 lb per hp.

Pearse claimed that this was the lightest motor in the world for its power. One cannot be sure that he was referring to the 'irrigation pipe' motor, rather than to his second, the four-cylinder model, for both would rate about 24–25 hp according to his yardstick for measuring horsepower. There are several frustrating things about Pearse's letter, and one is his lack of precision about which engine is which, but the inventor was known to be pleased with all his engines and their capabilities, so the distinction matters little on this score.

A wood and tubular steel frame resting on a tricycle undercarriage of cycle wheels with air-filled tyres supported the engine. The pilot sat over the undercarriage on a saddle which he could slide back and forth along a rail to adjust the plane's centre of gravity. Pearse also hoped that the seat's movement would help to absorb the impact of any crash.

Over the pilot's head was fixed the canvas-covered table-top wing. Witnesses recall that it was rectangular in shape and had a spread of about twelve to thirteen metres, though a span of seven to nine metres would have been, structurally, a sounder prospect. The wing's framework was of bamboo with neatly clipped metal joints for strength and lightness. Pearse is remembered making bicycle trips to the Temuka railway station to collect bundles of bamboo rods freighted to him from Christchurch.

The propeller of this first model, Warne recalled, 'finished with glass of a broken bottle and sandpaper, was eight feet long and beautifully made'. (No one else, apart from Warne, has any memory of Richard Pearse using this wooden propeller.) The propeller was attached directly to the driveshaft of the motor and it is thought that a small rectangle was cut out of the leading edge of the wing to allow the propeller room to turn. A propeller so positioned would be very hard to spin however, and the length of a surviving crankshaft suggests that he allowed later on for the propeller to turn in advance of the wing.

He later described his method of control: 'My system of balancing was to place a small horizontal rudder at the tip of each wing, which could be manipulated by a handle, for the purpose of preventing the machine from tipping over sideways. To prevent backward or forward tipping I used the usual horizontal rudder at the rear, while a vertical rudder was used for steering.'

This vertical rudder may not have been added till later experiments, for three witnesses to his first flight attempts, bearing in mind what planes later looked like, made a point of saying that the plane 'had no tail'. If so, the only way it could have been steered at this stage was by using the wingtip airbrakes to bank it. The controls were manipulated by handles which met directly in front of the pilot's head; one operated the elevator ('horizontal rudder'), and one dealt with the wing vanes. These controls were not linked but could be operated independently. Pearse steered the plane, while taxiing, by means of a long tiller leading back from the steerable nosewheel.

The plane was now ready to test. The motor and propeller had already undergone separate trials. Peter Hullen remembered the engine being mounted on a swing arrangement attached to a stand about three metres high so that the thrust could be examined. Harry Brosnahan, who believed that Pearse was experimenting with aircraft ideas before the turn of the century, recollected that the plane took a long time to build, and that he used to watch Pearse working at it on Sunday afternoons. Jack Connell testifies: 'I remember flight trials of this aeroplane and assisting Dick Pearse with it when he was experimenting. I remember a considerable amount of ground running and fast taxiing and hopping in the paddock in front of the house. It took two men to hold back the plane with the running of the engine.' Brosnahan and Dick Williams also saw some of these paddock trials.

Connell once saw Pearse trotting round behind his plane, holding on to the back of the wing. Another recalls him steering his plane around the paddock from behind, using reins attached to the controls, as if it were a horse. A third saw him taxiing about his property one day with a heavy sack of dirt dragging from the rear to anchor the machine down.

Fred Cone told Geoff Rodliffe of another ingenious way in which Pearse tested the pull or thrust developed by his engine. He would anchor the plane to a post by means of a 90-kg spring balance, run the engine, take a measurement, then alter the pitch of the propeller and try again. The spring balance was sometimes connected to a pulley block which gave a two-to-three gain. John Casey, too, recalled that Pearse tied his plane to a post while testing its engine power. A pull of 90 kg would be more than twice what was necessary to get a plane of Pearse's dimensions up to flying speed. It may be the block-and-tackle attachment which another witness had in mind: Alice Southby, who is seen handing out afternoon tea in Jimmy Orr's photograph of the Terrace Tennis Club's garden party of 1898, told her daughter — Mrs Harry Banks of Christchurch — that she saw Pearse one day test his plane 'at the end of an endless rope'.

It is not possible to date accurately the numerous observations of Pearse testing his engine or machine, but this hardly matters; his techniques would not have varied much over the years, and it is of more interest to know what his methods were.

Eventually, after about eighteen months' intermittent work on it, Richard Pearse wheeled his monoplane out on to the Main Waitohi Road near the school intersection. He was assisted by Warne, who was the only person present and who later dated the event at about June 1901. The plane was taxied briskly down the road towards Temuka but to the inventor's disappointment the machine would not lift off. So, for one reason or another, it was a case of 'back to the drawingboard'. There is, unfortunately, no way now of verifying this episode or the date suggested for it.

Miss Cissie Connell told Geoff Rodliffe of another flight attempt which might have been made a little later, in 1902, when she was twelve years old. 'I was told that Pearse would fly today so I climbed on to a haystack on our farm which was adjoining his and I was within 200 yards of Pearse when he made his attempt. He was assisted by my brother [probably Jack] and started from the vicinity of his house. The plane travelled across the paddock and crashed on to the gorse fence. This occurred a long time before the great snowstorm and the plane remained on the fence for a long time.'

Mrs Daniel Friel saw Richard Pearse's plane on the hedge at this time and also believed that it was well before the 'big snow' of July 1903. There is no way of dating these two observations except from the 'big snow' and one cannot place too much reliance on 1902 from this evidence.

Pearse's 40-hectare property was oblong shaped, running north to south, and was divided by gorse hedges into four 10-hectare paddocks. The plane evidently made its run from the workshop, set well back in his south-western paddock near the junction of the fences, and finished up in the gorse fence on his Main Waitohi Road boundary. All his hedges were of heroic dimensions, so it is not surprising that Miss Connell had to climb a haystack to get any effective view of the proceedings.

It is impossible now to estimate the number of trial flights that Richard Pearse made at this period or to date them. One witness believes he made some practice runs on the Orrs' farm which was situated eastwards along the terrace roughly halfway between Trewarlet and the Cones' property. The terrain on the Orrs' property was more level than on his own. Moreover, he would have had a well-informed audience in the Orr brothers, who were gifted mechanics in their own right. Joseph Coll believed that Jimmy Orr may have shown Pearse how to balance his propeller, using the same technique as for balancing a threshing-machine drum. Another witness thought Pearse used Galbraith Road for taxiing on. A likely explanation for all this is that Pearse used a variety of locales for his flight experiments, depending on the wind direction and the state of the ground or road surfacing.

As Pearse later admitted, most of time 'was spent in developing the light motor and in testing air propellers'. But he seems to have made other modifications to his plane. He changed the propeller to an iron-framed two-bladed model, with sheet-metal blades cut from sheep-dip drums. Like its wooden predecessor it was fixed straight on to the end of the engine crankshaft.

He also appears to have rounded off the corners of the wing to give it an elliptical or oval appearance, though there is some doubt about when he actually did this. This may have been to produce a streamlined effect, or perhaps to reduce any chance of the squared wingtips getting caught up in gorse hedges and other undergrowth. It is believed, too, that at this stage Pearse replaced the canvas immediately behind the propeller with a metal section made from the thin tin of golden-syrup cans opened out, flattened, and soldered together. During early trials he found that the canvas in this part of the wing kept buckling and flapping because of propeller turbulence. The metal insert may have slightly increased the weight of the plane, but it also improved its stability. In addition, it lessened any chance of the wing catching fire from sparks out of the engine exhaust.

After further testing on his farm to get the feel of things, Pearse was ready for the road again. The following seems to be what happened, collated from the soul-searchings of several who claimed to have seen him on this key occasion.

He first ran the aeroplane out of its canvas-roofed shelter, and with Warne's help pushed it to the school crossroads, about 800 metres away. There some two dozen curious spectators gathered to watch the fun. The stretch of rutted metalled road running from the Upper Waitohi School back towards his farm was still the best runway he could find locally. Though the road was officially 20 metres wide, high gorse hedges growing on top of sod fences jutted out on both sides, and the grass verges would also be a hazard if he drifted on to them.

The state of Pearse's front fence warrants some further explanation here, before the action starts. On a well-tended property of the period, a gorse hedge was cut annually and would have been about one and a half metres in height and one metre in width. A delinquent gorse hedge flourishing on top of a sod wall could reach a height and breadth of three metres or even more. Pearse's hedges are clearly remembered as being of such dimensions.

According to Mrs Daniel Friel, Pearse made several attempts in the late afternoon to get airborne but, despite much pushing, shoving and revving, got nowhere. Eventually the crowd dwindled, leaving only a handful behind. Most of the others who had returned to their farm work nearby kept an eye open for developments. Then came the last all-out effort. One or two volunteered to give the contraption a push when Pearse was ready. The signal was given. 'I had the pleasure of pulling the propeller for starting,' recounted Warne in 1954. 'She was a wonderful engine and started with very little bother.' It took two men, plus boulders in front of the wheels, to restrain the plane. It was held back for a short time until the motor had picked up speed, then Warne kicked the boulders free and Richard was helped on his way. 'Mine was the last push and off she went. There was no silencer — and talk about a breeze! As he whipped past me, my hat flew in the air.'

The plane taxied for a considerable distance, keeping very well to the centre of the road. Then Pearse accelerated, and the machine rose sluggishly into the air, sounding 'rather like a giant chaffcutter'. It was travelling at an estimated 30 kph.

Mrs Louie Johnson, in a 1961 affidavit, described what happened next: 'As soon as it got into the air it started pitching rather badly and the climb was very slow. The aeroplane then veered badly to the left and landed on top of the hedge.' Warne Pearse and Mrs W. Barker in separate affidavits also remarked on the plane's pitching and wobbling action in the air and its final leftward swerve on to the gorse fence fronting Pearse's property. Estimates of the distance covered range, with these and other witnesses, from 45 metres to 400 metres. They average about 135 metres.

Mrs Inwood remembered later how 'goggle-eyed with amazement' those present were at this spectacle. One of the Connells ran to the fence to help Pearse and in doing so caught his pants on the gorse and tore out the seat.

According to Warne and others, Richard fell to the ground when this plane crashed and hurt his shoulder. He was taken to the Temuka cottage hospital (since burnt down, with all its records) to see if his collarbone was broken, but it was not, and he returned home next day. A Temuka professional photographer apparently went to Waitohi the next day and took a snapshot of the plane, but his complete stock was destroyed in the 1945 flood. It is thought that the Orr brothers also would have taken photographs of the plane at some stage or other, but all their photographic plates and most of their albums were lost or destroyed when the family left Waitohi 40 years later, a decade before there was any interest in Pearse.

Richard Pearse's feelings as he became airborne can only be guessed at. Self-possessed and taciturn as he was, he has left behind no written impressions of this feat, though he sometimes talked of it in later years. One can imagine that his elation at leaving the ground would have changed to consternation as the pitching started, and near-panic as a rough descent seemed inevitable. But most likely he was so busy manipulating rods, wires, levers and the sliding saddle that he had no time for serious reflections of any kind.

Though his boisterous seconds aloft may not have been in terms of control and duration a true 'flight', they did at least amount to a 'powered takeoff'. The distance travelled was not measured and we are entirely dependent on years-after estimates by the witnesses concerned.

The most conservative of these is 45 metres and it would be the safest calculation to work from. It would also most closely approximate Pearse's own judgement on his flying attempts in the first plane as recorded in his Christchurch *Star* letter of 1928. There he tells of his difficulty in controllng the plane, which used to spin round broadside-on as soon as it left the ground. The duration of a 50-yard (45-metre) flight, at the 20 mph (30 kph) Pearse writes of in his letter, would be a little over five seconds.

It is clear from his remarks that Pearse did not himself regard this as flying. Nor, apparently, did he regard the Wright brothers' efforts on 17 December 1903 as true flights because they used a launching rail. Pearse told his nephew Richard 30 years later that what he wanted was a plane which could get him to Temuka and back. Hops and leaps did not therefore interest him.

Nevertheless the switchback performance down the Main Waitohi Road was an impressive effort. Of the seven powered takeoffs which preceded the Wright brothers, Pearse's attempt would have completely outclassed five of them (Du Temple's, Mozhaiski's, Maxim's, and Langley's two), and almost equalled Ader's and Jatho's. If Pearse's distance airborne was greater than the minimum estimate cited above, and this is quite possible, it would constitute the most ambitious *flugsprung* made at that time by any pilot flying a heavier-than-air machine in any part of the world. Additionally, it was (apart from Ader's) the only successful flight attempt made from level ground without the use of ramps, slopes, guiderails or a catapult.

And the date? In all likelihood, Tuesday 31 March 1903.

8. Takeoff testimony

As Richard Pearse roared into the air above the Main Waitohi Road, two young women were sitting on the hillside a few hundred metres across the paddocks. They were the Fraser girls, later Maggie Esler and Annie Casey, and they were bagging potatoes being dug by David Stumbles. Maggie and Annie arranged a little pile of potatoes around themselves and made up their minds that if the aeroplane came their way they were going to 'pelt that crank Pearse with spuds'.

Other witnesses remember, too, that it was potato harvest time. Country folk are apt to date events by connecting them with the state of the crops or with various farm routines, and in Waitohi it is usual to get the potatoes in by late March or early April, before the weather turns uncertain and frosts begin to harden the ground.

However, what clinches the time of year is a conversation recalled by Pearse's two youngest sisters who were attending Waitohi Flat School at the time. Digory had moved the girls away from Upper Waitohi School in 1898 when Mr Hugh McIntyre — a most popular and respected teacher — transferred to Lower Waitohi (Waitohi Flat).

Florrie and Ruth Pearse, the Bourn twins — Elsie and Ellen — and a younger sister Ethel were walking to school one morning. Florrie and the twins were in front, and Ethel and Ruth walked behind. The exact dialogue is uncertain, but it went something like this, Ruth Pearse exclaiming:

'Oh, Ethel, Dick flew his plane yesterday.'

'Tell me another!' retorted Ethel. 'It's the first of April today.'

'It's quite true, Ethel,' chipped in Florence from up front, 'he really did fly.'

The Pearse sisters and Ethel Bourn have all signed affidavits to the effect that this conversation did take place, and the April Fools' Day reference pinpoints the date of the flight concerned as 31 March. At the time Florence and the twins were fifteen, Ruth and Ethel were nine.

A Temuka man, William Edgeler, was working in a nearby field on

59

the afternoon of Pearse's crossroads 'flight'. Years later he was still telling his children what happened. 'I heard a terrible noise coming along the road and looked up just in time to see this plane careering towards a gorse hedge. It was the day before April the 1st. Had Dick Pearse waited another day he would have been a proper fool instead of just a bloody fool!' Edgeler was cracking this joke years before George Bolt publicised the other April Fool's anecdote, so here is further support for a 31 March dating.

It is a much harder task trying to isolate the year of this flight and 1902, 1903 and 1904 all have their advocates.

In support of 1902 is the evidence of Harry Brosnahan of Auckland, who believed that the flight attempt took place soon after a very bad flood in the Waitohi district that year. Many farmers lost stock at the time. The meteorological records confirm 'heavy rainfall over most of Canterbury' and bad flooding on 23–24 March 1902. At Fairlie, 107 mm of rain fell, the heaviest downpour recorded there in 70 years. Timaru experienced 62 mm, and Orari suffered the most severe flood since 1868. As the Opihi River, which has its origins near Fairlie, forms one of the boundaries of the Waitohi district it is quite certain that the flooding of the Waitohi riverflats would have been extensive and memorable. Thus the flight attempt might be dated to an approximate degree by means of the flood. But Brosnahan's memory of how close the two events were could be at fault after such a lapse of time and his evidence, though useful, is inconclusive. Harry Brosnahan also dated the takeoff in autumn 'because I remember that I was sowing green feed on the farm and that was always an autumn operation after harvest was finished'.

Jim Hoskins of Christchurch contributes a second argument for a 1902 dating. An uncle of his, Ernest Hooper, once spoke of being picked up by Richard Pearse between Timaru and Temuka. Pearse was driving a wagon loaded with willow wood and cane. He told his passenger that it was needed to repair his flying machine which had crashed the day before. And the old man — he lived to be nearly ninety-three — was quite sure of the date: the encounter had taken place shortly before he got married. The Registry of Births, Deaths and Marriages shows that Hooper was married in Christchurch on 30 July 1902. Here again the evidence is tantalising. The wedding date can be vouched for but there is no way of ascertaining that the incident took place before the wedding — not after. So Hooper's wedding, like the flood, can serve only as an approximate guideline.

Hooper's anecdote was reported also by Ellen McAteer, a niece. Furthermore, Miss McAteer recalled seeing Pearse's plane on top of the hedge 'in 1902' as she was going to school in her second-to-last year. The McAteers lived up on the Downs overlooking Pearse's property and saw a good deal of him. Miss McAteer remembered her father saying the plane would take off some day but 'The cussed thing will come flying up the hill when I'm taking the mare to town!'

Nellie McAteer was an alert witness with an unswerving memory, and most emphatic about her dates. In the above instance, though, there is no positive method of proving which class she was in when she saw the plane on the hedge.

Her most substantial contribution towards the dating of the crossroads flight relates to the conversation between the Pearse and Bourn sisters, recounted already. Nellie McAteer avers that Florence Pearse could not have taken part in that conversation if it had taken place later than 1902. Florence and Nellie were in the same class, and Miss McAteer has her Education Board Certificate to prove that 1902 was her last official year at the school. This certificate, signed from 1898 to 1902 (her Standard 6 year) by Hugh McIntyre is lodged with the Early Settlers' Museum in Timaru.

The point is made quite emphatically in an affidavit signed by Miss McAteer before a Timaru Justice of the Peace in 1969: 'I had all my education at the Waitohi Flat School . . . I passed Standard 6 on the 26th August 1902 and continued in Standard 7 until after the school became a one-teacher school with Mr McIntyre as sole teacher. According to a statement requested and received from the Canterbury Education Board . . . the school became a one-teacher school from the 1st April 1903. I was the only pupil left in Standard 7 for some months as the others who had been with me in Standard 6 had left before the end of 1902. Their names were Elsie and Ellen Bourn (twins) and Florence Pearse. I was the only one to remain in 1903. As Florence Pearse and the Bourn twins left school before the end of 1902 it is quite obvious that this conversation took place on the 1st April 1902.'

When Maria Hill, doing research for a television *Survey* documentary on Pearse, interviewed Miss McAteer in a Timaru hospital in August 1970, the latter was still of the opinion that she was the only one in Standard 7 in 1903 and that both Florence and the Bourn twins had left school. She recollected sitting over to one side of the room by herself and said that if she had had more company she would have finished the school year — which she did not. Pressed further, Miss

McAteer conceded that Florence and the Bourn girls just might have been at school in 1903, but only for the first few weeks.

There is, therefore, despite Florence Pearse's independently sworn testimony that she did spend a year in Standard 7, some likelihood that the April Fool conversation took place in 1902 when both these witnesses were quite definitely still at school and in the same class. All class rolls and school records from 1899 were later lost in a fire so this aspect of the flight dating may never be proved conclusively. Ellen McAteer herself died only a month or two after the interview with Mrs Hill. Miss Ethel Bourn and her twin sisters have also died and, since the original publication of this book, so have the Pearse sisters. (Geoff Rodliffe was sufficiently convinced by this and the foregoing evidence for a 1902 dating that he confidently asserted in *Richard Pearse: Pioneer Aviator* (1979), that Pearse 'flew his aeroplane' in 1902, no ifs or buts.)

At best the dialogue indicates a 1902 flight. At worst it dates from 1903. But there are more grounds than this to suggest a 1903 dating for the first takeoff.

Others who watched the episode from higher ground were William Charles Bedford, his wife Mary, and her sister-in-law Mrs Louie Johnson. Richard Pearse had advised them of his intention to fly and suggested that they climb up on the hillside nearby to watch. Richard had once proposed to Mary Jane Johnson, but she married Bedford instead. (This is the only indication on record that he ever took a girl seriously enough to want to marry her.) The three named above ' . . . stood on the hillside and saw him fly his aeroplane and land on top of the hedge. It was March 1903. Dog daisies covered the ground. The certainty of the date is known because Mary Jane was about to have her first baby who was born on 6.6.03, named Basil Charles Hayes Bedford.' This statement was sworn to by Basil Bedford's wife at Kirwee in 1967, and supported by a birth certificate. Bedford himself signed a sworn statement along similar lines at the same time. To further substantiate the year, it can be shown that William Bedford sold his Waitohi farm in December 1903 and went to live at Apsley, Darfield, where he resided for the rest of his life.

The Waitohi Flat Library next to the school used to be open each Monday evening. Thomas Edwin Hide clearly recalled the excitement at the next library night when 'all the talk of the meeting was about Pearse's flight'. He thought the meeting was on the same day as the flight attempt. If this were confirmable it would be further evidence for

1902, when 31 March did fall on Monday. Hide also remembered that Pearse was taken off to hospital 'in a slightly dazed condition' after hitting the hedge.

A retired publican of Timaru, Michael McAteer (Nellie's brother), remembered the time of the flight for he was taken by his father to see the plane perched on the hedge. 'I am able to date it because it was the year I started school at Waitohi. It was just after the harvest in 1903.' Miss Ethel Bourn of Timaru who went to school at Waitohi at the end of 1899 believed — without documentary support — that she had spent three years at school when the flight took place. So (independently of the April Fool conversation) this puts the date at about 1903. Ted Hide, who knew Pearse well, was firmly of the opinion that the flight took place in 1903, judging this — again without confirmatory data — from the time he went to Waitohi after leaving school.

Mrs Louie Johnson, before the Bedford affidavit was filed, gave much useful evidence to George Bolt about the flight, especially about the behaviour of the plane in the air, and proved to be one of the most alert witnesses interviewed. She believed that the takeoff took place well before she left Waitohi to live on the Rosewill Estate subdivision in May 1904. The Timaru and Temuka papers show that applications were invited for the Rosewill block in January 1904 and the ballot took place on 18 March. So while Mrs Johnson was of the view that 1903 was the year, her sighting could have conceivably been (in terms of the Rosewill deadline) in 1904.

Warne Pearse settled for 1903 without giving reasons. Tom Wade of Rangitata Island said that the flight took place in 1903 because he was still at school and being taught by Miss Crowley — who left the distrct in September of that year. Steve Smith was sure the event was before the 1903 snowstorm. Michael Friel was positive it happened within a year of the end of the Boer War. (The plane Friel remembered had a wing span of about six metres and a chord of about two and a half metres. He also thought the canvas covering was stretched under the wing rather than over it. So this may be a later configuration.)

The anecdote about the potato pickers is itself a useful indication that 1903 (or 1902) may have been the date, for contemporary newspaper reports suggest that the South Canterbury potato harvests of 1904–5 were virtually wiped out by Irish Blight. The Fraser sisters themselves remembered that the incident happened before the Rosewill Estate was subdivided.

Frank Biggs of Taiko remembered his teacher at Fairview School,

Mrs Ritchie, telling the children that Pearse had flown. Biggs, later to marry a Hullen from the farm next to Trewarlet, thought the date was about 1902–4. Frank Agnew and Mrs Alice Pettigrew recalled that pupils from Pleasant Point heard about Pearse crashing and some crossed the river to have a look for themselves. Neither could date the occasion. Jim Connell, Jim Chapman, William Moore and John Fraser remembered the flight attempt but could not date it. Mrs Dan Friel (neé Connell) also testified: 'I saw the flight of Pearse's aeroplane from the road from a distance. I clearly remember the machine in the air.' But she could not be sure of the date either.

Neither George Bolt nor any of those who probed the territory later have turned up much evidence to confirm a 1904 dating for Pearse's first flight attempt. Warne Pearse describes one episode which might date from 1904, but it is uncertain. Bolt in interviewing Daniel Connell was told of one attempted takeoff which Connell thought took place when he was about twelve. As Connell was born in 1892 Bolt assumed that 1904 was an approximate date, but enquiries since then have shown that Connell was referring to another flight trial on the road by Pearse's farm and the date was more likely 1906. James Campbell of Geraldine remembered two flight trials but could not date them closer than between 1904 and 1906.

Several others from Waitohi and elsewhere who either saw the flight or heard about it at the time would not commit themselves to any date at all. Nearly all those interviewed have maintained that Pearse got his plane off the ground well before any news of the American flights reached them — not that this clarified the position much, for news of the Wright brothers' achievement was not common knowledge until about 1908, even in the United States.

From all this evidence, both documentary and circumstantial, it would appear that Tuesday 31 March 1903 is the most likely date for Richard Pearse's historic takeoff. This is the conclusion George Bolt had tentatively arrived at by mid-1958, and none of the research since has done anything but consolidate that view. It was the discovery of the two letters by Pearse, the only written statements known to have been made by the inventor on his own part in flight history, which completely upset Bolt's calculations. They also discouraged him from making any further serious study of Pearse's achievement.

The offending letters were found late in 1958 in an old scrapbook belonging to Mrs Ruth Gilpin, Richard's sister. For some years no one was able to tell when or where these letters had been published. Eventually the author (having borrowed the scrapbook) took the step of steaming the cuttings off their cardboard mounts. It was then possible to date and locate each letter from newspaper evidence on the reverse side. The first of these letters was written in 1915, during the First World War, to the editor of Dunedin's *Evening Star*. Pearse was then farming near Milton in South Otago. The second letter was written in 1928 to the editor of the *Star* in Christchurch, when Pearse was living at Woolston. The Milton letter was written in answer to two science articles published earlier by the *Evening Star* on the evolution of aerodynamics, whereas the Christchurch letter was in response to an article on the history of New Zealand aviation. Both letters are reproduced in full in Appendices I and II.

Pearse's motive in writing each time is apparently 'to show that New Zealand brains anticipated the essential features of the aeroplane', a possibility which the two journalists seem to have overlooked. He also claims that all his own 'experimenting in aerial navigation' was pioneer work 'and deserved to be recorded'. His tone in these letters, which add up to a little over a metre of column space, is reasonable, unassuming and frank. The letters are well written and show that the writer is an orderly thinker and able to write with detachment about matters that intimately concern him.

He concedes at once that the Wright brothers beat him to it as far as extended and controlled flight was concerned. Modestly he refers to his own performances as experiments rather than flights. All he wishes to take credit for is being the first to use ailerons, a pneumatic-tyred tricycle undercarriage, nosewheel steering, and direct transmission to the propeller. These claims will be studied later; the critical issue to be investigated here is the date which Pearse himself gives his first trials.

At this point Richard Pearse of his own accord seems to torpedo any case for a 1903 flight. Both his letters give 1904 as the year. 'After Langley's failure in 1903,' he wrote from Milton, 'I was still of [the] opinion that aerial navigation was possible, and I started out to solve the problem about March 1904.' In his Christchurch letter he changed the month but not the year. So he deals 1903 a double blow. One, with his reiterated selection of 1904 as the year he began his experiments; the other, with his reference to Langley. Langley's *Aerodrome* crashed twice in 1903 — on 7 October and 8 December — and Pearse suggests he did not start work until after this.

If we are to take Pearse literally on this issue, it is hard to imagine even a 31 March 1904 takeoff. It would have been virtually impossible for him with shearing and the summer grain harvest to cope with as well, to have constructed his engine and plane by such primitive work-shed methods and had it airborne within that space of time — not unless he had already done a great deal of preliminary work which he does not mention. It is otherwise difficult to account for the many months of preparation and testing of which witnesses speak. If he was relying on the *Scientific American* for details of Langley's flight experiments, an account of the first crash on the Potomac (in the 17 October 1903 issue) would not have reached Pearse until nearly Christmas 1903 — giving the inventor only some three months to get his machine built and mobile. In fact, if Pearse started only after he had heard about Langley it would be hard to accept even 1905 for a 'flight' date.

Gibbs-Smith, with some justice, initially took the hard line on any suggestion that Pearse could have been in the air as early as 1903. 'No one will ever accept that his memory was at fault when he twice says that 1904 was the date of the first experiments and ties it in with Langley. No so-called eyewitness statements can ever stand against those remarks he made about himself.' It was for this reason, too, that George Bolt appears to have thrown in his hand, though he had less evidence than we have now and little corroborative dating for it.

Eyewitness accounts and years-after recollections certainly have to be treated with a healthy scepticism, and if there were only one or two such reminiscences to pinpoint the issue they could be written off as the errors of old age. But we cannot lightly shrug off the datable testimony of the much larger number of persons who claim to have seen Pearse perform in 1903; or who remember and can date the reaction in Waitohi at the time. Only one of the witnesses mentioned (Warne) was related to Pearse and none of the others could be described as a devoted friend or suspected of partisanship. Most were highly sceptical of the aviator and his ambition, and one or two thought to the end of their days that he was quite crazy.

Moreover, the witnesses, who had dispersed to many parts of New Zealand, were interviewed separately by several researchers between 1954 and 1972. There was little chance of collaboration anywhere, and none of the witnesses had any special reason to perjure himself. All were of sound mind when questioned, though undoubtedly elderly. What is more, a surprising number of the recollections can be dated by one means or other.

A historian may well be dubious about testimony which maintains that something happened 'just before' or 'just after' a particular event, even if that event can be accurately placed. At best such dating methods can only be approximate, although an accumulation of such estimates — as with Pearse — can be of use. If the dating device involved a 'cut-off point' (such as Nellie McAteer's Education Board document, Basil Bedford's birth certificate, or Miss Crowleys' departure from Upper Waitohi School) then it has to be taken seriously. And there are later flight attempts during this same year which one can end-date by a similar means. Thus 1903 cannot be dismissed categorically despite Pearse's own words on the subject.

But there is no case for pressing on regardless unless some attempt can be made to explain why he dated his experiments as he did in his letters. These are some possibilities.

For a start, Pearse himself might have got the year wrong. He too was, after all, trying to recall this pioneer work from a distance. When the Public Trust Office at Christchurch itemised his belongings after he had been taken to hospital in 1951, there was no sign anywhere of a diary, private letters, photographs, plans, blueprints, farm logbook, or any other documents dating from the times in question. Nor was there any way of dating the material which had survived on his second plane. Pearse simply did not keep records of this sort and was working from memory just as all the other witnesses have been. If he had any firm dates to work from he himself would not have been so tentative. His use of 'about' to prefix both dates he gives scarcely makes the statements definitive.

Next, it is likely that he discounted his earlier experiments as not being worthy of mention for they had not been, in his opinion, a success. In his Milton letter he implies quite clearly that he was working on a plane of his own before the Wright brothers' maiden flights. 'I only built one aeroplane, which was designed before anyone had made a flight.' This utterance by no means lessens the possibility that he may have been testing his flying machine as early as 1901. As Warne later explained, his brother would talk to no one about his experiments until the results came up to his expectations. And they hardly ever did. 'Dick wanted to make the job a complete success first.' In a 1961 affidavit Warne states: 'My brother worked entirely on his own and did not desire in the early stages to show anyone what he was doing, nor did he wish at that stage that the newspapers be informed.'

The suspicion that Pearse may have discounted his 1903 experiments as a preliminary to a more earnest attempt to perfect his aircraft

in 1904 is strengthened by his refusal to acknowledge the Wright brothers' 1903 flights. Elsewhere he describes their first attempts to fly as
unsucccessful as he believed (erroneously) that they had used 'a special
launching apparatus'. So he writes ' . . . I started out to solve the problem about March 1904. The Wrights started at about the same time.'
There was quite enough known after 1908 about the Wrights' four
flights of 17 December 1903 for Pearse to have included them in his letters of 1915 and 1928 if he had thought they deserved it.

Even the use of the word 'solve', in relation to grappling with the
problems of powered flight, implies a late stage in the process. It suggests that the preliminaries were over and the final effort (possibly the
drawing up of the patent specifications) in sight. In other words, he may
have been dating what he believed to be the finalising of his aeroplane
rather than the preparatory work.

The reference to Langley now makes better sense in regard to all
this, for Pearse suggests that the Wrights did not set out to 'solve the
problem' either, until Langley had failed. Yet by 1915 Pearse must have
known that the Wrights had started experimenting long before this. If
he was subscribing to the *Scientific American* he would have learned this
from as early as the 22 February 1902 issue when an article on Wilbur
Wright's 'Some Aeronautical Experiments' lecture says that Wilbur ' . . .
was drawn to the study of aeronautical problems a number of years ago,
and his active interest dates back to the death of Lilienthal in 1896'.
The article goes on to mention that the brothers tried some experiments in North Carolina in 1900 (actually they had begun the year
before in August 1899 by building their biplane kit). James Collier,
whose articles provoked Pearse's letter, also refers to Wilbur Wright's
1901 lecture on wing-warping.

In short, by the time Pearse came to write his letters he must have
known that the Americans had been working on the problems of flight
since 1899–1900. Therefore, when he has them setting out to 'solve the
problem' in 1904 he must be deliberately disregarding all their preliminary experimentation. It is not unreasonable to argue, then, that he was
treating his own preparatory work similarly. And his early efforts could
just as easily date back to 1899, as there is evidence to suggest.

The phrase Pearse uses in his Milton letter about the impact on him
of Langley's failure, that he 'was *still* of the opinion that aerial navigation was possible', also would suggest that he was working on the idea
before Langley's two misadventures in October and December 1903.

To the average historian it must certainly be disconcerting to find the latter-day statements of witnesses being preferred to the document-ed words of the inventor himself. And the notion would be quite un-tenable if Pearse's words on the subject dated from the time of his experiments. But they do not. Thus his recollections scarcely have the same cast-iron certainty about them as the meticulous day-by-day records of the Wright brothers. Also, it is not so much a question of dis-believing Pearse as of trying to interpret what he meant by 'solving the problem' and 'flying'.

There are enough anomalies and contradictions in the texts of his two letters to make it a risk for anyone to be over-dogmatic about their meaning. Though no one should prefer other forms of evidence to the words of Pearse himself, the doubt still lingers that he made a mistake or that he has been misunderstood.

Unless some totally new data turn up — a diary reference, a dated letter, an undiscovered newspaper report, a lost notebook, an inscribed photograph or something else of an irrefutable nature — the question of when Pearse first got aloft will never be resolved to everybody's satisfac-tion. But in the meantime there is a more than healthy chance that 31 March 1903 was the date.

9. Further trials

Nor is this the end of the possibilities for 1903. It is almost certain that other Pearse takeoffs or tentative flights took place. One of these, witnessed by the late J.W. Casey of Waipawa, reads as though it might have been the most vital flying episode of Pearse's career. The only present evidence for what happened was submitted to the Geraldine County Council on 22 August 1967 by John Casey in the form of a letter which answered questions put to him by Geoff Rodliffe on behalf of Joseph Coll.

According to Casey, who was a lad of only seven at the time, quite a crowd gathered in the vicinity of Pearse's farm to watch this flight attempt. 'I should think about thirty were present but I'm not too clear on that . . . ' It was not long after Pearse's first takeoff and the news had got around that there was to be another free show. Casey remembered that Miss Crowley, then the teacher at Upper Waitohi School, let her pupils out to see this 'flight'. The *Temuka Leader* of 17 September 1903 records Miss Crowley's departure: 'The Social held in the Waitohi School room recently was an unqualified success. Mr R. Williams presented Miss Crowley, the teacher, who is leaving the school for a well earned promotion, with a gold bar brooch, and a greenstone and gold charm pin.'

John Casey thought this particular 'flight' was in March 1903, but it is unlikely to have preceded Pearse's first effort down the Main Waitohi Road. It is more probable that, allowing Pearse time to get his plane off the gorse hedge and patched up a little, it took place in April or May before the winter started. At any rate it must have happened before Miss Crowley left in September 1903.

Richard Pearse's 40-hectare property was situated in the angle of Main Waitohi Road and Galbraith Road and the 'flight' in question was made from the corner paddock. John Casey's evidence is that Pearse's plane, after a short run of about three chains (60 metres), took off from a slightly elevated part of the paddock. It then rose to about eighteen

70

metres and flew two and a half circuits of the field before landing on top of the gorse hedge separating the corner paddock from his workshop paddock. Casey thought the whole episode lasted 'about ten minutes'. J.D. Coll, who located this witness and who subsequently questioned Casey more closely about the evidence, believed that the distance Pearse covered was about two and a half kilometres and that this was a controlled flight. When Pearse hit the gorse he was actually bringing the aircraft into a landing, but apparently misjudged the height of the hedge. Coll did not think that this landing — which caused no damage to the aircraft — disqualified Pearse's performance from being termed a controlled flight. Miss Wanaka Hullen remembered being shown, as a child, Pearse's plane perched on this paddock fence with the undercarriage deeply embedded in the gorse.

Although John Casey thought that about thirty persons witnessed this flight trial, his version is the only one that has so far been recorded. His testimony covers other details that are interesting: Casey was the first to describe the syrup-tin insert in the plane's wing; he believed the plane had a three-bladed propeller (Pearse tried several sorts of propeller so this may have been so); he noted correctly that the tricycle undercarriage had its single wheel in front. But his estimate of the time taken to fly the distance described seems greatly excessive. So, indeed, does the distance itself and Pearse's height off the ground. And, rather perversely, Casey describes the engine as being behind the pilot, rather than in front. He later changed his mind on this point.

As Richard Pearse's paddock is nearer to the downs than are the school crossroads, there is a possibility that the potato incident refers to John Casey's 'flight' rather than to the first takeoff. There may even be a chance that this is the occasion Warne Pearse spoke of where the 'flywheel' flew off. Casey believed it was Warne who spun the propeller but Warne never mentioned any flight of Casey's dimensions. If Warne had seen anything as impressive as two and a half circuits of a large paddock he would surely have referred to it somewhere, even if he had only heard about it. But apparently he did not and had not.

John Casey suggested that Dan Connell, Stewart Baxter, Robert and Tom Wade and Frank Friel may have seen it happen. Connell, Baxter and the Wade brothers described different flight attempts, however, from Casey's; and Frank Friel died before he could be questioned.

It is most tantalising to have so little testimony on this performance by Pearse. One, as yet, uncorroborated account is not nearly sufficient to clinch the case. If Casey's description could be authenticated,

Richard Pearse's round-the-paddock flight would have to be taken as the first controlled flight in the world by a powered aeroplane. It would also predate the first circular flight, which was made by Wilbur Wright on 20 September 1904. But there seems little chance of such authentication.

The principal objections to Casey's evidence are his extreme youth at the time and the fact that Pearse himself made no mention of such a flight. It is understandable that a 71-year-old witness might distort, exaggerate or misrepresent something he saw at the age of seven; but there was no need for him to completely invent what he saw. He had not seen Pearse since 1904, was no friend of the aviator's and had no personal axe to grind. There is no doubt that he saw Pearse's aircraft airborne to some extent or other, even if the details of what he thought he witnessed are arguable. Gibbs-Smith thinks that Casey may have been watching Pearse experimenting with a model plane, or with a ballasted plane guided by pre-set controls. These explanations are feasible, though there is no supporting evidence for Pearse ever having worked in this way.

There are two methods of end-dating what Casey saw. The first is his belief that Miss Crowley was his teacher at the time. (Two others with memories of Pearse's first experiments — Tom Wade and Stewart Baxter — have recalled independently that Miss Crowley was their teacher then.) Miss Crowley left the district in September 1903. The other deadline is Casey's own departure from the district: both Casey's parents, William and Margaret, balloted for a farm property in the Chamberlains subdivision some thirty kilometres inland from Waitohi, near Albury. Lands and Survey Records show that 'Mrs Margaret Casey's application for Section 3 (Chamberlains) Block II, Opawa Survey District (211 acres) was successful as from 19 March 1903.' William went to Chamberlains on his own, stocked the farm and got a home built. Margaret Casey and eight children stayed for a while with a neighbour in Lower Waitohi before shifting to the new farm in June 1904 once the house had been completed. John Casey did not see Pearse again.

Soon after Casey's sighting, another flight is alleged to have been made by Pearse. This time it was from a nine-metre terrace on what is now Malcolm Cone's property near the cutting that leads down to the Saleyards Bridge, which crossed the Opihi River from Lower Waitohi to Pleasant Point. Robert Gibson, later of Auckland, witnessed this flight as a child of about nine. He was fairly sure it took place on Easter Saturday 1903, which fell on 12 April in that year.

Gibson had, since April 1964, when he made a statement to the Museum of Transport and Technology, been interviewed by Joseph Coll, Geoff Rodliffe, d'E.C. Darby, and Hamish Keith of the New Zealand Broadcasting Corporation (NZBC). Gibson, a sprightly and alert septuagenarian, acquitted himself confidently on all occasions and the following are excerpts from his conversations with Darby and Keith:

How did I see the machine flying? I used to muck around with my brother Ramsay, the brother older than myself. The youths of the village had followed the construction of this machine and they evidently knew that Pearse was going to fly it from a paddock, so of course about half a dozen of those boys gathered round to see Pearse — what shall we say? — break his neck, and I was with Ramsay.

Well there were a couple of horses and a dray and this contraption. Pearse started his machine and ran it down hill. I suppose his idea was to get it into the air but he didn't. He got it into this clump of gorse. He didn't leave the ground at all. Well the boys pulled it out of the gorse fence and straightened the prop which had been bent and then they got it back about fifty yards from the cliff face along the Opihi River. Apparently he reckoned if he could get off the ground he could fly and that was the reason why he went over the cliff. They had a good inspection. All the boys and him walked over it [the ground] for half an hour.

Then he got the engine going which was a frightening noise, and the boys started pushing to get him some speed up, and about halfway towards the cliff — that would be about a chain — it was going too fast for them to keep up with it and away he went and we watched him until he turned. We saw him in the air over the cliff, turning. He turned to go up the river. Well then we cut across the paddock diagonally about halfway from where he started, to where he landed. We could watch from the cliff where he was just gradually going downwards. He flew anything up to half a mile from where he was pushed, up the river, and eventually fell in the river just alongside a pine plantation. Pearse clambered out of that — of course we didn't see that — but we saw him climbing up the river bank into a clump of blackberries.

In his description filed with the Auckland Museum of Transport and Technology, Gibson estimated the flight as lasting 1200 metres and said the plane broke up on landing.

This 'flight', if it did take place as narrated, may best be described as a powered glide, with the plane descending all the while. Gibson could not remember whether there was a gain in height at takeoff, so it is safer to assume that the plane just shot straight off the edge of the terrace. But it must have had enough speed and stability for flight, otherwise it would have plunged straight down into the riverbed. The course to the right is significant, as the plane had on previous occasions shown a tendency to veer to the left. Somehow Pearse may have learned to correct this aberration, perhaps by a refinement of his flight control system. Robert Gibson recalled a vertical rudder at the back of the aircraft which, in combination with his steering airbakes, could have made the difference. Pearse mentions such a vertical rudder in both his provisional patent specification of 1906 and in his letters.

How did Gibson pinpoint the date so confidently? 'If you could find out the date Ramsay shot Alex Agnew's bull, you have the date. It was in the same school holidays. I am certain it was 1903 because Ramsay turned fourteen just shortly afterwards and had to go to work straight away . . . Also that snowstorm was shortly after this flight.'

Robert Gibson had a photo in his possession showing Ramsay skinning dead sheep in the Mackenzie Country following the disastrous snowstorm of July 1903. There is a reasonable chance, on this evidence, that the Terrace 'flight' took place when Gibson said it did.

Obviously, the researcher cannot make much use of Gibson's bull-baiting recollections, and this part of Gibson's dating system cannot now be confirmed. Yet the events of the day are described in such convincing detail and they match the locale so well that it is not easy to dismiss them as a youthful hallucination.

If Pearse does not mention this occasion either it is not surprising, for it was not a flight according to his own criteria. When asked what had happened to the other witnesses Gibson replied that they were mostly older than he was and had since died or he had lost track of them.

It has long been a legend at Waitohi that Pearse made a 'terrace flight'. Hearsay accounts, quite unrelated to Gibson's, have come in from several sources in the district. Gibbs-Smith, like others, believes that Pearse would have been quite crazy to attempt to fly off a cliff with such little experience. He suggests, as with Casey's 'flight', that Pearse may have been using a model or a ballasted aircraft. Again this is feasible, though there is no corroborative evidence for such experiments.

The most puzzling aspect of Gibson's recollections is his description of the plane. His comments, added up, point to a much smaller plane than elsewhere reported and constructed along different lines, more like a Blériot, perhaps. He told Darby in 1970: 'All the frame was iron and the wing was covered with a piece of an old canvas tarpaulin. That I am sure of. The engine [which] he built himself was down low and he drove the propeller with bike chains. It was a monoplane [and] he was sitting above and in front of the wings and actually looking through the propeller and the engine was in front of him again. The whole thing wouldn't have been more than twelve feet across the wings. The tail was very much after the present style.'

Gibson gave Joseph Coll other details: that the ends of the wings were rounded though the leading and trailing edges were straight, that there were two wheels to the undercarriage and a skid under the tail; and that the wing frame was of tubular piping.

Though Pearse is known to have modified the shape and style of his first plane a number of times it is hard to believe that he could have altered it so drastically in the short time elapsing between his school crossroads takeoff and the terrace episode. It can only be concluded that Gibson's present memory of what he observed as a boy is faulty, or that his recollection of the plane has been affected by what he has seen of other planes since, or that the event took place at a much later date. Dan Connell recalls a Pearse aircraft somewhat similar to Gibson's dating from about 1906.

This terrace takeoff may be the 'flight' which Arthur Tozer claims he saw from the Opihi riverbed. Pearse 'flew' over his head and Tozer thought he landed back on the terrace, but Stratford's plantation probably cut off Tozer's view and he was merely speculating. Other than a few stumps, there is nothing left of the plantation now, and a new traffic bridge replacing the old Saleyards Bridge has now been built across that part of the river in which Pearse is said to have crashed his plane.

George Bolt unearthed another account of a flight attempt from the Opihi terrace. According to this description by an unnamed witness, the flight covered about 400 metres down the bed of the river. It appears that the plane was controlled to fly along the winding course of the river, between the willow trees which lined both banks, but it was unable to climb over the trees. As the takeoff was from a high bank and as the aircraft flew downstream there may not have been a gain of height during this flight. It is not known when this particular terrace takeoff took place. But for the fact that the directions taken in these two flights are diametrically opposite, it might be suspected that they are different versions of the same event. It is hard to doubt, however, that Richard Pearse at some time or other made at least one attempt to fly off the river terrace.

As he preferred to work without an audience, most of his taxiing and hopping was done within the secluded limits of his own farm. There are, accordingly, several reports of takeoffs which he made on his farm possibly between 1902 and 1904. But the surface of his farm was too undulating to make taxiing easy, so he tried his plane out in various localities nearby. Bert Smart, who was an in-law of the Pearses, understood that Richard made a takeoff from a farm paddock higher up Galbraith's Road where it begins to ascend Spur Hut ridge. Running his plane downhill Pearse managed to get airborne for a short distance before crashing into a fence. This episode cannot be accurately dated, but it is thought to have been one of his early flight attempts.

It may be the same exploit recorded by D.A. Gregan of Te Aroha in a letter to Bolt. Gregan grew up at Pleasant Valley near Geraldine and his family were friends of the Hallys, who lived at Waitohi. The Gregans drove over to Waitohi to visit the Hally family one autumn about Easter time. No year was mentioned.

> Anyway on the second day of our visit we all drove up to Mr Pearse's farm to have a look at the flying machine which had been tried out a few days before we inspected it. Mr Tom Hally explained to me that the machine had been towed up to the highest point in a nice sloping paddock by a horse. When the machine was all ready it started off down the hill and after a chain or two it rose off the ground and flew for about forty yards. The wind had blown it off its straight course, it hit a wire fence and landed in the neighbour's paddock. The propeller was damaged and other parts of it were badly strained. When we saw it, it was laid up awaiting repairs. He, Mr Pearse, had often tried flying before we inspected it but that was the most successful flight he had made up till then.

The last comment is not to be taken too seriously. Most witnesses seem certain that the particular 'flight' they were associated with was the best effort Pearse made, or the first, or the final one.

Harry Stoakes of Temuka was brought up in Lower Waitohi and

remembered seeing Pearse make two flight attempts down the Galbraith Road edge of his south-east paddock some time — he believed — in 1903. Stoakes was about ten at the time. Watching from the road he saw Pearse make one run down the fence line, rise briefly into the air and taxi to a stop. Apparently not satisfied with the performance he made an adjustment of some sort to the propeller, pushed the plane back to its starting point at the end of the paddock and tried again. This time the machine sailed higher into the air but did not clear the gorse fence on his Main Waitohi Road boundary and crashed on top of it. Harry Stoakes' sister was riding her horse up the road towards Upper Waitohi next day when they came upon the crashed aeroplane. The animal got such a fright at seeing the strange device on the hedge top that it refused to go past.

Apart from a difference over the paddock used, this takeoff account bears some similarity to the one recorded by Cis Connell which she dated at 1902. But it is likely that Pearse made several flight attempts from within his farm and the fact that so many of his efforts were thwarted by gorse hedges is not to be wondered at. The whole of Waitohi, like any other pioneer Canterbury settlement of this vintage, was crisscrossed by gorse hedges — the only form of fencing most farmers could afford. Not only were the narrow roads lined with gorse but most of the farms were also fenced off into four- or eight-hectare paddocks by gorse hedges. It would be difficult to fly in any direction at all without making the acquaintance of one gorse hedge or another. Certainly by the time Pearse had finished with his flying career, he must have acquired a far more intimate knowlege of gorse hedges than was agreeable to him.

The last 1903 sighting is presumed to have been in May. Alexander Amos Martin of Temuka, shortly before his death in 1970, vividly recalled the occasion he was returning home down the Main Waitohi Road past Richard Pearse's farm after spending a day chaffcutting at Dick Connell's: 'I noticed a weird construction in Pearse's paddock composed of bamboo rods and bike wheels. It taxied fifty yards, rose ten to fifteen feet, flew fifty yards, then crashed into a hedge. I got on my bike and hightailed it off!'

In a celebrated *Town and Around* interview for CHTV3 in 1969, Martin was asked what he thought of Richard Pearse.

'I thought he was a silly bugger,' replied Amos, after a well considered pause.

Amos Martin left Temuka for Nightcaps in Southland in August 1903 and was convinced that the crash he witnesssed took place on the afternoon of 3 May 1903.

One resident with a particular interest in what Pearse was trying to do was Hugh S. McCully. Waitohi has produced several inventive souls in its century of settlement, including the Orr brothers, Dick Southby, Peter Hullen and Norman Chapman — all of whom showed a preference for farm machinery. But the most ingenious apart from Pearse was certainly Hugh McCully, Irish born, who bought a farm on Palm Hills in 1901 and later on in 1907 moved to Downlands in Lower Waitohi. Though he left the district in 1922 and lived thereafter in Temuka, Peel Forest and Timaru, he was at Waitohi during Pearse's first creative years.

Hugh McCully later acquired a considerable reputation through his writings on archaeology and for his knowledge of Maori prehistory in South Canterbury. But while he was at Waitohi his principal passion was farm mechanics. In 1917 he invented the hustler (a new type of drag harrow) and followed this up in quick succession with patents for a plough lift, combined cultivator, sower and intercultivator, nine-tine hustler and tractor attachment. He also devised his own seed-cleaning plant, a browntop stripper, a bird trap and a hydraulic water ram.

It appears that McCully was one of the few in whom Richard Pearse was able to confide. In truth he was at that time the only neighbour apart from the Orrs with enough mechanical insight to follow what Pearse was trying to do. He spent quite a lot of time watching Pearse tinkering about in his workshop. Once Pearse asked him if he would like to fly the plane but Hugh, who was going to get married shortly, declined the offer. He had too much to lose if the machine landed on something less pliable than a gorse hedge. Department of Justice records show that Hugh McCully was married at Temuka on 17 June 1903.

On 11 July 1903, Pearse took off again in his aircraft. The episode was not observed as far as is known, but the plane was later seen by witnesses resting once more upon the gorse hedge at the bottom of his farm. It must have been late in the day when he crashed because he left the plane where it was. That night a snowstorm struck unexpectedly after a mild day, coating Waitohi in 30–45 cm of snow, the only fall of any kind between 1902 and 1905. The snow and subsequent frost led to bitterly cold weather for some time and old residents remember how it killed off both stock and bluegum trees in the district. The 'big snow' it is still called. The *Timaru Herald* and local meteorological records date the snowstorm accurately, and thus the flight attempt. The snow depth at nearby Temuka was described in the *Timaru Herald* as being the worst in living memory. At Pleasant Point, just over the river, it was 22 cm deep. At Orari, it lay on the ground for a fortnight.

So the machine stayed on the hedge for several days until the snow-drifts melted, and it was seen stranded there by several people. It cannot be discovered whether Pearse, on this occasion, had taken off from his farm or from the road, but as it was midwinter the road would have pro-vided a firmer surface. Steve Smith was one who remembered Pearse's plane on the hedge in the snow. The memory was vivid as he had some trouble coaxing his horse along the road past the stranded aircraft.

If Pearse was keeping an eye on the *Scientific American* he might have seen in the 17 October 1903 issue already referred to, the full-page account illustrated by four photographs, of the failure of Langley's *Aerodrome*. The attempts by C.L. Manley to launch Professor Langley's plane off the top of a houseboat moored in the Potomac are described with some vigour, and suitable consolation is offered: 'Prof. Langley, despite his failure, deserves his full meed of praise for the earnest attempt which he has made to solve a problem which has puzzled in-ventors ever since the days of Icarus . . . That it should have failed is to be regarded simply as one step in the solution of the problem of aerial navigation, and not altogether as an abject failure.'

After further repairs and modifications, Warne remembered that his brother ' . . . then decided to try to take off in his paddock instead of the road, because there was a slight bank over which he hoped to take off. However, there was a mishap with a flywheel [propeller blade?] which flew off and cut a swathe forty-five feet through standing wheat'. This is how Warne Pearse managed to place this incident in or near the month of February 1904.

The anecdote resembles one from Stewart Baxter, who described how he and his brother were ploughing a paddock near where Richard Pearse was working on his plane: 'We put it in oats for him. I was talk-ing to my brother afterwards and he reckoned one of the blades from the propeller shot off and cut a swathe through the paddock of oats where he was testing the machine. It is not clear from either story whether the plane was in the air or on the ground at the time the blade flew off.

When Richard Pearse learned (possibly by way of the *Scientifc American* of 11 June 1904) that the Wright brothers had flown it was, in Warne's words, 'a sad awakening'. A bitter disappointment might be nearer the mark.

A studio photograph of Richard Pearse taken at about this time shows a young man in his twenties dressed for a formal occasion in a tall butterfly collar, broadly knotted tie, high lapelled jacket and with an extremely determined look on his face. He was quite handsome in a lean, intense sort of way, with short curly brown hair, thin lips, straight nose, strong jaw, and a penetrating visionary gleam in the eye. Certainly not the kind of person, at first glance, who would abandon a cherished project easily.

Pearse now concentrated, it seems, on the theoretical side of his work: getting it down on paper. The aviation experiments continued, though at a diminished level. Witnesses remember the paddock trials he made intermittently, and his attempts to improve the control of his aeroplane lasted at least until 1906.

A flight attempt witnessed by Daniel Connell, later of Christchurch, seems to date from 1906. The Connells lived by the Upper Waitohi School crossroads and Dan was the youngest. In 1906, when the Upper school closed down temporarily owning to a shortage of pupils, Dan was transferred for his last year or two of schooling to Waitohi Flat School. It was about the time of the transfer, Dan Connell believed, that he saw the takeoff concerned.

The event took place, as Dan remembered it, just a short distance down the Main Waitohi Road from Pearse's farm, near the Terrace Road turnoff. Dick Williams and Jack Connell helped Richard to push the plane across his workshop paddock to the road gate. They then lifted the machine through the gate to clear the gateposts and wheeled it down towards a dip in the road. Jack Connell does not think that the plane weighed more than 77 kg. Pearse swung the prop himself while Dick and Jack held the plane back. When the propeller was turning fast enough they let the machine go. The plane took off and after taxiing a short distance Pearse took off, hopped about forty metres, then swerved leftwards and crashed into yet another gorse hedge.

Pearse was disappointed but unhurt. With the Connells' help he hauled the plane out of the hedge and wheeled it back to the farm. Dan Connell remembered that the plane was about three and a half metres across, that it was easy to lift, that it had a four-bladed propeller and that its slender rectangular wings were covered in grey canvas. In all, it sounds somewhat like Gibson's account of the plane. Richard Pearse himself was at that time 'tall, dark and slim, with a little moe [moustache]. Nice and quiet. You would pass him by on the road and he would hardly see you. Thinking all the time. We all thought him a bit silly trying to fly.'

Mrs F.H. Halligan wrote to Bolt about her father, T.P.D. Mee of the Levels, who was a government inspector of stock and noxious weeds. For the latter reason he probably had to do regular business with Richard Pearse: 'Many many times my Dad spoke of an aeroplane he had seen in a shed at Waitohi and how interesting it was . . . And my father always spoke of the plane in an awed voice.'

Bert Smart remembered visiting Pearse at his workshop shortly before travelling north to the Christchurch Exhibition in 1906. Bert was with the Allen brothers, who usually got the contract to cut Pearse's oat crop. The aviator offered to show the boys how his plane worked and he put it through a static test. The plane was held fast by ropes attached to posts driven into the ground. 'Dick Pearse got the engine started and revved it up. The whole thing shook so much I thought it would fall to bits.'

On 19 July 1906, Henry Hughes Ltd, the patent and trademarks agency in Wellington which had earlier handled Pearse's bicycle invention, submitted to the Patent Office on its client's behalf a patent specification of considerably greater daring and potential. It was for 'An Improved Aerial or Flying Machine'. The preamble ran as follows:

I, Richard William Pearse, of Upper Waitohi, Temuka, in the Colony of New Zealand, Farmer, do hereby declare the nature of my invention for 'an improved aerial or flying machine' to be as follows;

My invention relates to aerial machines, and it is my object to provide a machine that will be capable of floating in the air, without the aid of an attached balloon.

To carry the invention into effect, I employ an aeroplane [i.e. wing] and means whereby same may be adjusted to any angle to suit the conditions of the atmosphere, as well as provision for a light engine to enable the machine to be propelled.

Pearse was at last in business. Or aiming to be.

10. The 1906 patent

To obtain a New Zealand patent in 1906 under the terms of legislation passed in 1889 and 1890 it was usual first to file a provisional specification. This reserved the rights of applicants long enough for them to investigate the practical and commercial aspects of their inventions. A provisional specification did not need to be detailed provided that the nature and purpose of the invention were described.

The complete specification of the invention, which was to be filed within nine months from the date of filing the provisional specification, had to detail the construction and operation of whatever was being patented. It also had to conclude with the claim or claims which gave the invention its uniqueness, so as to define precisely the scope of the monopoly to be afforded by the eventual patent. Where possible an illustration of the invention was expected. This illustration had to satisfy the requirements as to clarity, size and mode of execution, but did not need to be a full working drawing of the invention, nor did exact dimensions have to be supplied. If the complete specification fairly described the invention and conformed to other criteria laid down by the Patent Office, the application might then be approved for grant of a patent.

Richard Pearse filed his provisional specification for 'An Improved Aerial or Flying Machine', Patent Application No. 21476, on 19 July 1906. The complete specification was filed on 19 April 1907, the last day of the available nine-month period, although a one-month extension of this time was permitted. The Wellington firm of patent agents, Henry Hughes Ltd, prepared both specifications for him. One would expect a relatively complicated invention such as Pearse's plane to be illustrated by a formal drawing, but none was filed at this stage. Perhaps there was no sketch or photograph available for the patent firm to work from, although the language of the specification strongly suggests that there was. Or there may have been a sketch or photographs available on which a drawing could have been based but it arrived too late to be of use. This could have been because Pearse changed his mind or was uncertain about some aspects of the plane and sought to take full advantage of the time to clarify his thinking. Another possibility is that the patent agents simply decided not to file a formal drawing. (Unfortunately, there is no record of Pearse's correspondence with Henry Hughes Ltd. The firm's files were purged in 1950 before any interest in Pearse had developed.)

In July 1907, some three months later, a substitute complete specification was submitted to the Patent Office by Henry Hughes Ltd. This specification was accompanied by a formal drawing of the aeroplane. The text was altered in a minor fashion to include references to this drawing, and a system of lettering in both text and diagram served to identify particular features of the plane.

There are some differences between the provisional and the complete specifications. The latter covers certain features that are not described in the provisional application and omits other features which are. In the main the complete specification is more precise, more detailed and more helpful, as it was meant to be. Where the two texts differ most is in the nature and purpose of the control surfaces described. In other matters — the basic wing construction, carriage construction, undercarriage, pilot's seating position, keel, wing incidence control, airbrake construction and engine — the aircraft described in the two specifications are fundamentally the same machine.

Pearse's substitute complete specification of July 1907 continues to describe the plane as 'An Improved Aerial or Flying Machine' and the opening statement sums up the nature of his patent aircraft:

This invention relates to an improved construction of aerial or flying machine of the aeroplane type, which has been designed in order to provide for the more effective handling and directing of the machine. The invention consists in a special construction of frame for the sail or sheet of the machine by which construction the machine may be put together and taken apart with ease and quickness. In order to provide for its transport from place to place and by which, also, it may be freely adjusted upon the wheeled car which supports it while on the ground. Other improvements relate to the use of rudders or hinged vanes by means of which the machine may be guided while afloat in the air, to the use of a central keel piece extending along its top for assisting in the maintenance of its equilibrium, and also to a special construction of propellor [sic] by means of which the machine is propelled.

This specification sets out first of all to describe the wing, which is to be rectangular in shape and 'constructed of bamboo or other like material'. The drawing shows a rigid framework composed of straight boundary rods which are braced by intersecting double-rodded trusses. Both rods of each truss are arched outwards towards the middle so that when the fabric is attached to the upper surface of the framework 'it will assume a correspondingly rigid form that will cause it to somewhat resemble the form assumed by a bird's wings when soaring'. At the centre of the wing structure described in his earlier specification, where there is greatest distance between the bowed rods of each truss, the distance is stated to be three feet (90 cm). With a wing covering on the upper surface of the frame this would provide a maximum camber of 18 inches (45.7 cm).

The proportions of this rectangular wing, in which the chord is half the span, show it to be of low aspect-ratio. Though no dimensions are given in specifications or diagram, the size of the wing would be somewhere between three-metre chord with six-metre span and a four-and-a-half-metre chord with nine-metre span, calculated from the height of a hypothetical pilot seated in the carriage. These proportions are rather surprising in view of the research which Lilienthal, the Wrights and others had revealed, much of it based on the observation of bird flight. Most other aircraft inventors were aiming at a much more efficient ratio of five or six to one.

One feature of this wing which Pearse considered worth mentioning is that it can be 'taken apart with little trouble for packing purposes'. The provisional specification refers to 'adjustable pins' for securing the wing framework and bracing. Both Pearse's first and last planes could be dismantled for storage. Undoubtedly, he was thinking of his own convenience as much as anyone else's here, for neither at Waitohi nor Woolston did he have more than shed space for his planes.

The wing's covering is referred to in the complete specification as a 'sail', 'cloth' or 'sheet', but in the provisional 'some light material such as calico' is specified and calico is the material described in the *Temuka Leader* report of 1909. In any case calico is a much more appropriate wing fabric — in terms of both cost and weight — than the canvas of which some witnesses of his early flight attempts speak. The provisional specification indicated that the 'supporting surface' is stretched across and fastened to the framework, and the avian aerofoil effect Pearse was striving for could be achieved only with a covering over the top of the frame, in view of the apparently diamond-shaped cross-section of the wing. The central panel on the leading edge of the wing would be left uncovered to permit rotation of the propeller. The next panel back, situated over the engine, was in danger of catching fire each time the motor started. It is this panel which one witness described as being constructed of beaten-out syrup tins soldered together. As well, such a covering would better resist air turbulence from the propeller. The engine exhaust was probably angled upwards, through or over the wing, to prevent the pilot from being either gassed or scorched.

The only major discrepancy between the accounts in the two specifications of the basic wing structure is to be found in the provisional. There it is written, with reference to the wing, that 'the sides of same are slightly turned upwards so as to resemble a bird soaring with its wings raised at the tips'. It is difficult to imagine how this effect could be created with the basic wing structure described above, unless the fabric were attached to the undersurface of the wing instead of the upper, but this would not provide an efficient aerofoil. In addition, it would be hard enough, structurally, to achieve the camber effect without dihedral angle as well. Two possibilities are that Pearse did mean what the provisional specification said but changed his mind before the complete version was submitted; or that the specification writer misunderstood what Pearse meant about bird flight and how the covering was to be secured to the wing.

The wing of Pearse's aircraft was hinged to the apex of a triangular-shaped framework carriage, or 'car' — to use the language of the specification. The carriage in the patent diagram is drawn from a difficult angle and it is likely that the two rear members of the framework were angled backwards rather than being vertical as shown in the diagram. Otherwise, with the pilot seated to the rear of the carriage, the plane would have tended to tip over backwards.

In both the patent specifications the 'car' is equipped with an undercarriage 'preferably provided with pneumatic tyres and arranged in tricycle fashion', that is, with a single front steering wheel. The size of the wheels is not specified, but the diagram suggests they were smaller than the cycle wheels most contemporaries of Pearse remember. They seem more akin to the 'small wheel on a penny-farthing' which is the dimension which Warne Pearse recalled that his brother once toyed with, or the front wheel on an errandboy's bicycle.

A control arm led from the nosewheel to a rack attached between the front members of the carriage. By using this tiller, Pearse steered the plane while it was taxiing. The rack could hold the nosewheel in a fixed steering position when necessary.

Pearse planned to accommodate the pilot in this manner: 'A seat for the operator is provided in such a position that he will be able to oper-ate the guide wheel of the car, the arm for operating the three rudders, the keel, and control the engine. This seat is made in such a manner that it will be capable of sliding backwards or forwards or of moving to either side, in order that the operator may shift his weight to control the equilibrium and operations of the machine.'

The patent drawing shows that the pilot was seated to the rear of the 'car' on a bicycle saddle secured to a bar extending fore and aft in the centre of the carriage and supported on two crossbraces. Jack Connell, who remembered Pearse's experiments, said that the inventor sat on a 'sort of saddle under the wing, almost in an upright position'. Further confirmation is in the *Temuka Leader* description which has the pilot's seat 'underneath the engine and a little to the back'.

As to the motor itself, the complete specification is of little help: ' . . . the oil engine employed for driving the propelling mechanism . . . may be of any of the approved forms, but preferably of the two-cylinder type'. The engine is said to be located in the centre of the wing, as shown in the patent diagram and supported by a framework not shown in the diagram. The framework supporting his heavier four-cylinder engine in 1909 is known to have been of steel tubing. How-ever, the wood screws attached to the mounting of one of the 'irrigation pipe' cylinders from his first motor suggest that the framework supporting the engine of the pre-1906 model was mainly of timber.

While the complete specification dismisses the engine in two sen-tences, the provisional gives it a more comprehensive description. At that stage the writer evidently believed that the motor was an impor-tant aspect of the invention, but by the time the complete specification was prepared his chief interest had switched to the wing construction and control surfaces. This engine, which has already been described, was ingenious enough in its own right, but Pearse must have seen by July 1907 that it was not the most original feature of his aircraft. When he first constructed his motor there were very few internal combustion aero engines in existence. By 1907 there were many.

'To propel the machine,' reads the provisional specification, 'I use a propeller . . . and mount it near the front of the machine, and preferably mount the propeller direct on the crank axle. By this construction, the propeller will act as a flywheel and thus save gearing.' In the complete specification, the propeller is described in greater detail. It is unusual in two respects; its blades are of canvas and their pitch is adjustable.

However, as the propeller pitch adjustment could be made only when the plane was stationary and its engine switched off, Pearse's airscrew cannot be called a variable-pitch propeller in the modern meaning of the term.

Pearse evidently came to regard his propeller as novel enough for it to merit illustration on his patent drawing, though it was not made part of his claims. Oddly enough no witnesses of his flight experiments have recalled his using a canvas prop, though a wooden model and various metal types are remembered. But the inventor himself wrote of the time he spent in developing different sorts of propeller, and his secretive working methods did not give local residents much chance of seeing all the ideas he was working on. Understandably, with a patent pending he would be careful to keep most of the novel features of his plane under cover.

One further feature of the wing is covered in both specifications. The complete one describes it thus: 'The car is provided with bearings at its top in which the main framework of the aeroplane is articulated in such a manner that it may be tipped forward or backward to any desired angle, and a handle is provided to so adjusting it.' In other words, wing incidence control. Pearse could tilt the wing to vary its angle of attack. It could be adjusted to either a positive or negative incidence setting.

As with the propeller adjustment it would be praticable to manipulate the incidence control only when the plane was motionless. Moreover, the arrangement would contribute to structural weakness in the aircraft. The control lever, which fitted into notches or an arc-shaped rack to the left of the pilot, probably had to be tied firmly into position once the incidence setting had been selected.

Next to the wing and the carriage, the most conspicuous feature of the plane is its keel or vertical stabiliser. Both specifications and the diagram substantially agree on its nature: 'To assist in maintaining the machine in equilibrium,' reads the complete specification, 'a keel piece is attached to the top of the frame and extends centrally from the front to the back thereof. This keel piece is made of a light rectangular frame hinged by the side members of the main frame so as to be capable of lying flat, while, should a cross wind be encountered it may be lowered so as to lie flat against the main sail of the machine.' The provisional specification suggests that calico or a similar material be used to stretch over the keel framework. It also enlarges on the function of this vertical stabiliser: 'This construction enables the aeroplane to maintain its upright position as whenever it is caused to tip sideways, the pressure caused by the resistance of the air against the side of the keel will tend to carry the aeroplane into its normal and upright position again.'

Neither the texts nor the drawing show how the keel is to be supported in its vertical position. Pearse must have therefore had in mind a fairly uncomplicated method, probably involving wires, levers or springs. The pilot could have operated the keel, from his saddle, by use of a handle, lever, rods or wires.

No one who remembers Pearse's first plane mentions this stabilising keel: perhaps he developed it in secret. But it is also likely that he found it of little value and kept it in the horizontal position, or that he did not have one at all. Its use on his patented plane might be entirely theoretical.

One device hard to account for is the horizontal stabiliser described in the provisional specification: 'Two suitable rudders are attached horizontally to the car and are connected together by a lever, in such a way that when the car swings when travelling, the pressure of the wind upon one of the rudders, which is preferably made smaller than the other, will operate the larger one, the normal position of which is horizontal, and in that position is held by means of suitable springs. This method of construction prevents the car from swinging sideways during flight.'

It seems that the smaller rudder, deflected by airflow to a non-horizontal plane, would act as a servo and cause the larger rudder to be moved accordingly. The airflow against the larger rudder was then to have some effect on the directional control of the aircraft, but it is hard to imagine how an arrangement of horizontal rudders could in any way effect directional control. Another mystery about this horizontal stabiliser is its intended location. Was it to be attached to the 'car' at the front of the plane or at the rear? The most likely position, where the stabilising device would receive an uninterrupted airflow and be least in the way, was forward of the 'car' at a height midway between the wing and undercarriage.

Pearse, at any rate, did not persevere with this contrivance, for it receives no mention at all in his complete specification and is not shown on the patent diagram. The *Temuka Leader* reporter describing the 1909 version of the plane says that 'in front there is an arrangement to lift it up into the air or lower it as desired'. This may be a modification of the horizontal stabiliser whose function the reporter misunderstood; it is more likely that it was Pearse experimenting with a form of forward elevator such as the Wright brothers had popularised.

Finally, the control surfaces. Here there has been much confusion and there is more controversy associated with Pearse's proposals for controlling his aircraft than with any other issue except the date of his first flight attempts. The chief bother is that he changed his mind about both the mode of operation and function of his control surfaces between submitting his two specifications. And, to complicate matters, the diagram which was filed with the substitute complete specification shows a further deviation which disagrees with the accompanying text.

At the heart of the problem are what Pearse describes as 'vanes' in his provisional specification, 'wing rudders' in the complete specification and, misguidedly, 'ailerons' in his two newspaper letters. Possibly 'spoilers', 'airbrakes' or 'steering airbrakes' would be appropriate terms to use nowadays. Gibbs-Smith has suggested the use of 'elevons', which are control surfaces combining the functions of elevator and aileron.

The construction of Pearse's airbrakes is clear enough, and the two specifications appear to agree on where they should be sited. These 'vanes' amounted to two rectangular calico-covered flaps, each hinged to an upper truss rod of the wing framework, and situated one at each wingtip. They normally lay flat on the upper surface of the wing and were retained in that position by means of springs. A bellcrank lever was provided at the hinged edge of each airbrake, and could be pivoted so that one of its arms would serve to raise the adjacent airbrake. Each lever was linked by a flexible connection (such as a wire or rope) to a control handle within reach of the pilot, which in the case of the complete specification also operated the rear elevator. It was intended that the airbrakes be operated individually or simultaneously, and the movement of each 'vane' was upwards almost as far as the vertical plane.

However, the arrangement depicted in the drawing shows each of these 'wing rudders' to be trapezoid in shape and hinged to the lower rod of the appropriate truss so that the rudders operate below the wing rather than above it. The vertical arm of each bellcrank lever to which the connection was made extends above the wing so that the operating wires or ropes would have to be passed through apertures in the calico wing covering. The arrangement of the 'vanes' shown in the drawing is quite operable, but it does not accord with the description of their siting in the two specifications.

It is hard to account for this discrepancy between the text of the complete specification and the formal drawing filed three months later.

Though both airbrake systems are workable, it is clear that either the drawing is in error on the arrangement of the 'wing rudders' or that the text is. Or alternatively and perhaps more probably, the difference represents a change of mind on Pearse's part which was not remedied in the text. This may have been because he overlooked notifying his agent of changes that needed to be made to the wording of the specification. It seems unlikely that the different location of the airbrakes could be attributed purely to error on the agent's part. The sketch or photograph provided by Pearse to enable preparation of the formal drawing itself must have shown the arrangement of the 'vanes' and controls depicted in the formal drawing. Whatever the wording of the two specifications might say, the diagram probably reflects Pearse's latest thoughts on his 'side rudders'. However, so that his flight control methods as explained in the two specifications may be intelligible, it will be assumed in what follows that the airbrakes were, as a matter of general preference, to be located on top of the wing.

As if it were not enough of a puzzle deciding where Pearse wanted his 'vanes' to be located, the inventor also presents us with two entirely different systems of flight control. In the first, according to the provisional specification, flight control is to be achieved with the airbrakes and with a vertical rudder. The second method, described in the complete specification, combines airbrakes with a rear elevator to produce similar results. The airbrakes have a different function in each case.

In his provisional specification, Pearse describes the purpose of his airbrakes as follows: 'These vanes are so arranged that whenever the aeroplane is tipped sideways by the wind, the angle of the vanes is altered at the will of the operator by means of the aforesaid rod [connected by flexible controls to the vanes]. These latter means are also used to alter the angle of the aeroplane longitudinally, and by shifting the rod aforesaid, either forward or backward, the front of the aeroplane will be lowered or raised accordingly.'

Thus the airbrakes at this stage were to be used independently for lateral control and simultaneously for longitudinal control. Directional control was to be achieved by means of a vertical rudder: 'A rudder is also attached vertically to the rear of the aeroplane, and is used for steering the machine.'

In the remark that his 'wing rudders' would raise or lower the front of the aeroplane (or wing) there is a further problem. Elevons will produce the above effect, but if Pearse's vanes were in the form of airbrakes and were located on the upper surface of the wing they would not serve theoretically to raise the front of the wing when operated. In order to raise and lower the front of the wing in Pearse's theory, his vanes would have themselves to be capable of moving upwards and downwards. Pearse was, in other words, anticipating the elevator described in the complete specification. Unless the vanes were sited at the trailing edge of the wing they would then have to operate through apertures in the wing surface and be activated by a much more complicated system than his free-pivoting bellcrank levers. The inventor might, at this point, have had some such system in mind but it is more likely, perhaps, that a mistake was made in the description of his longitudinal flight control system.

Pearse gives no account of what his plane's vertical rudder was to look like but it is reasonable to assume that it resembled in shape and size the rear elevator shown in the patent diagram. It could have been hinged to the rear vertical support of the overhead keel and operated by means of a control rod or wires. Because its task was taken over by the airbrakes, Pearse dropped all mention of this vertical rudder in his complete specification and diagram, although at least one witness (Robert Gibson of the 'terrace' takeoff) remembered that his plane had one at some stage.

The inventor later recalled his use of a vertical rudder in the Milton letter: 'In the specifications I recognised that when the rudders at the wingtips were actuated there would be a drag at the particular wingtip that was being operated upon, tending to turn the machine round; but I proposed to counteract this with the vertical rudder at rear.' He also pointed out that he did not employ an automatic connection between the two. Rudder and airbrakes could be worked independently. The letter states, too, that this rudder was used in conjunction with a horizontal elevator. Pearse may mean by 'horizontal elevator' the horizontal stabiliser already referred to, but neither of the specifications mentions a combined use of rudder and elevator, so he may have been recollecting a configuration he used either before the specifications were written or afterwards.

In the complete specification, his flight control system underwent a significant change. The side rudders were to be used as before for lateral control — to deflect a wingtip upwards if it flipped down. But they were now to take on, as well, the job of directional control performed in the earlier specification by the vertical rudder. Functioning as steering airbrakes and operated with more angular adjustment they would provide drag at one wingtip or the other to deflect the course of the aircraft.

Longitudinal control in flight was now the job of the rear horizontal elevator, whose mode of operation was quite straightforward: 'Articulated upon the back edge of the main frame and at its middle is a rudder composed of a light rectangular frame arranged in the same plane as the main frame. This rudder is employed for deflecting the course of the machine upwards or downwards when flying, and it is controlled by an arm connected to it in such a manner that as the arm is moved longitudinally in either direction the rudder will be raised or lowered on its hinges.' The pilot could also slide his seat back and forth to assist longitudinal control during takeoff, flight and landing. Likewise he could shift from side to side to aid lateral control. Surprisingly, he does not suggest using the elevator to assist in the takeoff.

As it was required to do, the complete specification gives near the end a description of how the invention was to be operated. 'In use, the machine is first caused to run along the ground on its car by the revolution of the propellor [sic]. When it has gained sufficient speed the operator will throw his weight backwards so that the front of the machine will be tilted up thereby causing the machine to rise from the ground, until it reaches the desired height when it will be placed in equilibrium by shifting the operator's weight forward agin. The propellor being kept going, will keep the machine moving in the air, its course and the actions being controlled by the several means already described. It may be caused to descend by adjusting the rear rudder or by tilting it forward.'

Finally, the complete specification ends with four claims relating to the wing construction, to the overhead keel and to the aeroplane generally. The historical importance of these claims and of Pearse's ideas as a whole will be asssessed in a later chapter.

One can only speculate as to how controllable the aircraft of Pearse's patent would have been in actual flight.

The configuration described in his provisional specification, where there is a rudder but no elevator, would have been most unstable about its pitch axis. Such a plane would probably dive into the ground after takeoff or pitch up, stall, then dive. With an elevator but no rudder, as in the complete specification, the aircraft would still be unstable but its instability could be reduced to a series of fore-and-aft oscillations. Shifting the seat back and forth would not be a practical means of dynamic control, as it would be too slow to counteract rapid pitching movements. The incidence control if operated in flight would probably

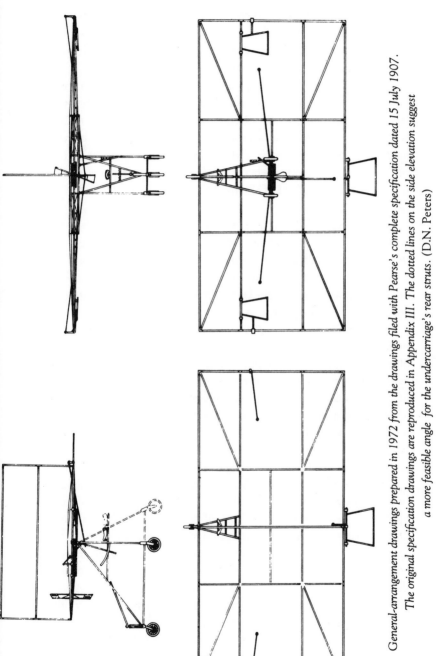

General-arrangement drawings prepared in 1972 from the drawings filed with Pearse's complete specification dated 15 July 1907. The original specification drawings are reproduced in Appendix III. The dotted lines on the side elevation suggest a more feasible angle for the undercarriage's rear struts. (D.N. Peters)

move the 'car' in relation to the wing, rather than vice versa. In any case it would, like the sliding seat, be too slow a remedy for violent pitching. The wing incidence control and sliding seat would be of more use in trimming the plane generally.

As far as yaw control goes, Pearse's aeroplane would have little 'weathercock' stability, for the centre of its vertical keel is shown to be forward of the centre of the aircraft, not behind it. Consequently, air-brakes above or below the wing would yaw the aircraft considerably. A rudder would slightly improve the plane's 'weathercock' stability and yaw the aircraft as required, but it would also roll the plane in the opposite direction on account of the rudder probably being above the centre of gravity.

Any sideslip following yaw would produce a strong rolling couple between the plane's high keel and low centre of gravity. Thus a yaw to the left would produce side thrust to the left on the keel and consequently the aircraft would roll to the left. The effect of the keel on sideslip following roll would be to tilt the aircraft back again strongly and set up a lateral oscillatory motion like that of a leaf falling.

If the airbrakes were above the wing as described in the specifications, and either airbrake were raised, there would be a small reaction in lift and a large amount of yaw. Raising the left airbrake, for example, would produce yaw to the left plus leftward roll, followed by further roll to the left and eventually a turn to the left.

Airbrakes below the wing, as suggested by the patent drawing, would produce a small lift increase plus a lot of yaw. So, though the pilot might be hoping to bank to the right by lowering his left airbrake, he would yaw left, roll slightly to the right, then roll left and turn left.

Situated above the wing, the airbrakes were likely to be more effective. The plane would also experience less yaw-roll effect with the vertical keel lowered, and Pearse himself seems to have had it this way. Overall, with air-brakes, elevator and rudder (a combination of the two specifications which Pearse's Milton letter suggests that he eventually arrived at), his plane would possibly be controllable in the hands of a skilled pilot. But almost certainly not so with an unskilled one. It has been suggested that Pearse's airbrakes would merely succeed in flipping the plane over on its back and wrecking it. This is unlikely to have happened, however. The vanes were too small and the plane's centre of gravity, airspeed and height were too low to readily permit aerobatics of this sort.

On his own admission, Pearse could not control the plane in flight adequately. Yet it would not have been particularly difficult to get air-borne in such a plane, powered by either the two- or four-cylindered engines and assisted by 'ground effect'; and the evidence seems quite irrefutable that Pearse did so. Three eyewitness accounts of Pearse's first takeoff mention how the plane behaved in the air, making particular reference to its pitching, wobbling and swerving. These observations are largely supported by independent theoretical speculations about how the patented plane would have performed. So it is not at all un-likely that the plane Pearse tried to fly was along the lines of the version patented in 1906–7.

It has also been agreed that some of the plane's erratic behaviour in the air might have been caused by Pearse trying to teach himself to fly. Orville Wright's first 36-metre flight on 17 December 1903 was an undulating one. The rise and fall, in his case, has been put down to Orville's inexperience with the elevator, which was too evenly bal-anced, and to consequent over-correction. Something of the sort may have happened with Pearse.

In both cases the erratic flying could be ascribed to the pilot 'getting the feel' of his aircraft. Even in these sophisticated days, a trainee pilot handling the controls for the first time tends to overcorrect his errors, and it is hardly surprising that both Pearse's and Orville Wright's flights were, respectively, 'swerving' and 'undulating'.

Be all this as it may, by 15 July 1907 the New Zealand Patent Office had on file an invention of considerable interest and usefulness to any who knew where to look, or cared to know. And this patent specifica-tion is the only tangible record which survives of the aircraft Pearse attempted to fly in the early years of this century.

11. Diversions

Though Richard Pearse applied for his patent on 19 July 1906 it was not until 15 July 1907 that the substitute complete specification was filed at the Patent Office in Wellington. Meanwhile he worked away quietly at his plane, improving its design and taxiing it about on his farm a great deal.

He also kept up his other interests. He was a member of the Waitohi Flat Library, enjoyed the occasional euchre or crib game there on Monday evenings, played draughts with Jimmy Orr, chess with Warne, and a few rounds of golf at Temuka. He also played 'ping-pong' for the Upper Waitohi club and turned out with the rest of his family to tennis matches in the district.

Pearse went regularly to the Waitohi Flat Library but he was not a heavy borrower. In his last three years in the district he took out only seventeen volumes, ten in 1908, none in 1909, seven in 1910. The titles of his borrowings may still be seen in the issue book and they indicate a fairly catholic taste. Borrowings range from Volume I of Gibbon's *Decline and Fall of the Roman Empire*, *Canada*, *Engineering Tools*, and *With Kitchener to Khartoum*, to *Hearts in Exile*, *Petticoat Government*, *Berenice*, and *Elusive Isobel*. Four of these books including Gibbon and the handbook on tools he appears not to have returned, and three others turned up in 1912, a year after he had moved south to Milton.

His chief interest seems to have been in scientific magazines. If he wanted other reading he could fall back on the numerous volumes brought back to Trewarlet on library nights by his father and brothers. Warne was a particularly voracious reader and in 1896–7, when Richard was fast developing his interest in things mechanical, borrowed several volumes which may have been useful to his older brother. These included *Stories of Invention* and *The History of the Steam Engine*.

Occasionally, Richard would attend the local dances but, increasingly, he seemed to find these occasions a strain. He was not given to horseplay or social chitchat, and generally stood apart from the other

Trewarlet, South Petherwin, Cornwall. One of the properties owned by Richard Pearse's grandfather.

Richard Pearse at Waitohi Flat School in 1887, seated front row fifth from left.
Jack is fourth from left in back row; Tom stands at left of third row;
Annie is second from right in third row.

The Upper Waitohi School senior classes, 1893. Richard Pearse stands at left of the back row
alongside his head teacher, Charles Goldstone. Warne is fourth pupil from left
in back row; Maggie third from left in centre row.

Waitohi Terrace Tennis Club afternoon tea, 1898. Standing, left to right: Alice Southby, Jim Chapman, Dick Williams, (unknown), Hugh McIntyre, Richard Pearse, Jim Connell, Tommy Orr junior.

Tennis Club group, 1898. Richard Pearse near middle, holding lapel; young Warne on his left, Jimmy Orr junior behind his right shoulder, Jack second from right in back row. Mrs W. Barker, later an important takeoff witness, is seated front left in white.

Digory Pearse's Waitohi home, Trewarlet, a few years after being built in 1888. This stone house replaced an earlier sod cottage and — substantially altered — is now occupied by Jeffrey Pearse, a great-grandson of Digory and great-nephew of the aviator.

The Pearse family orchestra at Trewarlet circa 1897. Back row: Digory, Jack, Tom. Middle row: Richard (with cello), Margaret, Sarah, Warne, Annie. Front row: Ruth, Florrie, Reg.

A newly discovered photograph, taken around 1907, showing Richard Pearse (far left) with close friends Major George Irwin (centre) and Irwin's fiancée Mary Lambert (far right) at a picnic near Waitohi. The other two women have not been identified. Richard's brother Warne probably took the photo.

A 1993 view of the Main Waitohi Road from the Richard Pearse Memorial. After being a short time airborne, Pearse crashed onto the overgrown gorse fence that once grew along the line of the present wire fence.

Certify that **Ellen McAteer**

PASSED EXAMINATION as under:—

Passed the First Standard 26 Aug 1897
at Waitohi Flat School,
in the Education District of S. Canterbury

Signed:

Passed the Fourth Standard 28 Aug 19..
at Waitohi Flat School,
in the Education District of S. Canterbury

Signed:

Passed the Second Standard 31st Aug 1898
at Waitohi Flat School,
in the Education District of S. Canterbury

Signed: Hugh McIntyre

Passed the Fifth Standard 30th Aug 1911
at Waitohi Flat School,
in the Education District of S. Canterbury

Signed: Hugh McIntyre

Passed the Third Standard Sept 1899
at Waitohi Flat School,
in the Education District of S. Canterbury

Signed: Hugh W.

Passed the Sixth Standard 28th Aug 19..
at Waitohi Flat School,
in the Education District of S. Canterbury

Signed:

Nellie McAteer's Waitohi Flat school certificate, one of the
documents used to date the flight attempt. Hugh McIntyre is the teacher.

Richard Pearse in 1903.

Warne Pearse, Richard's younger brother, was a key witness to the early flight experiments. This photograph was taken in 1914.

A replica of Richard Pearse's first aeroplane. Constructed from his patent description and eyewitness accounts for a television documentary, it became airborne when towed.

The late George Bolt, photographed in 1958 with remains of Pearse's second aero engine, plus metal propeller, recovered for him from an Opihi riverbed dump by Maurice Cameron of Temuka.

In 1971 the author (left) assisted by Tom Bradley (centre) and Maurice Cameron relocated the Opihi dump and excavated further remains of Pearse's first plane.

young men. His serious and withdrawn manner made him easy game for clowns and pranksters and, to make matters worse, he had little sense of humour. Bert Smart recalled the time at a tennis club dance when a local lad, Dan Fraser, leapt on Pearse's back and attempted to bronco-ride him. Dick did not see anything comical in this: 'You're nothing but a big fool,' he said tersely, and left.

The Pearse family orchestra, in which Richard played until he left Waitohi, also absorbed a lot of his attention. This ensemble was so able and so well esteemed that it performed all round South Canterbury at concerts, parties, charities and musical evenings. The Pearses played music both light and serious, especially imported by Digory from the 'old country'. Though Tom was overseas and Mrs Pearse did not play, that still left nine players: Maggie on the harp, Annie on the piano, Florrie on the flute or clarinet, Ruth on the piccolo, Richard on the cello, and Digory and the rest of his sons on violins. Florence was also, for many years, official accompanist at the Temuka Competitions, but this was in later years.

It may well have been Richard's wish to perpetuate the sound of this unique group that led him to experiment with sound-recording devices at this time. He was not satisfied with the cylinder-and-earphone type of gramophone then fashionable, so he made a huge phonograph and trumpet, and the results could be heard a quarter of a mile away. He used to recite into the machine. 'I remember one recitation,' related a sister. 'It had some tremendously big words, real jaw-breakers. "Professor Snuffles" it was called.'

On several occasions, according to Warne, Richard recorded items performed by the family orchestra. Unluckily, no further details of this invention survive, and nothing of the machine itself. The records were wax-coated and it seems that Pearse worked on both disc and cylinder recording methods. He continued with the work later on in Milton, and in Christchurch.

Another recording gadget was a music box which Richard's sisters describe as being round, its wooden barrel made from three-ply wood and bound by hoop iron. It could play 350 notes, had its strings underneath and was played by keys on top. You could register any three tunes on it that you fancied. You then wound up the machine, selected one of the melodies and could hear it played back.

Warne Pearse also described a sound-reproducing machine based on a clockwork mechanism and lengths of barbed wire. By attaching a series of guitar strings Richard made the barbs press on a cylinder which revolved at the instance of the clockwork motor. A tune could be play-ed on to the cylinder, possibly by plucking the wires, and then played back any number of times, the barbs picking up the original marks they had made on the cylinder, thereby plucking the correct strings of the guitar in their original sequence. Nothing remains of either of these machines.

Every year Richard Pearse used to go on a fortnight's holiday to Christchurch. The Canterbury Museum, the Canterbury Public Library, and music were what generally lured him north. He was also a keen filmgoer in the early days and predicted talkies long before they came. His youngest sister, Mrs Ruth Gilpin, remembered that 'Richard was very fond of Williamson's theatricals and Florrie and I would look after his sheep to see that none got down on their backs. He would always bring back a present for us. Once it was a kaleidoscope and a large box of oil paints. He knew we were very keen on drawing or dabbling with colours and it was really this gift that started us on our art careers.'

To appeal to their artistry, Pearse also made his sisters a 'movie view-er' or 'zoetrope', a round disc shape with several successive pictures of objects in action, such as a man on a jumping horse. You peered through an aperture, moved the disc with your fingers, and saw the action come alive.

Florence and Ruth Pearse later showed as much ingenuity in art as their older brother did in his various sidelines. Oils and watercolours were just a beginning. Inspired by exhibits at the 1926 Dunedin Exhi-bition they went on to experiment with a wide range of styles and materials: indian ink sketches; barbola and tarso work; pictures worked in wool, silk, raffia, human hair, crushed paper, coloured tinfoil and satin; eggshell mosaics; gesso work; hand-painted porcelain brooches; feltwork and cone work. Their artistry won awards in New Zealand and Australian shows and was exhibited in England and Austria.

Richard Pearse, meanwhile, continued to work away patiently at his aeroplane. Somewhat belatedly, the *Temuka Leader* got on to his trail in 1909, and the following brief item appeared on 6 November: 'A young South Canterbury farmer, who has for some years past been working in secret in an endeavour to perfect a flying machine, considers that he has nearly reached the goal at which he is aiming. He intends to make a trial of his airship at an early date. The framework of the ship is of bam-boo, the wings all of calico, and the propelling power is a 24 hp motor. The inventor is Mr Richard Pearse of Waitohi.'

This piece of news earned a limited coverage in other provincial newspapers, but interest was then being concentrated on Oswald Coates of Christchurch. Coates had in July 1909 successfully tested a model plane which he believed could be greatly superior in speed and lifting power to 'Wilbur Wright's English [sic] machine'. He obtained a lot of publicity for his invention, demonstrated it before the Governor General, Lord Plunket, in Wellington, and was trying to form a syndicate to take the idea to the British Government.

An *Otago Witness* reporter, Sam H. Carter, visited Pearse in late November and his report appeared in the Dunedin paper on 1 December 1909. This newspaper item, discovered shortly before the first edition of *The Riddle of Richard Pearse* went to press, appears as Appendix VI.

Like the *Temuka Leader* story printed a fortnight later, Carter's report describes an aircraft that was radically different from the machine of Pearse's 1906 patent or the one recalled by early witnesses. It is so different, indeed, that Geoff Rodliffe and others argue quite persuasively that this was a second aircraft, not merely a modification of the first. This is despite the fact that Pearse wrote in 1915 that he built only one aircraft at Waitohi.

The inventor is said to have 'toiled for five long years' on this plane's construction, which would date it from 1904 or early 1905. So vast was its wing area that it could never have been manoeuvred through a farm gate or taxied down a narrow country road for a flight attempt, such as the one publicly witnessed on the date which most circumstantial evidence suggests was 31 March 1903. In short, for anyone trying to find easy answers to the riddle of when Pearse first tried to fly, where, and in which machine, Carter's report is nothing short of exasperating. It offers more confusions that solutions.

On 14 December 1909 the *Temuka Leader* reporter, having made a special trip to Pearse's farm workshop, filed this account of his bewildering experience. (Before the discovery of the *Otago Witness* report, this appeared to be the only publicity which either of Pearse's aircraft received in his lifetime.)

It has been known for some time that Mr R.W. Pearse, farmer, Waitohi, has been engaged in the construction of an aeroplane airship [sic], and curious to know what it was like, we paid him a visit recently. We had preconceived notions of what it was like, but we certainly were disillusioned. It was nothing at all like what we expected it would be, and it was nothing that we can adequately describe. One must see it to get an idea of it. When we saw it there was nothing to be seen but the skeleton framework and that looked much like an enormous spider's web, with the engine taking the place of the spider in the centre of it. The most practical way to convey to the reader's mind any idea of it is perhaps to begin on the ground, but before doing so it may be as well to indicate the principle on which it is worked. The idea is to run it along on wheels till it gets a good speed on, and then it is expected to rise like a kite into the air, and float away into space. To secure this result Mr Pearse had three bicycle wheels on the ground just like a tricycle, fixed on a frame of bicycle steel tubing which forms the central part of the whole machine. Some distance behind this is the engine firmly fixed in a frame of steel tubing and in front of it is the fan which is intended to serve the same purpose in propelling the aeroplane as the propeller of a ship does.

The remainder of the extra-ordinary mechanism is mostly made of bamboo cane, braced together by steel joints and steel wire. Underneath the engine a little to the back is the driver's seat and there are also cans to carry petrol in, and water for the cooling jacket of the engine. The engine is a four-cylinder one, of what is called the double opposed type, very compact, and very easily started or stopped.

It is a 4" stroke and a 4½" bore and develops 25 hp and is the lightest of the kind made. It is fully under the control of the operator, who can very readily make it go fast or slow, or stop it altogether.

It is an excellent motor but considered not powerful enough. Now the whole of the vast surface is covered with calico, and in front there is an arrangement to lift it up into the air, or lower it as desired. There are also side wings for balancing and guiding, but as these were not on when we visited the place we cannot describe them.

The whole idea is that she will rise up like a kite and the spread of calico will keep her afloat. The total weight with the man on board will be only about 500 lbs. She will have the largest floating surface and lightest weight of any kind made, and judging by results already obtained there is little doubt that Mr Pearse will before long be floating in the air.

He has already made some trials and has been off the ground

several times, but it is not easy to balance her. He has improved on previous performances every time, and in his latest effort he flew about 25 yards. We believe it is the intention of Mr Pearse to make a 50 hp engine and if he does he will have little difficulty in flying. Mr Pearse is not, of course, a trained mechanic, and has neither tools nor machinery necessary for such an enterprise. If he succeeds with the means at his disposal he will achieve an extraordinary feat.

The Temuka reporter seems to have been quite unaware that Pearse had already been airborne with an earlier version of this plane; he does not even seem to know much about flying at all. Though it might be said in mitigation that this was only a small country paper, it still seems surprising that the reporter knew so little about aviation generally. There had been, even by the end of 1908, over seventy powered takeoffs or aeroplane flights in various parts of the world. By December 1909 not only the Wright brothers but Alberto Santos-Dumont of Brazil, Henri Farman of France, S.F. Cody of America, J.A.D. McCurdy of Canada (the first British Empire citizen after Pearse to achieve a powered take-off or powered flight), and J.T.C. Moore-Brabazon of Britain had flown impressive distances. Louis Blériot in July 1909 had even flown the English Channel. Either aviation news was slow to get to Temuka or the *Temuka Leader* reporter was foxing for effect.

There are — despite its occasional clumsiness — several aspects of this newspaper description of Pearse's plane which are of particular interest. First of all, Pearse evidently told the reporter he had flown about 25 yards (23 metres) with this aircraft. Then, unless the reporter is viewing the plane back to front, Pearse seems to be experimenting with a forward elevator such as the Wright brothers and other early aviators used, but which he had hitherto done without. His plane's earlier configuration had the elevator at the back, the accepted position in present-day aircraft. Thirdly, this is the first documented reference to Pearse's second engine, the four-cylinder opposed motor now housed in a display case at MOTAT. Also, the total weight with the pilot aboard is 200 lbs (90.7 kg) less than Pearse mentioned in his patent specifications and press letters. But this is no surprise, as he was constantly altering his wing shapes. Finally, the airbrakes (or they may have been by 1909 authentic ailerons) seem to be detachable. At any rate, they were not fitted at the time. Otherwise there is not a great deal of difference between the *Temuka Leader*'s description and other accounts of the plane available elsewhere. The engine, however, merits special attention. It is a most ingenious contrivance and Pearse admitted that he spent a great deal of time developing it. He was evidently well pleased with the result.

This motor has been expertly analysed by George Bolt as follows. It was a four-cylinder opposed engine with a 4-inch (10.1 cm) bore and 4½ inch (11.4 cm) stroke. Its four-stroke action had the 2 to 1 wheels coming from one end of the crankshaft. The other end of the crankshaft was very long, with the propeller out about a metre in front of the engine and supported by a bearing of its own. The cam oscillated an unusual rocking-lever arrangement near the centre of the engine. From these rocking-levers the exhaust-valve pushrods went to the top end of the valve chamber and operated there with a rocker, like an ordinary overhead valve. In other words the valve gear was operated from a central point with pushrods radiating out to the individual cylinders.

On the head of each cylinder was a surface carburettor. This took the form of a small steel chamber bolted on to the head, fitted with concertinaed gauze with two pipes leading to it. One fed fuel and air in and the other went to the cylinder to supply the charge. This was the only cooling for the cylinder head. The middle part of each cylinder was waterjacketed. The connecting rod fastened to the crankshaft was such that one cylinder carried a master rod with an ordinary split big end. On the cap of this big end was a lug, and the opposing piston had a rod with a fork end fitting on to the lug. A small pipe came from the waterjackets to cool the exhaust-valve chamber. Lubrication was made from several points by small drip chambers. There was no crankcase, the cylinders being held together by spacer bars.

With the probable exception of the shaft for his first engine, Pearse had his crankshafts made for him by a Timaru engineering firm, Parr & Co. Ltd. In the late 1950s George Bolt managed to track down the man, Oscar Miller, who worked on this job. Mr Miller was then very old, but he remembered that five crankshafts were made altogether. Some of them apparently broke but the fifth one was successful. Roger Parr, a retired chief engineer of the Hawera & New Plymouth Freezing Works, wrote to Bolt in 1959 confirming this. He had been with Parr & Co. at the time and remembered that Oscar Miller made the first three crankshafts and Charles Dale the last two, the first one being produced in about 1908. (The *Otago Witness* report refers to seven such crankshafts.) As Miller went to sea in June 1908, his work for Parrs would have to predate that event.

'In those days,' Roger Parr recalled, 'we had to forge and temper our lathe tools from carbon steel. The engine these cranks were for was a four-cylinder 4-inch bore and 4-inch stroke from memory, and the con rods were slipped over the cranks to jam on the two-piece big end, being secured by flanges on the bearings by screws.'

Parr believed that the cylinders were of cast steel and that Scott Brothers Ltd of Christchurch did the work. Tom Hally thought that the engine was made by P & D Duncan, agricultural and general engineers of Christchurch. Robert Gibson maintains that Pearse did not have any work done in Timaru or Christchurch but got help from the Pleasant Point blacksmith, Billy Hayes. Others argue that Parrs of Timaru did the work on both crankshafts and cylinders. The question cannot be resolved, as all these firms' records dating back to this period have been long since purged.

Nor can it be established when Pearse built this engine. Though he may have started on the job before 1906 it is not the motor he describes in the provisional patent specification of that year. So at that stage, if the four-cylinder engine did exist, it was not completely constructed or was not then working as well as his two-cylinder model. The complete patent specification dated 15 July 1907 also states a preference for an engine 'of the two-cylinder type': therefore, the four-cylinder motor must have been perfected during the two and a half years separating the complete specification and the *Temuka Leader* report.

This seems to be the motor Pearse writes of in one of his letters, the 24-hp engine weighing 5 lbs per hp which he describes as not being powerful enough. This is the same comment that the *Temuka Leader* reporter made about the 25-hp engine, no doubt having being told this was so by the aviator himself. So it may be assumed that these two engines are the same one, especially as the first *Temuka Leader* report describes the engine as a 24-hp one anyway.

But one of the frustrating things about Pearse's letters is that he refers to the 24-hp engine as his first, not his second. Either he had forgotten about the two-cylinder motor, or did not rate it important enough to mention. Another possibility is that he did mean the two-cylinder engine when he referred to the 24-hp motor as his first. The letter does not indicate whether it is a two- or four-cylindered motor at issue, and according to the yardstick by which Pearse calculated horsepower, both these engines seem to have had about the same power output. However, if he does mean the two-cylinder engine as his first, the *Temuka Leader* engine is then not accounted for by Pearse, for it cannot

possibly be the 250 lb (113 kg) 60-hp motor which the inventor describes as his second engine. It is discrepancies of this sort which reduce
the Pearse researcher to near-despair.

There is no evidence to show that Pearse ever got the *Temuka Leader*
plane into the air again at Waitohi, but it seeems to be basically the
same machine that he later tried to fly in Otago. In his last year in
South Canterbury, he is thought to have experimented with yet another
idea, a circular wing. Joseph Coll saw this plane 'about half a dozen
times, during four of which I was alongside it and got a good idea of its
shape and dimensions. I was twelve years old at the time. The dates
were between the middle of June 1910 and the middle of the following
November. Pearse was trying to fly it during that time. I saw it from a
distance a few times making runs down the road in an attempt to fly,
but I did not see it even rise off the ground. Jack Cunningham, a former
Lower Waitohi resident, told me twenty years ago that he saw it rise
about a yard off the ground. I was a pupil at the Upper Waitohi School
at the time mentioned above.'

According to Joseph Coll's account of the plane itself, there was an
open space about two and a half metres in diameter near the centre of
the wing, in which the engine was placed. The pilot stood on the undercarriage framework with his head and shoulders protruding through
the space, a little above the engine. A dart-like tail was attached to the
rear of the wing, and the tricycle undercarriage had its single swivelling
wheel at the tail rather than the nose. The engine drove a four-bladed
propeller. The aircraft was tilted up at the front when it sat on the
ground, so the leading edge of the wing was about two metres above the
ground and the tail about a metre clear of it.

No one else, apart from Joseph Coll, has described this plane,
though Stewart Baxter remembers an 'egg-shaped wing' on Pearse's
plane at this time. The machine seems radically different from any
other of the inventor's variations on the basic pattern and it is hard to
know what to make of it. The four-bladed propeller is no problem, for
Pearse tried many propeller styles, but the tail wheel is a reversal of his
usual practice of employing a steerable nosewheel.

The circular wing is a complete mystery, for it was not a shape
Pearse had worked on earlier, neither is it mentioned in his patent or
letters. Either he found it unsatisfactory and dismantled it, or the witness confused this shape with the oval styling we have already observed.
The pilot's position, standing not sitting, and with his head protruding

through the wing aperture, is also an arrangement not come across else-where. It is not likely that Pearse persevered very long with this flying saucer lookalike. It could never have been more than an eccentric adaptation of his standard model and it was not the plane seen later at Louden's Gully.

Louden's Gully? Richard Pearse, by 1910, had reached his limit at Waitohi. His farm's condition had declined wretchedly in the twelve years he had leased it, and a 40-hectare property was too small to work profitably anyway. Not that his expectations were high: all he seemed to want was a sufficient income to meet the cost of his experiments.

The decision to move out of Waitohi was made by Richard himself in his usual brisk and independent way. Late in 1910 he became serious-ly ill with typhoid contracted through drinking contaminated water from a creek or water race on his farm during a hot spell. His parents had in 1909 retired to Landue, at Epworth, near Temuka, leaving Warne and Reg to farm the home block at Trewarlet, and Richard spent some six to eight weeks at Landue being nursed by his mother and Florence. Dr Crawshaw cycled over from Temuka to visit him every day and for much of the time Pearse was in a semi-coma. Sarah and Florence would take turns in watching over him for most of the night and if Richard came to he generally said, 'Why don't you go to bed?' He hated being dependent on anyone. Yet he was lucky to survive typhoid in these times. Wilbur Wright died from it on 30 May 1912.

Exactly a month after Wilbur Wright's, there was another death much nearer at hand and also of considerable interest — though indi-rectly — to aviation historians. Marie Lilienthal, sister of the great German flight pioneer Otto Lilienthal, died at Fairview on 30 June 1912. Fairview is a small country community about twenty-four kilo-metres due south of Waitohi and just inland from Timaru. Marie had emigrated to New Zealand, married George Squire of South Canterbury, and lived to the age of 55 years. Her grave, which Tom Bradley located in the Timaru Cemetery, had a memorial erected over it which is in memory of Marie, her husband and son: ' . . . also of her brother Otto Lilienthal first inventor of the flying machine, killed near Berlin August 10th 1896'. Lilienthal flew a whole series of monoplane and biplane gliders betwen 1895 and 1896, greatly increasing the knowledge of sta-bility and control in the air. He was on the point of developing a pow-ered glider when he died after a crash. His experiments considerably influenced the Wrights, and Richard Pearse must have at least known about them, but there is no indication that Pearse and Marie Lilienthal ever learned of each other's existence.

When Richard Pearse became strong enough he set off to Dunedin for a holiday, in April 1911. While there he went for a train trip further south to look at the countryside, and on returning to Temuka he announced to his astonished parents and sisters: 'I've bought a farm at Milton.'

'How long did it take you to decide to do that?' asked his father.

'Half an hour.'

Digory Pearse, who had become increasingly disenchanted with his son's agricultural blunderings, did not raise any further quibbles. He probably had the wisdom to see that at the age of 34 Richard needed a fresh start.

So ended Richard Pearse's Waitohi years. As a farmer he had been a disaster, but who now cares about that?

12. South to Milton

South to Milton went Richard Pearse. With him he took a few farm implements, one or two scientific books, his vice, lathe, phonograph, cello, a few tools, tennis racket and golf clubs, his bicycle and the latest version of his first aeroplane. His first two aero engines, spare cylinders, a metal propeller, and bits of wing and undercarriage were left behind in his Waitohi workshop.

The Milton railway station is much the same now as it was then — a long platform edged by the usual assortment of huts, sheds and conveniences with a main station building, a siding or two and a goods shed. Food could be bought there, for Milton was one of the refreshment stops on the run between Dunedin and Invercargill. It had been served by a 58-km railway link with Dunedin since 1875 and the town's prosperity in the early 1900s was largely due to its importance as a freight forwarding centre for farm products to Dunedin.

At this point, however, Pearse was more interested in freighting in than in freighting out. His wagonful of possessions was shunted into the goods siding and he contacted the nearest carting company to have the load shifted to his new farm at Louden's Gully. Alex Campbell Ltd responded and sent along a sixteen-year-old lad, Albert Paul, with a lorry.

Later retired in Oamaru, Bert Paul well remembered that sunny afternoon, probably the last Saturday in April 1911, when he ' . . . took the plane and all connected with it off a low-sided four-ton railway wagon and carted it to the Louden's Gully property and unloaded it into a stable. Mr Pearse, when unloading both from the wagon and at the stable door, told me to be careful and not put any pressure on any of the tubes around the engine. When we arrived at the stable to take the engine off the lorry, he tied a rope around it and fastened the other end to the manger after passing the top over a beam high up. He then tied another rope to a four-by-two just inside the door so as to save the engine from hitting the manger when I drew the lorry away.'

Bert Paul knew very little about engines at the time, and nothing at all about aeroplanes. His only recollection of the motor was of 'a mass of rubber tubes with a one-inch pipe running through it'. The plane was apparently in a dismantled state, with all removable parts stripped off. All the other material was just loose.

'As to Mr Pearse, he was a very reserved man and evenly built all the way up, without any extra bulges.' Mr Paul also used to drive the Royal Mail to Glenledi every Tuesday and Friday, and later on he quite often passed Pearse on the way to or from Milton 'riding his high-framed cycle'.

By the time Richard Pearse came to Milton it had been settled since 1850 and a municipality for 45 years. It was a substantial and handsome country town, in good heart, functioning briskly, and with a population of about 1500. Its flourmills and proximity to the Otago goldfields had early on given it prosperity. Compared with Waitohi, Milton must have seemed to Pearse a teeming metropolis. Even Temuka would suffer by comparison, for although the two towns were of much the same size, Milton had a far wider range of local industries and activities than its Canterbury counterpart.

The farm at Louden's Gully was also quite a different proposition from Pearse's flat 40 hectares at Waitohi. The road to Louden's Gully branched off Back Road at Salmond's Corner, crossed half a mile of gently rising pasture then wound up the bottom of the gully, keeping for the most part to the north flank. About half a mile further on, Pearse's 74.5 hectares began.

The property was originally taken up by Robert Melville in 1866 by Crown grant. At the time the property was in two parcels, one portion of 104.5 acres (42 ha) from the Akatore Survey District and 79.5 acres (32 ha) adjoining it from the Tokomairiro Survey District. Joseph Thompson and family had the property later, followed by Martin Klimeck then Hugh and Bob Thompson. For a short while Cassidy, an erratic horsebreaker, occupied the land before he took off suddenly for Australia, leaving behind numerous unpaid debts. The farm then returned to Martin Klimeck, who had been leasing it to Cassidy and the Thompsons.

Richard Pearse bought the cottage and land from Klimeck on 24 April 1911, for £556. In the Deeds Register at the Dunedin Lands and Survey Department Pearse describes himself as being 'of Temuka, farmer'. Presumably, he did not think Waitohi was an intelligible address.

With the road as its bottom boundary the farm took in a section of the creek and five or so hectares of flattish land at the bottom of the gully. It then rose up the western side of the valley taking in a long ridge which was his boundary with James Wood on the Milton side, a shallow gully (at right angles to the main valley) dotted with scrub, and another long ridge which was his boundary with Frank Barra, the next farmer up Louden's Gully. The lower boundary of Pearse's property was at an elevation of 30 metres and the farm rose to about 120 metres at its back boundary.

The cottage he moved into was a much more primitive abode than Trewarlet. It must have been one of the earliest wooden homes in the area. A plain rectangle 9 metres by 4.5 metres in size facing northwards across the valley, it was walled with roughly hewn weatherboards and originally had a shingle roof. Downstairs the cottage was divided in two with a kitchen-cum-living room to the left and a bedroom to the right. There was a small stove in the kitchen but no water was laid on. This had to be fetched by a bucket from a rain tank out by the barn. A lean-to at the rear was used as a pantry and storeroom, and there was an outdoor privy. Up a narrow ladder you climbed eleven steps to extra bedroom space in the low-peaked attic, which was also divided in two. Pearse later stored grass seed up there.

The interior walls of both attic and downstairs rooms were lined with newspaper, and in the attic especially there is still some good reading to be had if you do not mind a kink in your neck. The favourite literature of successive occupants during the 1880s and 90s seems to have been the *Bruce Herald*, the *Otago Witness*, the *New Zealand Tablet*, *Queen*, the *Illustrated London News*, and *Black and White*. The earliest decipherable issue is a *Bruce Herald* from 1878. On top of this journalistic backing, traces of faded floral wallpaper may yet be seen. Dim light reached the attic rooms through small square windows at each end of the cottage and downstairs there were five assorted windows of 'unbreakable' gauze glass.

There was a front door opening on to a view across the bottom fields to the creek and far side of Louden's Gully; and there were two back doors. The flooring was of unevenly laid totara and there were no floor coverings. A bed, one or two cupboards, a table and some wooden chairs were the remaining fittings, and a kerosene lamp provided light in the evening.

The only other facilities were a barn (Bert Paul's 'stable'), a shed, a few looseboxes sited east or up-valley from the cottage, and a sheepyard behind. A rough path led down to the creek, across a small bridge and up to the road on the other flank of the gully. Some old apple trees and an elderberry grew by the west end of the house, but there was little or no garden. A wire fence marked out the bottom boundary, and gorse hedges did the same service at the sides and rear of his property. The farm was not subdivided into paddocks by any further fencing. A willow or two grew by the creek and there was some stunted scrub, a gorse shelterbelt and some bracken in the middle gully. Close-cropped grass surrounded the cottage and most of the high land was clothed in grass or tussock.

All in all a mixed bargain. Pearse was certainly on his own now and able to please himself about what he did with his time. The property was a bigger one than he had leased up north, but the farm was on relatively poor country and in a rundown condition, and his living quarters were a great deal more rudimentary than those he had been accustomed to at Trewarlet.

Pearse stocked the property with 300 Romney sheep, bought a black-and-white collie sheep dog, then settled down to more interesting matters.

First of all, the aeroplane.

13. New life

Pearse's barn, which like the cottage is still standing, had a division down the middle. In the front end nearest the road he stored hay and the few bits and pieces of farm equipment he possessed. In the back end he had his workbench, tools, lathe, and other gadgetry. His plane was stored in the adjacent shed, dismantled. The shed was locked.

It is clear that he had to get flying out of his system before he could put his mind to other things. The indications are that the little work he did on his plane at Louden's Gully he did near the outset of his time there. There seem to have been no witnesses at all to any of his flight attempts, but he was seen preparing to fly on one occasion and the plane was seen crashed by several observers on a second. Pearse himself spoke of another flight, probably his last. Because of the way Louden's Gully curves, his flying attempts would have been out of sight of the neighbours on both sides of him, and there was little traffic on the road, then or now. Hence the shortage of testimony.

Andrew Hood's father had a 93-hectare farm on the other side of Mt Steep, a 120-metre hill which overlooks the northern approach to Louden's Gully. He was working on the property one day in the summer, he thinks, of 1911. Hearing an unusual clattering sound coming from Louden's Gully he climbed to the top of the intervening ridge and looked across to Pearse's property, where he saw the source of the row. Pearse had an aeroplane contraption working.

'He had the engine running. It was what I could hear from over beyond. He wheeled the plane up against the hill, turned it and got on. But I never waited to see any more.' Andrew Hood didn't know if Pearse got the plane to fly on that occasion. The plan was evidently to give the machine a good run on a gentle down-slope and hope it could lift off to clear the fence and creek at the bottom of the gully.

What Pearse expected to do then is not clear but he would have needed to bank fairly sharply to the left to avoid disaster. Hood recalls that the grass was very short and the day sunny and calm. He did not stick around to watch Pearse 'in case he had another crash', and anyway he 'wouldn't go near a madman'. News of the inventor's escapades in South Canterbury must have already got around.

From his vantage point on the other side of the gully it seemed to Andrew Hood that Pearse's plane had long rectangular wings, each about six metres long and that the pilot 'perched right behind the engine in the middle'. The machine was mounted on two 28 x 1.5-inch bicycle wheels and probably had a skid at the back. Looking down on it, the whole contraption looked 'a real crate of a thing . . . more like a framework than a plane'.

Pearse's second aeroplane outing (of those we know about) must have ended in a crash. Three witnesses — Mrs George Rekowski, Alan McLeod and Elliot Hogg — remembered seeing the plane hanging halfway over a gorse hedge well up his private gully. There was no sign of Pearse near the plane, which was left lying on the hedge for several days. Other passers-by on the way to Glenledi are known to have seen it, but are now dead. No one can date the event.

From the direction in which the machine was pointing all witnesses believe Pearse had taken off from the hill just behind his cottage. It is hard to understand how this might have been done, as it would have needed considerable effort to drag the plane up the hill, and the run in the direction of his gully is fairly risky. But any attempt to fly in those days was a risk, and this hilltop takeoff would have been no more hazardous than his trip off the terrace at Waitohi.

Richard Pearse's last experience of flight took place some time near the end of the following summer or even in 1913. The only account of this episode comes to us by way of Andrew Hood. Hood was at the time working for the Marshall & Summers cycle shop and garage. He used to serve petrol at 1s 3d a gallon to Pearse for use in his engines. Petrol sales were fairly infrequent with, at that time, only a dozen or so cars in the district.

One day Pearse turned up on his bicycle with one arm in a sling. He told Hood that he had made a flight down his front field and crashed. 'He was evidently off the ground but reached the bottom fence and attempted to get his wheels through the gateway. But he just couldn't make it and he hit the fence, crashed, and put his shoulder out. He told me he was annoyed because he couldn't play tennis with his crook shoulder. As far as I know this was his last flight.'

Andrew Hood thought that for this flight Pearse had coupled two four-stroke engines together with a universal joint of green leather. Jim

Barra, who was a teenager on the farm next door, recalls seeing a much larger engine on the inventor's plane when it was stored in the shed later. He believes it was a sixteen-cylinder horizontally opposed engine, eight cylinders to either side of the crankshaft. The cylinders may have been double-acting.

This is possibly 'the sixteen-cylinder rotary engine' which J.R. Parmenter of Temuka told Bolt about. Parmenter remembered seeing Pearse with a sixteen-cylinder engine of some sort on his Waitohi farm well before the inventor moved down to Milton. It also seems to be the 60-hp 250-lb engine which the inventor later mentioned in his letters. (The weight of the motor is certainly in accord with Bert Paul's recollections.) 'But with my 60 horse-power motor, which proved very reliable, I had successful aerial navigation within my grasp, if I had had the patience to design a small plane that would be manageable. But I decided to give up the struggle, as it was useless trying to compete with men who had factories at their backs.' In addition, powered flight was 'by then an accomplished fact'.

Pearse was particularly pleased with this engine for it weighed only 4 lbs per horsepower. He may have got the idea for an engine of this kind from the sixteen-cylinder 50-hp Antoinette which Blériot used in his 1907 *Libellule*.

This then is all the evidence there is for Pearse attempting to do any flying at Milton. There are several uncertainties. No one actually saw him fly. Jim Barra who lived next door did not think he flew at all. Andrew Hood's description of Pearse preparing his plane for a flight and his conversation with Pearse about the last crash are both unattested. The takeoff point for the flight that ended in the gorse is uncertain. The nature of the engines he used is open to doubt.

There is no documentary evidence to pinpoint the dates of those flight attempts either, but all witnesses, and others who had opinions based on hearsay, seem positive that they were early in the second decade. So some time during the first year or two of Pearse's tenure seems likely, and flight experiments would have been possible only in summer when the ground was dry and the grass short. The summers of 1911–12 and 1912–13 therefore seem the likeliest times. However, Pearse's *Evening Star* letter of 1915, written at Milton, gives the impression that he had not been experimenting with flight since he left Waitohi. The 1928 letter tells us he let his patent lapse in 1910 and the inference is that he lost interest in flying after he went to Otago.

Fortunately, it does not matter too much what he did or did not do with his aeroplane at Milton. His historic work had already been done back at Waitohi, and he was not yet on to the project which was to distinguish his last years in Christchurch. As far as aviation was concerned, the Milton years were an interlude. Pearse had other schemes and hobbies to preoccupy him and he put his plane into cold storage, dismantling it and housing it under lock and key in his shed. Holding his regular bicycle in reserve, he bought another, motorised it with a spare aero-engine cyclinder and thus improved his mobility in another kind of way. This is the machine which George Bolt later acquired from the Tai Tapu farmer for his Auckland museum.

Andrew Hood, dispensing petrol and allied services at the garage, used to do business with Pearse and his powercycle quite often: 'The bike had a long-stroke engine very similar to an ordinary engine on a big motorbike, like a Triumph, but a wee bit longer in the stroke it was. He only had a straight pipe and the exhaust stuck up in the air above his head. Just bang-bang-bang without a muffler. The belt he had on was greenhide, twisted to tighten it. He put a rim round the spokes like there used to be on Triumph and King Dick bikes driven with a belt. Oh, he was a shrewd customer, was Pearse.'

Wilson Elliott of Dunedin was chauffeur to a Milton doctor at this time and frequently saw Richard Pearse on his powercycle. 'Even now when I hear a helicopter go over with its put-put-put I still think of Pearse's motor driven bike which was very high geared and he had to run very fast to start it.' Henry Adam of Palmerston North confirms the latter point: 'It carried him down to Milton all right, but had to be pushed up the hills on the way home.'

Many older residents of Milton remembered this bike, its noise, and Richard Pearse's pleasure in it. Roy Jaffrey, who as a boy used to live along the Back Road beyond the Louden's Gully turnoff, recalled the machine well. Sometimes, biking home from school at Milton, young Jaffrey used to be overtaken by Pearse, clothes flapping and feet resting on the powercycle's pedals, one up and the other down. To try to race Pearse was a little fruitless, but Roy Jaffrey and other youthful cyclists often tried.

One dark night, returning from the Athenaeum, Pearse collided with Bill Hamilton, a near neighbour, on Back Road. Hamilton was on a pushcycle, neither had lights and, according to Alex Pringle who heard about it later, 'the air was pretty lurid for a while'.

Miss Mary Salmond remembered Pearse going up the Gully road past the Salmond home at night with coat tails streaming out behind and sparks flying in all directions: 'I often wondered why he didn't catch fire.' Warne Pearse recalled in a radio interview in 1954 how he once went to visit Richard at Milton. They decided to go off for a game of golf together: 'He got another bike for me and he just towed the two of us along and we arrived there on the links as happy as larks.'

A story, possibly apocryphal, used to go the rounds about Pearse getting a puncture in the main street one day. Seeing him stripping off tyre and tube and preparing to mend the leak, a passer-by asked him if he wanted a patch.

'Not a patch, a match!' replied Pearse. He borrowed a boxful, lit a match or two under the hole until the rubber was melting, pinched the edges together, refitted tube and tyre, pumped in some air and was away.

The motorcycle is now among the exhibits of the Auckland Museum of Transport and Technology. An Auckland engineer, E. Harding, has described the machine as follows:

> Richard Pearse adapted a standard bicycle frame to take a single-cylinder air-cooled four-stroke vertical petrol engine . . . The engine cylinder and separate head have the appearance of professional manufacture, being finned castings. [Evidently this is not the engine's original cylinder.] In contrast, the remainder of the engine is obviously the work of an amateur, lacking in engineering expertise but with good ideas and intentions. The cylinder has on either side, apparently riveted to its lower end, a flat steel extension, the lower ends of which carry the crankshaft bearings. The crankcase appears to be of sheet metal, and is secured to the bottom of the cylinder by screws. The admission valve is spring-loaded and automatic in action, while the exhaust valve, and a crude make-and-break, are operated by a two-to-one reduction gear. A conventional sparking plug is used, apparently supplied with current from a battery and induction coil. Vaporisation of petrol is by adjustable supply directly injected into the lower end of a rather long induction pipe laid alongside the exhaust pipe.
>
> Lubrication is by adjustable drip-feed into the side of the cylinder. There is no obvious supply to crankshaft bearings or bottom end, but detailed examination would probably disclose some provision for such an obviously important supply. An adjustable jockey pulley varying the tension of a belt drive serves as a clutch.

Mishaps aside, the powercycle was a great boon to a man who made far more trips to Milton than was helpful to the efficient running of his farm. Though James Gray & Sons ran a horse-and-van delivery service twice a week up the gully, Pearse did most of his shopping in town himself. But his living style was frugal, and he went to Milton for other reasons as well. One of them was to catch up on the latest scientific and engineering books in the reading room of the Milton Athenaeum. The Athenaeum was also the venue for evening classes, the chess and draught clubs, and various sports clubs' meetings. Pearse looked in for a game of chess or draughts occasionally but his chief target was the scientific reading on the shelves. Oldtimers in Milton still remember him sitting in the reading room, especially on Saturday evenings, completely absorbed by his books.

During much of the summer Pearse's mind seems to have been on tennis. He had played a lot of club tennis in Waitohi and the pattern was to continue at Milton.

His proficiency at the game must have been recognised at once, for in his first summer he was selected for the Milton Tennis Club team to play in seven matches. The first of them was against Balclutha in November 1911 and Pearse won all three of the games he played in — men's singles, men's doubles, and mixed doubles. It was a successful debut. This match was followed at fortnightly intervals, except for a break in January, by matches against St Kilda, Outram (twice), Lawrence, Kai-tangata, and the Hanover Club from Dunedin. Overall, Pearse won three-quarters of the games he played, even when his club as a whole was defeated.

Tom Lockhart, who was in the team with Pearse during these pre-war years, later told Alex Pringle that 'Dick Pearse was a really good tennis player.' Lockhart knew Pearse fairly well. These two were the only farmers in the club. Pringle notes: 'It struck me at the time that Lockhart must have been more intimate with Pearse than most persons I had met because he called him Dick Pearse, using the name Dick which I had never heard anyone else use around here. Most people just talked about Pearse, or Mr Pearse perhaps.' This is some indication of the respectful distance maintained between Pearse and other folk.

Others too remember his tennis skill. Jack Anicich heard from Jenny McPherson who sometimes partnered Pearse in club games, that 'if you had him for a partner you very seldom lost'.

Pearse was a familiar enough figure on tennis days: tall, slim, dark curly hair turning grey, swarthy complexion and somewhat stubbly. He cycled to games with his racket clipped to the handlebars, looking slightly neglected; straw boater on top, tennis gear a shade off-white and not often pressed, and soiled sandshoes. He often seemed preoccupied with thoughts unrelated to racket and ball. Alan McLeod recalled him biking into Milton one afternoon, on a Sunday by mistake: 'Didn't know what in hell the day was!'

Tennis club dances and an occasional Bachelors' Ball were his only frivolities. When properly turned out with his belted Norfolk jacket, cap and collar and tie, he was quite presentable company — nicely featured, of good bearing, and well spoken. He was always considerate and courteous. 'A real gentleman,' the ladies remembered.

But he was not an easy mixer. 'He was a bit of a hermit . . . We all thought he had a kink,' remembered one Miltonian. He had no small talk. He did not converse freely unless on a mechanical subject. He rarely started a conversation, and usually waited until spoken to, contributing little of his own accord. Though retiring and reserved he nevertheless liked company.

Miss Salmond remembered him at an evening function wearing fairly inappropriate clothing with as *pièce de résistance* a pair of hobnailed boots: 'Real clodhoppers. I don't think they'd seen Nugget [shoe polish] for many a day.' But the boots' owner joined in with the dancing amicably enough. His partners? Jean Littlejohn, Jean Salmond, and others. 'He had a special affection for the Moore sisters, two very attractive girls called Annie and Janie.' Wouldn't young ladies feel a little nervous dancing with hobnailed boots? 'Yes, but they were well-bred ladies and wouldn't have refused him.' According to another witness, women quite enjoyed Mr Pearse's company ' . . . but they used to reckon they could smell bachelor'. There was never really much prospect of marriage.

During the winter months Dick Pearse's fancy turned to golf. He had spent most of the winter of 1911 settling in to his new farm routines, but in 1912 he found time to join the Tokomairiro Golf Club, which had been formed only two years earlier. With a membership of about thirty-five persons, the club operated on links which were situated near the Domain grounds at the north end of the town on what was later the Government Poultry Farm.

Pearse had not played much golf in South Canterbury but at Milton he took to the game like a cat to salmon. In his first club match against Clutha at the Balclutha links, he played with a handicap of 24. This was in June 1912. By September his handicap was down to 20 and on the Toko Golf Club's closing day in November he had a field day. It was, as the *Bruce Herald* reported next day, 'Waterloo for the scratch golfers'. The first item on the programme was the ladies' and men's handicap putting competition. Richard Pearse, with a handicap of 4 for this event, won the men's section against eleven rivals. 'In the playoff, Mr Pearse's putting was deadly and he pulled off the first prize with the best gross score of the day, 20. After the cup that cheers and the sandwich that satiates had been dispensed, the Club President gave out the trophies.' For his trouble, Pearse collected a tobacco pipe. He did not smoke.

At certain stages of the year (particularly March, April, October and November), the activities of the tennis and golf clubs overlapped. Wednesday was a half-holiday in these times and Pearse invariably treated it as such. With Saturday matches as well and club games in Dunedin which sometimes involved the whole weekend, you could scarcely have called Pearse a full-time farmer.

During the 1912–13 tennis season the Milton club's membership rose to 48 but Pearse still held down his place in the select competition team of six. He played in two matches against Lawrence, two against Outram, and one each against Hauraro, Arthur Street (Dunedin) and Roslyn. He also played in the local club games and in a special match against ex-members, which Pearse helped his side to win. To end the tennis season he played with the Milton team in the Dunedin Easter Tournament in which Milton players 'acquitted themselves satisfactorily and gained experience which will help materially in the improvement of their play,' as the *Bruce Herald* reported. In other words, they lost.

Two months before this tournament ended the tennis season, Pearse had gone back to his golf as well. Jim Barra recalls him setting up a small course on his front paddock, and he evidently put in a lot of practice before the first Club Handicap Tournament of the 1913 season, held in February, for his handicap was dramatically reduced to 12 and throughout the next season hovered between 12 and 15. Monthly medal competitions and two games against Balclutha kept him going till October, shortly after which the season ended.

Tennis had begun again but no mention of Pearse appeared in the *Bruce Herald* for three and a half months. This may have been because of the shoulder injury of which Andrew Hood spoke or some other indisposition, or a crisis of some kind on the farm. At this stage, too, he was having some difficulty with a neighbour.

By February 1914 Pearse was back in the lists again, playing in the Milton Tennis Club match, Married versus Single. The latter lost, but

Pearse won his games. He finished the season strongly by winning all his three games in a match against Anderson's Bay.

The 1914 golf season did not begin very notably and in April the *Bruce Herald* had to rebuke the district accordingly: 'In Milton in the past, the microbe of indifference has killed many institutions. Let us hope it is not now on the trail of the Toko Golf Club.' But it was indeed. The Club played only one match during the year, against Balclutha, and lost it.

Meanwhile the First World War had started.

14. Press coverage

Though Richard Pearse was to be free of the war for another three years, there was drama for him looming on the home front.

In September 1914 his neighbour James Wood took him to court in a civil action for 'wrongful detention of sheep' — not quite sheep-stealing but perilously near it. The *Bruce Herald* recorded the ensuing trial in some detail and the gist of the matter seems to have been as follows.

James Wood was a farmer from Springfield who ran sheep on land adjoining Pearse's western and back boundaries. His statement of claim was that Pearse had illegally and wrongfully converted seven sheep and three lambs to his own use and that the value of these animals (£10) had to be paid to the defendant.

The hearing, in front of Mr E.W. Burton, Stipendiary Magistrate at the Milton Magistrate's Court, occupied several hours of fairly confused and acrimonious wrangling. Wood's case was this. One day late in 1913 he had been helping Pearse to shear his sheep, along with a shearer named Andrew Lilburne. Pearse in mustering his sheep into the yards noticed six 'strangers' and put them out. He later noticed another eight doubtful ones and put them out also. Pearse had then said that when he was earlier grazing sheep at Proudfoot's place some sheep must have been taken out of his flock and an equal number put back in. He accused Wood of knowing something about it, which Wood denied.

Pearse had then gone on to say that his brand had been stolen out of his barn and put on sheep in place of those taken from him. James Wood had retorted that the worst of the sheep he owned were better than the best of Pearse's, so why should he have wanted to take them? Pearse had again challenged his neighbour about the substitute sheep, saying that he believed some people were playing practical jokes on him and that Wood was among them. Wood had got angry and left off work, threatening to fight, but afterwards went on shearing. The charge was repeated by Pearse and this time Wood did go, much offended, saying he would sue.

In December of the same year Wood had approached Constable John Fox at Milton saying that Pearse had some of his sheep. Fox and Wood had gone to Pearse's farm and Pearse had allowed Wood to pick out any doubtfuls that might be his. James Wood could not do so, therefore Pearse had himself selected six or seven for Wood. Wood had driven these off down the road but after they had gone some distance, a dog had come behind and scattered the sheep and Wood had lost them, 'using some language about it'. It is tempting to think that the dog might have been Pearse's.

In answer to questions put to him at the hearing, James Wood said he had always looked on Pearse as a friend. Wood did not claim the seven sheep on the first day he was shearing because he intended to claim them the next day, but he had walked off the job and not returned. The trouble was that both Wood and Pearse used similar punch-holes in the ear to identify sheep.

Pearse's lawyer, Mr Reid, summed up by saying that all through, Pearse's conduct had been open and honourable. He had even asked the plaintiff to help shear his flock, which was not the action of a man fearing an inspection. Reid displayed a letter from Wood to Pearse threatening to sue for the price of three lambs only. This had been written three months after shearing yet nothing was said in the letter about the seven sheep. Therefore, Pearse's counsel asked for a non-suit as no evidence of conversion had been disclosed.

Despite considerable argument from James Wood's lawyer, who conceded that his case was not a strong one, His Worship concluded that the plaintiff's evidence did not seem sufficient. A verdict of non-suit was given but Pearse, however, was not awarded any costs.

In truth, the fault lay on both sides. It is hard to understand why farmers in adjoining properties would use the same earmarks on their sheep, but both were muddlers. James Wood was a well-read and intelligent man, but, like Pearse, his mind was too often on non-agricultural matters. His farm routines were not well organised and he had a tendency to start the day too late.

Dick Pearse's own farm was a shambles. It was poor land in the first place but most of it had at least been under cultivation. Pearse did next to nothing to it.

He had his bottom pasture ploughed once or twice — John Hogg and Edward Coleman did the job for him. Jim Barra sowed his turnips for him. Someone else put in his crop of oats and harvested them. The stooks were put down by the creek but rotted on the damp ground. As for his sheep, it was pitiful to see them.

Pearse had begun by overstocking his farm. With lively competition from the rabbits for what decent feed there was, his 300 Romneys just could not manage. Half of them, according to the Barras, died in the first winter. James Wood's scathing comment on the desirability of his neighbour's sheep would be no injustice. Mrs Jean Leslie used to pass by Pearse's farm frequently on her way from Milton to Glenledi, and sympathise with his sheep. 'They were terrible. He just didn't give them enough to eat, that was all. You know, you had to feed them, even in those days! He couldn't keep the lambs alive after they were taken away from their mothers. Those poor wee things, I can see them yet. It's stuck in my mind. He got rid of them after a while, I think. He didn't want them any more. He didn't deliberately neglect his sheep, he just didn't know any better. He should never have touched animals. Bikes and aeroplanes and things, but not sheep.'

Though there was a farmers' club in Milton, Pearse did not belong to it. He did not exhibit stock at local shows. He did not seek advice from his neighbours. In fact, he barely mentioned farming at all in his conversation. Miss Salmond thought that many Milton folk 'probably put a wrong construction on him as a lazy and incapable man as far as farming was concerned. So he was just left to himself. How he ever came to be a farmer or a landowner I don't know. Perhaps he just liked the seclusion. He should have been an engineer or something.'

Despite his mechanical ingenuity, Pearse was in some ways a curiously impractical man. Mrs Leslie recalled one classic instance of this: 'He found borer in some boards at the back of his barn. Wanting to kill it he took some boards off and put them in the creek. I suppose he hoped to drown the little beggars! Those boards never went back again, I remember that. They were still off the shed when he sold the place.'

Richard Pearse may have been a neglectful farmer but he was not likely to have been a dishonest one. The 'wrongful detention' case clearly arose out of mismanagement and confusion on the part of both men. There is no evidence of adverse reaction against Pearse locally: he was at the tennis club annual general meeting only four days after the trial and played in a match against Anderson's Bay within a month. Thereafter he eased off over the midsummer period, playing only in a Married versus Single match in January, and in the Easter Tournament team at Dunedin three months later. His golf during 1915 got a complete rest.

Pearse now put more time than ever into his workshop. Jim Barra from next door used often to visit him. Sometimes they went shooting rabbits together in the evening. Jim with his .22 rifle and Pearse with a double-barrelled shotgun. But Sundays were best. Jim used to watch him pottering about in his workshop, which was 'just cluttered full of junk'.

At one end was a workbench on which were set up the lathe and vice that Pearse had brought down from Waitohi. He also had the phonograph which he had constructed up north. Jim Barra never saw Pearse make one of his cylinder recordings, but heard him play the results back several times. The recordings were always of his cello playing. This would be the only recordable sound available and Pearse loved his cello. According to Barra the recordings 'sounded all right, but a bit grindy'. On homemade equipment — recording mechanism, cylinders, horn, the lot — that is not to be wondered at.

In the evenings, Pearse could sometimes be heard playing his cello to himself. He had had the instrument since he was about fourteen and he was largely self-taught. The music in him could not be suppressed and it remained a comfort to him till the end of his days. There is something deeply touching about this solitary cello playing. In a way it is reminiscent of that other lonely bachelor, Samuel Butler, playing his Handelian fugues on an upright piano in a remote sod cottage near the headwaters of the Rangitata River 50 years earlier. Pearse played for his own ear alone — 'mainly light classics like Ave Maria', recalls a relative. There was no instrumental group in Milton that could have used him. His name never appeared on local concert programmes. And if occasional passers-by like the Barra children paused down on the road below his cottage and listened for a moment to those melancholy sounds a cello habitually makes, it would have been unbeknown to the musician. The cello stayed with Pearse all his life and was the only personal effect left at his death that had any monetary value.

Andrew Hood believes that Pearse also constructed a huge harp inside his cottage. The instrument was so big, apparently, that he could not get it out of the door.

Pearse now turned his attention to devising farm appliances. One of these was a ridging device, made out of two slanted discs, for moulding turnips and potatoes. A second was a topdressing machine.

One of Pearse's most ingenious but most useless contrivances was his automatic potato-planter. This consisted of two mechanical arms fitted side-by-side to a framework at the back of a double-furrow plough. The jointed mechanical arms, each about two feet long, quaintly resemble those remotely controlled robot arms used to handle radioactive material in an atomic pile. These arms worked off a sprocket on the back wheel of the plough. By means of a cunning combination of cogs, wires, levers and plungers, the arms were obliged as the plough moved forward to dip into a long box of potatoes (carried on the rear frame), impale a potato each on spiked 'fingers', rise clear of the box, knock off the potatoes, and return to the box to repeat the process.

There must be a thousand less complicated ways of planting potatoes than this, but the engineering problems posed in constructing such a contraption would have appealed to Pearse enormously. At any rate this potato-planter, which may well have taken him weeks of workshop time to perfect, lasted less than an hour. Jim Barra, who saw him try it out, maintains that the inventor had done only two or three circuits of his paddock when the whole system seized up. Pearse never tried it again.

A fragment of the topdresser 'worm' and parts of the two potato-planters were still lying about the farm in January 1971, when Jim and John Barra located them among junk in Pearse's former workshop and presented them gleefully to the writer.

On Wednesday 7 April 1915 the Dunedin *Evening Star* published the one hundred and fourteenth in a series of syndicated science articles by the Australian journalist James Collier. It was entitled 'Evolution of Aeronautics' and gave an account of the history of flight up to the time of the Wright brothers. The feature covered the evolution of aerodynamic theory from Aristotle to Langley, and touched as well on ballooning, gliding, kite flying, the development of motors and the advent of powered flight. A fortnight later on 28 April, a follow-up article by Collier appeared entitled 'Mechanism of Flight'. This article detailed the practical advances in flight from box kites to the Wright brothers and ended with up-to-date information on wind science and military aeronautics.

Though Milton had its own newspaper, the Dunedin *Evening Star* and the *Otago Daily Times* were also freely available. Pearse read the articles by Collier and was displeased, especially, it would seem, with the amount of credit given to Langley.

After mulling the matter over for a few days he posted a letter dated 7 May 1915 to the *Evening Star*. The letter was published on Monday 10 May. In 1500 words Richard Pearse attempted to put the whole flight issue into perspective, and to show that 'the honour of inventing the aeroplane cannot be assigned wholly to one man; like most other inventions, it is the product of many minds'.

Collier had, quite correctly, ascribed to the Wright brothers the honour of being the conquerors of the air, and Pearse began by affirming the Wrights' place in history: 'Pre-eminence will undoubtedly be given the Wright brothers of America when the history of the aeroplane is written, as they were the first to actually make successful flights with a motor-driven aeroplane.' He then examined the Wrights' system of flight control, and described how Curtiss had fallen foul of the brothers by his use of ailerons, which was regarded as an infringement of the Wrights' wing-warping patents.

Then Pearse proceeded to the main point of his letter — his own use of 'ailerons' at a time when (before Curtiss) the Wright brothers were working at their wing-warping system. 'As a matter of fact, I patented a system of balancing almost identical with theirs, and just as effective in New Zealand on June 19 1906 . . . The Wrights used wings with flexible tips which could be warped to prevent the machine from turning over sideways, while I used rigid wings with small, moveable horizontal rudders mounted at the tips for the same purpose.'

He also explained how he used a vertical rudder, as the Wrights did, to counteract drag. He then summed up his position: 'As the Wrights' patent was not published at the time I took out mine, it cannot be said that I copied, and as the principle has been held to be the same it amounts to this, that it is a case of two persons living on opposite sides of the world arriving at the same conclusion; and, this being so, I can justly claim to having discovered it independently.'

The vexed question of 'who invented it first' was next dealt with and Pearse outlined modestly phrased claims relating to ailerons, undercarriage and direct transmission. He also referred to some of his engines and explained why he gave up his experiments. He concluded by apologising for the length of his letter, which was intended 'to show that New Zealand brains anticipated the essential features of the aeroplane' and that his own part in the historical process should not be overlooked. Several aspects of this letter are examined in detail elsewhere in this volume, particularly Pearse's comments on flight control, his engines, and the dating question. The overall impression this letter gives is of conscientious analysis. The writer is articulate, and generous in his recognition of other inventors' work. Though he had every right to feel neglected by history, even in 1915, there is nothing grudging or malevolent in his manner.

Pearse was well informed, up to a point. His knowledge of developments in aviation is sound enough when it concerns the Wright era but seems to peter out at about 1910, the year in which he let his 1906 patent lapse. Apart from the Wright brothers, Pearse mentions Langley, Maxim, Curtiss and Santos-Dumont, but he says nothing about Farman, Cody, Blériot, Voisin, Roe, De Havilland, Levavasseur, and other pioneers of the 1909–15 era. He also believed that, at the time he was writing, wing-warping was still as popular a means of flight control as ailerons. This may have been true in 1908 but was by no means so in 1915, nor was it still true in 1915 that the French were in the vanguard of powered flight. And Santos-Dumont was a Brazilian, not a Frenchman, as the correspondent supposes.

It is also clear that Pearse did not realise that the Wrights had applied for their patent a great deal earlier than 1906. He thought they had beaten him by only three months. In fact they had beaten him by three years, applying for their wing-warping patent in March 1903. Pearse's comments on the Wright brothers setting out to solve the problem of flight in 1904 may be the result of ignorance or error. But he may, as argued elsewhere, be deliberately overlooking their earlier efforts as not representing 'true' flights because of the launching rails they used. His reference in his letter to the British Government 'lately' awarding the Wrights £10,000 for use of their ideas was one means available, before the letter was tracked down in the *Evening Star*, of dating the letter sometime during the First World War. The transaction had taken place in 1914.

Pearse's Milton letter is the most important assessment he ever made of his work and his own position in flight history. His 1928 Christchurch letter is quite obviously an abridged version of the 1915 statement and shows little evidence of fresh thinking. There are enough anomalies and *non sequiturs* in the Milton letter, however, to make one wary of dogmatism. Some of Pearse's utterances relating to the engines, control surfaces and dating can be interpreted in more ways than are comfortable; and in these areas the researcher must tread with caution.

The *Bruce Herald* had since 1864 been one of the most lively and alert rural newspapers in Otago and all through the First World War years it gave a thorough and well-informed account of the way the fighting was going in Europe. The news columns were well filled with tales of valour and selfless sacrifice. Not only the editorials but the correspondence columns contained regular exhortations to enlist and fight. Casualty lists were published weekly; white feathers were alluded to. Every effort was made to stir the consciences of eligible men who had not yet responded to the call.

The editor must have considered that too many young men in the Milton district were still unmindful of their obligations, for he republished, with evident approval, a news item from the *Wanganui Chronicle*. This item is worth reproducing for it reflects well the feeling of these times towards supposed shirkers, and its impact seems to have put paid to all activity in the Milton Tennis Club for the next year. The date is January 1916.

> The enthusiasm of some of the young men for hitting a ball about on a certain country tennis court had given rise to the impression that they have not yet been acquainted with the fact that a war is in progress. Some of the settlers in that district were far too polite to offend the susceptibilities of the budding manhood thereabouts by suggesting such a thing as enlistment, but with a sincere endeavour to do something in that desirable direction they resolved on a unique plan. It so happened that on a recent afternoon when sundry young men turned up in flannels and carrying their racquets, they found the net posts pulled up and a rather conspicuous noticeboard on the courts which stated: 'Closed until after the war.' This gentle and courteous hint may possibly bear good fruit.

Not that Pearse was playing much tennis now. He had not played in a club match for a year, and would not play again till after the war. Meanwhile another agricultural implement was taking all his attention: this time, a motorised plough.

Though in the following newspaper report, and in evidence Pearse later gave before the Appeal Board, the machine is referred to as a 'motor plough', Jim Barra is positive that it was motorised discs that Pearse was working on. He might have tried out both possibilities but, more probably, both descriptions apply to the same machine. First, here is the *Bruce Herald* item from the local news column of 10 February 1916:

> Reports have been received of the successful trial one day last week of a motor plough made by Mr R.W. Pearse, of Louden's Gully. We understand that the engine, made by himself, after one or two minor defects had been overcome in connection with the belting, had no difficulty in drawing the plough straight up a forty-foot

ridge with two men sitting on it for ballasting purposes. The trial demonstrated that with the engine in use there was an abundance of power available which will necessitate an increase in the size and weight of the plough attachment. With horse feed at its present price, we wish the inventor every success.

As Jim Barra was one half of the ballast referred to (Pearse was the other half) his description of the machine and its eventual fate is worth mentioning:

> These discs were powered by Pearse's sixteen-cylinder engine taken off his dismantled plane. He fitted the engine to a framework built on to a back-delivery oat cutter and drove the back wheel with a belt running from the motor. There was a clutch. And he had this half set of discs fitted behind the back delivery. The towing shaft of the back delivery had a bicycle wheel attached to it on ordinary bike forks, and a tiller arrangement led back to Pearse, who sat on the framework next to the big wheel. I heard this engine start up and rushed down to the paddock from home. Pearse was trying to get his machine up the hill across his gully. He couldn't get up because the bike wheel reared up in front and he got me to sit up in front to hold her down. He then drove it up the hill some distance to a paddock on the ridge. When he got to the paddock he put the cut on his discs, but when he started off again the whole thing went round and round in circles. Of course he stopped then. The front wheel was the trouble. He took it all back down the hill, removed the bike wheel and welded the coulter of a plough on to the front end of the shaft instead, so it would cut into the ground and go straight. He drove it back up the hill, went four times round the paddock and at one fairly steep place the pole broke. That was the finish. He stopped there. Took the engine off and just left the rest on the hillside. Didn't bother about it again. He didn't have enough money. Everything was built too light.

Older residents of Milton still recall seeing the abandoned implement on the hillside. The remnants of Pearse's back delivery and discs were visible there for years. Some of the larger bits were taken away for scrap and the rest just rusted and rotted away. Occasional fragments are still turned up during cultivation of the hill.

Another invention still remembered by early residents of the district is Pearse's power generator. Upstream slightly from his cottage where some willow trees are at present growing, he dammed the creek and diverted a strong flow of water into a narrow race cut into the upper bank. The race at the point where it curved back to rejoin the creek dropped vertically for a distance of about three metres. At the foot of the drop was a waterwheel made from the small wheel of a binder. It was about a metre across with six or so blades attached at an angle to the spokes. This wheel was housed horizontally and the falling water drove it in the same way as air will turn a propeller. A long shaft of galvanised iron piping, acting as the axle, rose up above ground level, and attached to the top end was a bicycle wheel with the tyre off. A belt connected this wheel to Pearse's dynamo. He could stop the flow of water along the race with a board if he wished to halt the wheel.

Many people knew about this generator and all witnesses agree on the detail of its construction. Mains electricity was not laid on in Milton until 1918, so Pearse's use of electric power was something of a novelty in the district. Some witnesses are sure that he produced the electricity to light up his cottage at night. He may have tried this idea out, but Jim Barra disputes the notion: when the Barras took over the Pearse cottage there were no signs of wiring or electrical fittings within. The inventor used a kerosene lamp for illumination. Rather, it seems, the dynamo was used to charge Pearse's powercycle battery; the motor had coil ignition and he needed the battery to give the system life.

Jack Anicich remembered a talk Pearse gave at a patriotic gathering about this time. It was on the subject of electricity and seemed to last for hours. Everyone got restless, as the subject was incomprehensible to most listeners, and the majority of those present were more keen to get at the supper than to hear Pearse describing how his generator worked, and how he 'bottled the electricity' as he termed it.

The waterwheel was still lying around, badly corroded, until the late 1960s, when Jim Barra buried it along with other useless rubble in the foundations of a new culvert.

15. The conscript

Richard Pearse played a little golf during the winter of 1916. He attended the sixth annual general meeting of the Toko Golf Club in May 1916, and there seconded a vote of thanks accorded to the secretary for his services during the previous year. He played in the club's medal competitions in June and August on a handicap of 12. Shortly after, on the same handicap, he came fourth in the Club Trophy Competiton with a net 84.

But now the summons to war service was being sounded more stridently than ever. The war was going badly and casualty lists were lengthening. In May 1916 the Military Service Bill had been passed to ensure general compulsory service till the end of the war. A single man between the ages of 20 and 46 and without dependants — it was only a matter of time for Pearse. The enrolment of First Division Reservists was advertised for 1 September.

Numerous notices posted up publicly and printed in the press warned eligible men everywhere of the risks of evasion: 'Loss of self-respect, loss of liberty, may be the punishment of a man who does not comply with the provision of the Military Service Act . . . Prompt action is the only way to avoid trouble.'

As soon as all the names of eligible men, both single and married, had been collated throughout the country, balloting began. There was one draw a month, about 4,000 at a time. The *Bruce Herald* reported in January 1917: 'As each fresh ballot is drawn, the interest becomes keener, particularly among those liable to be drawn, as every ballot brings the First Division men nearer the camp.'

The original strength of the enrolment was 84,986 men, and the *Bruce Herald* calculated that it should be at least ten months before the supply was exhausted. It might have been even longer but for the fact that only a third of the men drawn actually went into camp. The Clutha Recruiting District quota was put at 1081.

Pearse's moment came sooner than predicted. In the *Bruce Herald* of

10 May 1917 came the unhappy advice that his name had been drawn for service under the provision of the Military Service Act. 'Pearse, Richard William, farmer, Milton' appeared along with 34 others. He had survived until the last ballot.

Naturally, he did not want to go. It was quite in order to appeal against the draft and scores did so. Every month the Military Service Board held a sitting in the Milton courthouse to listen to objections, and Pearse made his appearance before the chairman, Mr V.G. Day, on Friday 16 June 1917. The *Bruce Herald*'s account of the proceedings reveals most graphically Pearse's predicament.

On that other occasion in 1914 when he had appealed at this court, he had had a lawyer to represent him. Before the board he was obliged to manage the case himself. He began by handing to the chairman a written statement. In it he explained how he had turned his place into a small sheep-run. He did not grow crops and he depended on contractors to get his turnip work done. He had four brothers. One (Warne) had just returned from the Front wounded, one (Jack) had just been turned down, one (Reg) was in camp and the other (Tom) was a doctor in England. He had no relatives within two hundred miles who could look after his place while he was away.

In answer to questions from the chairman, Pearse said he had not tried to lease his place but he had tried to sell. All his time was occupied in keeping the weeds down.

'I understand you are of a mechanical turn of mind and devote a good deal of your time to mechanical inventions in your workshop?' said Captain Barratt, the military representative at hearings on this circuit.

'Well, I do spend some time on research work, which is for the benefit of the farm for the purpose of eliminating the contractors.'

'I also understand you have invented a flying machine?' said Captain Barratt.

'Yes, but that was in Canterbury. I have been engaged on a motor plough lately, for which I do not receive any assistance from the Government.'

'I also understand you spend a good deal of your time playing golf?' continued Baratt, who seems to have done his homework well. 'Of course, I do not wish to suggest you should not play golf. It is a very fascinating game, I believe.'

'I do play golf,' admitted Pearse, 'but I have not averaged half a day a week this last season. All the work I am doing on the farm is for the benefit of the country. The work on the agricultural motor is to make me independent of contractors.'

The chairman then suggested that the case be adjourned until the next sitting for a report from the Efficiency Board, which investigated the validity of appeals such as Pearse's.

'I am willing to sell my farm to the Government, for returned soldiers,' was Pearse's response, 'and I am willing to go if they take over my liabilities.'

The chairman did not comment on this and the case was adjourned. A month later, on 19 July, Pearse heard the result of his appeal. The chairman, Mr Day once more, explained to Pearse how advice had been sought from the Efficiency Board, who had replied that the property could be leased and the rent should prove sufficient to pay expenses.

But Pearse was not giving up so easily. He explained how he was trying to go in for more intensive cultivation. He disputed the Government valuation of the property which was only two-thirds of his. Though the place had all been cultivated at one time a lot of it had reverted to scrub and gorse. He had recently cleared about thirty hectares of this and was endeavouring to bring the place under cultivation again.

'It comes to this,' he argued. 'If I have to go to camp I am going to sell off the stock and shut the place up and I shall be fighting at a loss. I only want five shillings a day.'

'You will get more than five shillings a day,' replied Mr Day.

'Yes, but it will all go in expenses and I'll get nothing for depreciation. If the Government will pay for depreciation I will go.'

Though Pearse's second statement on what he was trying to do with the farm contradicted his first, and though his estimate of the size of the area he had cleared appears a little optimistic, his case was a good one. But it was by no means good enough. His appeal was dismissed and he was instructed to join up with the draft leaving on 18 August 1917.

There was little time left. Pearse seems to have sold off his sheep, as threatened, and just locked everything up and left. There was no farewell.

He entered camp on 20 August with the service number of 63410. A photograph, the last known to be taken of him, shows him with 25 other conscripts posed in front of their hut at Trentham. He embarked for Britain on 21 November with the 32nd Reinforcements of the 1st New Zealand Expeditionary Force. On 8 January 1918 he was posted as a private to the Otago Infantry Regiment and trained in England with the 3rd and 4th (Reserve) Battalions. During training he was troubled by a recurring illness arising from a pre-enlistment complaint, probably the typhoid attack, and in June 1918 he was admitted to the 3rd New Zealand General Hospital, Codford. The following month he was classed medically unfit for further service.

He returned to New Zealand on 25 October 1918 and was discharged on 22 November, after a total service of 1 year and 95 days, including 388 days overseas. For his service he was awarded the British War Medal.

By the time Pearse got back to Milton the war had been over for a fortnight and the armistice jubilations had ebbed. There was no special welcome at the station. Servicemen had been returning in dribs and drabs for some time now and it would be several months yet before the rest got back. It was impossible to send a deputation to the station every time a train came in. The *Bruce Herald* was full of angry correspondence from local residents protesting at the town's lack of gratitude towards its returned men. The Mayor was being asked to do something about it or resign. He said he would wait until all the servicemen got back then welcome them *en bloc*. At one of his council meetings the mayor got involved in a heated exchange with one or two councillors over his delaying tactics, and the *Bruce Herald* reported that in the middle of it all the newly installed electric lighting fused. The debate continued in darkness and the mayor held his ground.

So there was no hero's welcome for Pearse. Instead he made his way back to Louden's Gully under his own steam and found that his cottage and workshop had been burgled during his absence. Many valuable tools had been stolen.

Jack Salmond met him on the road returning to Milton, and invited him in for something to eat. 'My brother was pretty upset,' recalled Miss Salmond. 'He thought it was a pretty shady trick to have played on this man. So Mr Pearse came home to tea. I remember that he was quiet. He wasn't aggressive. He didn't berate anyone for his bad fortune. He just took his meal and seemed to be very grateful. He didn't volunteer much. That was the only time I ever remember Mr Pearse coming into our house.'

No one ever discovered who burgled Richard Pearse but the district was disgusted by the business, according to Miss Salmond, and very sorry on Pearse's account.

He now bought some pigs and a few more sheep and tried to settle back to the old routine. By 15 January 1919 he was playing club tennis once again. Two years earlier, almost to the day, he had been selected to play in an Old Buffers versus Young Duffers match. Pearse had been chosen for the latter team but did not play. Now he was an Old Buffer, and the Buffers lost. Pearse had not mislaid all his former cunning, though, and won his own singles match convincingly.

But he was now 42 years old, not terribly fit, and slowing down somewhat. His hair was turning distinctly grey. Nothing more is heard of him until the end of the year, when a Welcome Home social was held by the Helensbrook and North Branch districts. These districts are a mile or two north-west of Louden's Gully, but Pearse had not been welcomed home anywhere else and it is possible that the organising committee took pity on him.

The evening was held at the Forsyth residence on the first Friday of December 1919 and took the form of a social with presentations made to returned soldiers and friends or relatives of the fallen who had enlisted from the area. A large gathering of more than two hundred was present. The proceedings began with speeches of welcome and a short concert followed. Then 'In Memoriam' medals were presented to the relatives of all local soldiers who had failed to return, and medals and sovereign cases were given to the returned men. Among the 17 in the latter group was Private R.W. Pearse. Young ladies from the audience presented these souvenirs, and the *Bruce Herald* remarked later that 'the whole proceedings were marked by a fervour and enthusiasm which marked the event as almost historical'.

A dance in the Forsyth barn followed: 'During intervals in the dance, recitations were given. One of these by Mr Pearse deserves to be rescued from oblivion. The dance broke up in the early hours of the morning with *Auld Lang Syne*.' Here is a side of Pearse not so often seen. He may have been reserved by nature but he was by no means misanthropic at this stage, nor incapable of impressing an audience if given the chance. Roy Jaffrey thought that the recitation was a humorous one — on the subject of magnetos.

The last time Pearse made any sort of public appearance was on the occasion of the Prince of Wales' visit to Milton in May 1920. There was a civic reception at the station to greet Prince Edward as he passed through by train that morning. A parade was made up of 35 returned servicemen under Captain Gilroy, 3 Boer War veterans and 60 cadets. The wait at the station proved very trying. There was a bitterly cold blustery sou'west wind and the train was three-quarters of an hour overdue. Alex Pringle was at the reception and recalled the occasion very well:

I called at the Returned Servicemen's Association rooms on the way to the station and asked about the parade. I was told we were to parade in mufti and that overcoats would not be worn. So I decided there and then that I wouldn't be on parade. I watched it as a bystander instead and had quite a good view. The train was late and everybody had to stand and shiver in the bitterly cold wind. Pearse was a tall fellow in comparison with most of the other men and he stood out quite conspicuously to my sight and memory. I would say that he had a felt hat on and looked a bit shaggy about the hair. He wore a Norfolk coat — a square-cut jacket with a belt — which was habitually worn by Pearse on formal occasions. He looked as though he had got into the clothes which he had left behind before he was called up. I always think of him as being a little oddly dressed. He didn't follow the crowd.

In the line-up with Pearse as the Prince of Wales shook hands with all on parade was Alex Currie, who recalled not only Pearse but the fact that the Prince's right hand was so tender from the handshaking that he performed the operation with his left hand instead.

Pearse's last year at Milton was a quiet one. He played no more competition tennis or golf. His farm, which had become badly overgrown with thistle, scrub, gorse and other weeds after he left for the war, must now have been a real headache to him. Prices were falling, and though he could probably live on five shillings a week there was no sense in his staying on at Louden's Gully. He was weary of the land. His heart had never been in farming, and he now resolved to make another fresh start.

He offered the land to Frank Barra next door, a price was settled, and on 17 May 1921 Pearse parted with his property. The payment was £615, a mere £59 more than he had paid for it ten years earlier. But it could not be helped. The market was falling.

Jim Barra clearly remembered Pearse's last day at Louden's Gully. He went up to Pearse's cottage to say goodbye but saw through a window the occupant stark naked at his washbasin. Jim did not linger. He went back to the boundary fence and continued hacking at the gorse. Pearse left a little later by lorry for the Milton station, saying farewell to nobody. According to Miss Salmond, there were later some regrets in the district that nothing had been done by way of a sendoff for him, but it was too late: he had gone, and he would not have wished for ceremony anyway.

He took little with him, just his lathe, vice, hammers, hacksaw, stocks and dies, some kitchen utensils, a few gardening implements, a bicycle pump, his powercycle, cello and recording apparatus. His dynamo, potato-planter, moulding machine, topdresser, motorised discs, sixteen-cylinder engine and aeroplane remnants he left behind.

The Barras used to have their harvesting done by Bill Hamilton. Every time Hamilton came on the job he took away a bit of Pearse's machinery for scrap metal. Duncan Allison took off other remnants. All but a few fragments of the topdresser and potato-planter have now completely vanished. The big engine was last seen many years ago in a shed on a farm at Wharenui. For a while Mrs Barra used pieces of bamboo from the aeroplane framework for curtain rods, but now even they have gone. The cottage has since been converted into a shearing shed.

He set off north for Christchurch where he had a sister and brother living. It is hard to say what his thoughts must have been, but it is likely that one exciting prospect sustained him — the chance to get back to his first love, aeroplanes. Even before he went to Christchurch he seems to have devised a way of living whereby he could have his hobby and an income too.

While overseas he had become interested in flying again. He later told Warne that his few months abroad had given him a chance to see the significant way in which aviation was developing. His enthusiasm for air machines had been rekindled.

In his last year at Milton the town had had exciting visits from Captain Euan Dickson and 'Bert' Mercer. A Balclutha reporter on the *Bruce Herald* covered Dickson and commented on 'the steady and graceful passage of the first aeroplane to be seen in this part of the world'. Captain Mercer of the New Zealand Aero Transport Company of Timaru later gave a demonstration at Milton in one of the DH-9s given to New Zealand by the British Government after the war.

However, Pearse was not an orthodox thinker and the plane he had in mind was totally different from anything else in operation. Roy Jaffrey remembered him talking about it to the mechanically minded Hamilton brothers at the Welcome Home in December 1919. Pearse's scheme was nothing less than to construct an aeroplane capable of vertical as well as horizontal flight — to make practical a dream that dates back to Leonardo da Vinci.

16. Bungalow building

Christchurch in 1921 was a city of 105,670 persons, the chief town in Canterbury Province, the largest in the South Island and the third most populous in New Zealand.

Pearse's activities during his first six months in Christchurch are unknown. His sister Maggie had lived in the city since 1908, married to Charles Galt, a draper. His brother Reg was farming at Ohoka, near Rangiora, thirty kilometres out of the city. But Richard Pearse did not stay with either. He probably took cheap lodgings somewhere and looked about for a suitable property.

One part of Christchurch that was being opened up at this time was the north-eastern sector between the city and New Brighton. Linwood North, Wainoni, Aranui, Burwood and Bromley were sand-dune areas, undulating wildernesses of lupin and broom and very sparsely settled up to 1900.

Although there was no public road to New Brighton until 1902 a small community now known as Aranui grew up alongside the tram route where Pages Road was later formed. The first settlers there used the New Brighton tramline as a right-of-way. Their land was cheaply bought but it was almost pure sand and infertile. Wainoni, situated west of Pages Road in between Linwood and Aranui was another such area. As a district its chief claim to fame up till then had been Professor Bickerton's Wainoni Park, the most extraordinary entertainment area Christchurch has ever seen.

It was on Breezes Road, Wainoni, that Pearse had decided to make his fresh start, only a block away from Bickerton's former land. He had spent all but 18 months of his 44 years in rural areas and Wainoni was suitably quiet at this stage: yet if he wanted to go to town the New Brighton tram route was only a few hundred metres' walk to Pages Road.

On 28 November 1921 Pearse, describing himself as a farmer, paid John Hutchinson of New Brighton £45 for a section of one-quarter acre

(0.1 ha). It was situated on the south side of Breezes Road, the next section but one from the Wainoni Street corner. Pearse, who had built nothing larger than a shed before, now set about constructing a house.

He did the job on his own, in a deliberate and methodical manner. Much of the timber he used was secondhand and he wheeled it to the section on a bicycle. He lived on the site. There were only three or four other houses in the vicinity and Pearse kept completely to himself. Occasionally, neighbouring children would visit him to see what was going on, and Frank Roberts remembered that several times he recorded their voices on his recording machine and let them hear themselves back. Now and again he used to go next door to the Roberts' house and size things up when he was not sure what to do next. Frank remembers Pearse sinking his own well behind the house. He had a gantry and pulled the monkey up and down himself. In sandy coastal suburbs like Wainoni the water table is apt to vary with the tides and seasons of the year. But nevertheless, water is never very far down — usually within three metres — and Pearse got to it quite easily.

The house he built still stands. It was formerly 4 Breezes Road but in renumbering it has become no. 164. In style it is a single-storeyed weatherboard bungalow with a livingroom, three bedrooms and entrance hall, passage, scullery, bathroom and detached washhouse and toilet. The construction is reasonably solid still, and has lately been restyled, but originally it was far from an artistic performance. Pearse did everything himself, even to installing the lighting and plumbing. He planted a macrocarpa fence and front hedges but did not put down paths or garden. The land remained sandy and uncultivated until his death, though there was a rough attempt at a front lawn.

As soon as the house was finished, Pearse put in a tenant and lived off the modest rental.

Barely two years after he had bought the Wainoni section he bought another, at 68 Wildberry Street in Woolston. Woolston was by 1923 a well established south-eastern suburb skirting the lower Heathcote River and Ferry Road, the main route to Sumner and the eastern Port Hills. It had been part of the City of Christchurch since 1921.

Pearse must have been keen to get started on his second house. He had applied for a building permit on 4 December 1923, over a fortnight before the purchase transaction was completed on 20 December. Wildberry Street branches off Richardson Terrace on the Heathcote River two blocks upstream from Radley Bridge, which is situated where the Christchurch Quay used to be.

Paying Albert Coleman £80 for the one-fifth acre (0.08 ha) property, Richard Pearse described himself on the title deed as a builder. He used the same description when at the beginning of 1924 he entered his name on the City of Christchurch district electors' roll. So for the time being, anyway, farming was not on his mind. The Wildberry Street section had been owned by Coleman since 1913, when the street frontage was first subdivided for close settlement.

On his permit application Pearse stated his intention of building a house to the value of £500 and paid a fee of 30s for the privilege. Again he set about the job quite unassisted. The result, after another two years' effort, was a second single-storeyed bungalow.

This house was better built than the Wainoni one, but it still bears the mark of Heath Robinson. It is a weatherboard structure with corrugated iron roof and low concrete foundations, one livingroom, three bedrooms, kitchen, bathroom, sunporch and detached laundry. Pearse put in the septic tank himself and all the plumbing and wiring, as with his first house. He also laid paths and put up a paling fence and gate along his frontage.

A few years later, a tenant tried to lay some linoleum: 'On putting the lino down in the front room I found that one end of the room was six inches or more wider than the other. I drew his [Pearse's] attention to it. He told me he had built the house for himself and had never used a ruler.'

These building operations absorbed so much of his time that Pearse had no chance to enjoy his former hobbies. Though there was a tennis club handy to his Woolston house he did not join it, nor did he keep up his golf. While thousands of ex-servicemen had joined the Returned Servicemen's Association Pearse did not, although his brother Reg had since 1921 been a member of the Christchurch RSA. Freemasonry did not attract Pearse. Workingmen's clubs did not either. He was essentially an 'unclubbable' man, by Dr Johnson's definition, and the Christchurch Public Library seems to have provided his only relaxation.

When 68 Wildberry Street was habitable Pearse undertook his last property deal. A block further along Wildberry Street from the river was a vacant section on the Dampier Street corner. On 7 May 1926 he bought the one-eighth acre (0.05 ha) property from John Nash, a railway employee, paying £105 for it. Pearse reverted to describing himself as a farmer, so perhaps he felt that carpentry was not his long suit after all, yet there is no sign of this in the briskness with which he once again started building. He had been issued with a building permit a fortnight before the land purchase was finalised, paying once more a 30s fee for permission to erect a 'dwelling' which he estimated would be worth £500. The same calculation as before.

So after little more than a two-year interval, Richard Pearse, now aged just under fifty, was about to build his third and last house. As soon as he began work at Dampier Street he leased his Wildberry Street home and — as was by now his custom — lived on the building site.

For protection he erected in one corner of the house foundations a smaller shelter of boards and sacking, roofed with corrugated iron, and he later converted this into the kitchen of the house. There was a copper but no hot water, no electricitiy, no stove, no drainage. Pearse slept on a pile of sacks; in his work clothes, neighbours thought. He lived as austerely as a troglodyte, mostly on bread, cheese, milk and cheap biscuits.

Through the butt end of the 1926 winter and on into spring he plugged away at the house, getting framework and weatherboards up. He worked largely by rule of thumb. A former neighbour was asked to recall the house being built, and its builder: 'That funny old man! He used to tack each board up at either end then walk out into the middle of the street and study it carefully before hammering it on.'

Slowly and methodically he worked at the job, completely absorbed. His dress was generally an old white shirt buttoned up to the neck, long trousers tied in at the ankles, lace-up shoes, and no socks. In cold weather he would put on a cloth cap and his venerable Norfolk jacket, fastened at the throat with a nail. His long curly grey hair made him seem much older than he actually was, and his lean and lined features and a generally neglected look fortified this impression.

During the year new neighbours moved in alongside Pearse in Dampier Street — Joe and Alice Birchall, a couple who had come out to New Zealand from Lancashire before the First World War. The Birchalls were kindly folk who did their best to be neighbourly to the man next door, but though they tried to engage him in conversation he remained reserved and preoccupied. He kept strictly to himself. Now and again he accepted a cup of tea. Mrs Birchall would pass it through the fence and Pearse used to leave it on the Birchalls' front lawn when he was finished. Despite numerous approaches, he declined to go next door for a meal.

Christmas Day 1926 was wet and cold. Pearse seemed not to realise what day it was and worked away as usual on his house. Thinking that the Yuletide weather might make Pearse more sociable, Mrs Birchall went to her spare-room window which looked out on Pearse's section and called to her neighbour through the rain.

'Happy Christmas, Mr Pearse. Would you like to have dinner with us today? I have a lovely hot meal ready with peas, new potatoes and all the trimmings.'

'No thank you, Mrs Birchall. I don't want any charity.'

'But this isn't charity, Mr Pearse. It's Christmas time.'

'No. Don't want it, thank you.'

So dinner at the Birchalls was a fairly tense affair. Joe Birchall was so wild at Pearse's refusal he couldn't eat a thing.

'You please yourself,' said his wife, 'but I'm eating mine. If I hadn't asked him, though, I couldn't.'

Later on in January, the Birchalls became alarmed at Pearse's apparent disappearance. It was not his custom to leave the site except for essential supplies, and he never seemed to go on holiday, but now he was nowhere to be seen. Mr Bassan, living nearby, thought he heard groans coming from Pearse's lean-to, and the Woolston police sergeant was sent for.

Forcing his way into the shelter he found Pearse stretched out on his makeshift bed, gaunt, unkempt and more dead than alive. There was nothing edible in sight except a stale crust and half a tin of mildewed condensed milk. Bassan's car was used to take the sick man straight to the Christchurch Public Hospital. Pearse's only plea was that Mrs Birchall be put in charge of his cello, still his dearest possession. The cello case, a large, black wooden box, was secured by three locks; and Mrs Birchall gained the impression that there was more of value in it than a cello alone.

On the way to the hospital the policeman asked Pearse why he did not get help earlier.

'I have good neighbours,' replied Pearse, 'but I won't accept their charity.'

Nor did Pearse really need their charity. He was receiving the income from two rented houses and was by no means destitute. When he was being examined on his arrival at the hospital, the doctor found a money belt strapped round his waist. He had enough to live on in reasonable comfort but seemed quite oblivious of his basic needs. By nature he was frugal, and as with other lonely old bachelors, self-neglect was the real problem.

The medical notes on Richard Pearse's sojourn in hospital are still on file. He was admitted on 27 January 1927, giving his occupation once more as builder, and stayed in hospital for twenty days. For ten of these he was treated for stiffness of the legs, for a week he suffered severe pain in his legs whenever he stood, and for six days he experienced loss of appetite and nausea.

No diagnosis was made despite a large number of investigations. A barium meal examination disclosed an irregular filling in the upper portion of the stomach. This was thought to be either gaseous distension or malignancy. The report concluded rather dolefully that 'if the filling defect is due to malignancy, the disease is beyond the zone of operability'.

But Pearse was sent home again on 15 February, much improved, and it now seems likely that he had been a victim simply of malnutrition compounded by fatigue. It was certainly not cancer.

Mrs Birchall saw him in town soon after he had been discharged and he now looked so well she did not recognise him at first: 'He was really nice-looking, his head a mass of curls, and he told me he was feeling very much better.'

Pearse returned to Dampier Street, reclaimed his cello and settled down again in his lean-to. While he was in hospital a cord of timber had arrived and been dumped on the footpath outside his property. The Birchalls had moved it out of harm's way and Pearse now got back to work on his house with renewed energy. He finished it sometime in mid-1928.

The result this time was a wooden bungalow on low concrete foundations and with a corrugated iron roof. It had a livingrooom, a kitchen, two bedrooms, a bathroom, washhouse and detached toilet. The property boundaries were marked by a mixture of paling and privet fences, and a concrete path led from the front gate to the entrance porch. Much later on a garage was built and the house itself finished in stucco.

Pearse's bungalow building was at an end. He now had another matter to attend to.

17. Obsession

Early on the morning of Tuesday 11 September 1928 a large and tense crowd gathered at Christchurch's Wigram Aerodrome, then the largest in the country. They were there to see history being made.

Sharp at 9.15 came a shout of 'There they are!' Outlined against a thin band of white clouds rising from the northern horizon could be discerned five tiny specks, one blacker than the rest. Soon they were distinctly visible to all. There was no mistaking the silhouette of Kingsford Smith's giant tri-motor Fokker monoplane and its escort of four RNZAF Bristol Fighters which had taken off half an hour earlier to meet and escort it.

A kilometre from the airport, the *Southern Cross* broke from its escort. To an anthem of sirens, factory whistles, car horns, and frantic cheers, Kingsford Smith and his crew touched down safely.

This was, to date, the most dramatic illustration of aeronautical progress in the southern hemisphere but, up till 1928, there had been several feats of daring to focus attention on developments in aviation in New Zealand. Will Scotland, in his Caudron biplane, flew the 157 km from Timaru to Christchurch in 1914. Between 1919 and 1920 George Bolt established four distance records, using Auckland as his base and flying a B & W floatplane. Euan Dickson in his Avro 504K was on 25 August 1921 the first man to fly across Cook Strait. Dickson also made the first flight into the Mackenzie Country, being forced to land en route — ironically enough — on Warne Pearse's property at Waitohi to refuel. Bolt in 1921, aboard a Supermarine Channel flyingboat, became the first to fly from Auckland to Wellington, a distance of 614 km. And three weeks later 'Bert' Mercer eclipsed all previous single-day long-distance records by flying from Timaru to Auckand aboard his DH-9 in just under seven hours, a distance of 1000 km.

Nevertheless, the aviator who stole the largest headlines, by a wide margin, was 'Smithy'. Squadron Leader Charles Kingsford Smith's plan to fly the Tasman in his Wright Whirlwind-powered Fokker had received a great deal of advance publicity in the press, and when the event happened the excitement was phenomenal.

Christchurch had a grandstand view of the climax and both press and public made the most of it. The Christchurch *Star* on Tuesday 11 September 1928 scooped the news and did itself full justice. 'Southern Cross Makes Historic Flight' ran its banner headline: 'Huge crowds welcome daring aviators to New Zealand in early landing at Wigram Aerodrome. Aviators have at last conquered the Tasman Sea. After a thrilling flight through gale and rain at an average speed of more than eighty knots the *Southern Cross* arrived over Christchurch shortly after 9 am today and then landed on the Sockburn Wigram aerodrome amid the excited cheers of tens of thousands.' It does not require a very bold imagination to picture Richard Pearse in the crowd.

One feature article written for the occasion concerned pioneers of aviation in New Zealand. It implied that there had been nothing done in the country before Arthur Schaef of Wellington built a plane 'somewhere in 1911' and that 'it was not until 1913 that any real attempt was made to fly in New Zealand'. The article also touched on the early work of New Zealand pioneers Percy Fisher and Joe Hammond. It finally gave a witty account of how Emile Vershuren duped James D. Walsh and how both these Americans attempted in 1914 to short-change New Zealand's first aviation syndicate.

Pearse must have been both disappointed and hurt to realise how little anyone knew about his own pioneer work. Within two days he had composed a letter to the editor of the *Star*. It was published in that paper on Saturday 15 September 1928, and began: 'Dear Sir — the article in your paper entitled "Pioneers of Aviation" does not do justice to New Zealand brains as to the amount of pioneer work New Zealand inventors did and originated, and so I am writing this in the interests of history.'

He then went on to describe the plane he patented in 1906 and explain — as in his Milton letter — the differences between his 'ailerons' and the Wright brothers' wing-warping. His account of these control surfaces and Curtiss's legal problems seems to be derived from the earlier letter. So do his description of the engines, his claims on behalf of the undercarriage and direct transmission, and his account of when he began and finished his experiments.

All in all it is a concise and even-tempered restatement of his Milton position. The only hint of regret or frustration comes with his mention of the monopoly which the Wrights gained in the aircraft business with their wing-warping patent:

Ailerons would have given me a monopoly in New Zealand if I had kept the patent covered, but I let it lapse in 1910 because I did not know the Great War was coming, and I did not see much prospect of selling aeroplanes in New Zealand. So I came to the conclusion that to keep it covered would be only throwing good money after bad. It is the Great War that made the aeroplane and had I kept my patent covered I had the New Zealand Government in my power . . . But I decided to give up the struggle as it was useless to try to compete with men who had factories at their backs.

Perhaps the most interesting information in this letter, and it is not given in the earlier one, is his brief reference to the early takeoffs:

My aeroplane was of enormous size, having 700 square feet of wing area, and it was extremely light, being mainly of bamboo, and weighed, with man on board, under 700 lb so each square foot of wing area had to support 1 lb. At the trials it would start to rise off the ground when a speed of twenty miles an hour was attained. The speed was not sufficient to work the rudders, so, on account of its huge size and low speed, it was uncontrollable, and would spin round broadside on directly it left the ground. So I never flew with my first experimental plane, but no one else did with their first for that matter.

The fact that this letter had obliged him once more to consider carefully where he stood in relation to others in the evolution of powered flight, coupled with the enormous enthusiasm for flying which Kingsford Smith's tour of New Zealand now generated, probably did much to set his inventive mind ticking over again.

He had by now moved into his house at 68 Wildberry Street and it is presumed that the tenants there shifted over to the new dwelling on the Dampier Street corner some two blocks away. Pearse was now 51, with an assured income from his rents. For the first time in 30 years he did not have to worry about where the next shilling was coming from. He was virtually in retirement and could devote all his time to that which mattered most — pottering about with his mechanical ideas. He had had little chance to break fresh ground since before the war, but now he began to work on the idea which had been in his mind since Milton.

Warne Pearse told Bolt how the idea developed: 'When [Richard] came back after the war, after some considerable time I met him in Christchurch. I asked him what he was busy at. "I'm building a new plane which I call the Utility Plane because with my engine on a swivel I hope to do away with much runway and be able to hover and settle on a lawn."'

The Christchurch Public Library now became almost his second home. He spent a great amount of time in the reference room poring through tome after tome on engineering, aviation, mechanics, aeronautics and science. Gradually he brought himself up to date with developments in aircraft design and performance since the war. Henry Adam, who had known Pearse at Milton, once spotted him in the Public Library when passing through Christchurch. Pearse was dressed in the same clothes that he used to wear down south and was reading with rapt concentration, but Adam left him alone: 'As I thought that his hearing might not be very good, I hesitated to explain who I was.'

Every few months Pearse took a train south to Temuka to spend a weekend with his elderly parents at Landue, but in the main he kept to himself, seeing very little of anyone, even Maggie and Reg, who were reasonably handy to him in Christchurch. As his plans for the Utility Plane gradually took shape, he became more and more engrossed in the project — draughting, jotting, calculating, and researching. He also became increasingly secretive about it all. The sort of aeroplane he had in mind — an all-purpose convertiplane, an aircraft for the masses — then had no equivalent elsewhere and obviously had commercial possibilities. That is, if he could construct, test and demonstrate what was so far only a vision, an ingenious idea on scraps of drawing paper.

Though he had been thinking about the matter since the First World War ended, it is difficult to say when he first began work on his Utility Plane. He would have had little opportunity to do so before his house-building projects ended in 1928, but in that year he may have made a definite move to get the scheme started, on paper anyway. His comments in the *Star* letter of September, about his 'first' plane, strongly suggest that he had the details of another plane in mind at the time of writing.

However, he could not have made much headway with the actual construction of his aircraft until his garage was built late in 1932. It is likely, when he did start, that he began work on the motor first, for on the construction and performance of his special engine depended the success of the whole operation. One of the drawings for his engine is pasted on to a document dated 1933, and this is the only indication of when he got under way. In a letter of February 1944, one of the many he later wrote to the Patent Office in Wellington, Pearse told how he had spent eight years constructing his plane. This indicates that he began building it not later than 1936, but he seems to have been referring here to the airframe whose design he was then trying to patent. The engine and its accessories he had decided to patent separately, on the advice of the Australian Patent Office. Therefore, one may surmise that he was considering his design in 1928, that he began constructing his engine in about 1933, and had started on the airframe by 1936. But more of this later.

Digory Pearse died at Temuka on 17 March 1932, leaving his estate to his wife Sarah. Digory and his son Richard had seen little of each other since Richard left home in 1911. In personality, character and interest they had little in common other than their shared liking for tennis and music.

Digory's last years passed fairly quietly. He spent a lot of time in his billiard room and went to the local stock sales; otherwise he stayed at home with Sarah, who rarely left Landue for any reason. After Digory's death Richard kept up his intermittent Temuka visits to see his mother and his two youngest sisters, Florence and Ruth, who looked after her.

On 27 April Richard Pearse was granted for 5s a permit to build a garage to the value of £12. The structure he subsequently built was 4.2 metres by 2.9 metres, with corrugated iron walls and roof, and a concrete floor. The workshop which backed on to it was slightly larger, 4.5 metres by 2.9 metres, and was built of wood with an iron roof and earth floor. The workshop end of this compound structure was more primitively built, probably from offcuts from his Wildberry Street home, and was most probably put up in the mid 1930s, soon after the garage. At any rate the workshop did not long survive Pearse's death in 1953, as a later owner of the property tore it down. The garage alone stands now, and the back end, which used to be connected to the workshop, has been walled off. Even this garage is a masterpiece of improvisation, scrap tin and packing-case boards being the chief components.

Evidently, his first notion of what his garage should be like was different. His tenant at Wildberry Street from June 1930 to June 1932 was L.L. Preston, at that time a railway signalman. Preston wrote to George Bolt in 1959 telling him: 'When I was leaving Christchurch on transfer to Dunedin he [Pearse] told me he was going to build a garage on the section behind the house. I said it would be a good idea. He said he was not going to put a roof on it. I asked him why not. He said he was going to build an aeroplane that was going straight up. I asked him what he was going to build it out of. He said steel bicycle tubing. Next I asked him who was going to fly it and he said he was. As he appeared to be a man of about fifty and suffered terribly from indigestion, I admired his courage.'

Preston, who wrote to Bolt from Mosgiel, near Dunedin, largely to express his 'appreciation of Mr Pearse as a man', discloses that there was a kindly nature behind Pearse's gruff facade: 'As it was Depression time, every time we got a cut in wages, Mr Pearse reduced our rent accordingly, without [our] asking, from 25s a week to 17s 6d, an act that was much appreciated . . . Whatever the result of his labours, I will always regard him as a gentleman and a credit to New Zealand.' Pearse had also spoken to Preston about his early flight experiments: 'What he told me was in line with what I have read in the local papers, re getting on top of a twelve-foot hedge etc.'

However, it was the convertiplane which now absorbed all the inventor's energies.

Whenever Pearse went down to Landue to see his mother and sisters he seemed completely preoccupied with his new undertaking. Sometimes Warne and his three children — Richard, Margaret and James — would come across from Trewarlet for an evening with them: 'Uncle Dick used to talk of nothing but his plane in Christchurch,' his nephew Richard remembers. 'He was not interested in farming, politics, the weather or the economy. Just his plane.' A plane for everybody . . . mass-produced . . . one you could go to work in . . . that you could operate from your back lawn . . . with folding wings and tail so you could store it in your garage like a car. He would do for the aeroplane what Henry Ford did for the automobile.

'He had no small talk,' recalls his nephew. 'He was pretty deaf and he used to shout, quoting figures by the hour on length of stroke, compression and so on. He was very proud of his engine and its horsepower-weight ratio. He achieved this through his double-acting cylinders. He told us how it took nine solid months just drawing up the blueprints alone. Apparently he spent a great deal of time at the library working everything out as scientifically as possible.'

Margaret Pearse, later Mrs Dudley Gardiner, remembered her Uncle Dick's visits too: 'He was tall, leanly built with snow-white hair — long and curly — and a white moustache. He used to arrive at Grannie's with his cello. He would take it everywhere with him, like others take a suitcase. We were rather in awe of him. He was not a bit interested in children. He talked a lot about his plane, loudly and in a deep voice. He carried himself well with his back straight as a ramrod, and he was reasonably tidy. He didn't smoke or drink — except perhaps for a sherry occasionally. As the evening wore on he would mellow a bit. When the music started he would quite change. As he played the cello he seemed to lose his gruffness and became a different person — far more approachable. He favoured the light classics; Strauss waltzes and that sort of thing. Forence and Ruth would accompany him on piano and piccolo.'

To his neighbours in Woolston, Richard Pearse was always an enigma. No one was very sure where he had come from, what his connections were, how old he was or what he did for a living. Frequently he used to be seen cycling back from the local rubbish dump, his bike laden with junk. Timber, wire, tin, wheels, piping, scrap metal, rope, old doors, window frames, roofing iron and specially selected debris of all sorts. Naturally, there was much speculation about what he was up to; a lot of the material would go into his housing projects, but the rest was a puzzle.

The garage-workshop was evidently the key to it all. Pearse spent most of his time there. Occasional hammering sounds could be heard behind the garage doors, which were never left open, and the neighbourhood became more and more curious. He must have sensed that his operations were attracting more attention than was desirable so he put up a 1.8-metre corrugated-iron fence which stretched from the side of his house right across the garage entrance to his left-hand boundary. Nothing could now be seen of the garage-workshop except the top of the double doors and the roof.

The feeling developed in the district that 'old Mr Pearse' had a kink of some kind. He rarely spoke to anyone, except to return a greeting. Children were very wary of him. Even now, they still recall 'Mr Pearse' with awe and respect.

'I remember him best as a gaunt old boy riding round on a fixed-wheel bicycle very slow and very erect,' recollects Ian McBride. 'He was usually pretty gruff. I got the message somehow that he was a crazy old bloke and to keep out of his way. We used to peer at his place from across the other side of the road. Through his front picket fence we could see grass growing up to his windowsills. He had no garden at all. His paths seemed to be just tracks beaten through the twitch and cocksfoot. The front windows of the house had torn blinds, always drawn, and tatty bits of curtain. Pearse himself looked rough and dressed rough. But we did not treat him lightly.'

These were depression times, the early and mid-1930s, and there were a lot of strange characters in the Woolston area; eccentrics, drifters, and unemployables. Richard Pearse was by no means the only object of curiosity around Wildberry Street. Another old fellow nearby used to go about in sandshoes and silk stockings, and Pearse would sometimes exchange greetings with him. But Pearse remained the centre of interest, especially when word got around that he was building some sort of strange aeroplane in his workshop.

One of the few to gain the confidence of Pearse at this time was Richard Savage, a neighbour for twenty years. On several occasions Pearse allowed him to see the engine running. This motor had been made by the inventor in his workshop and he explained how he had shaped the two double-acting cylinders on his lathe.

Neighbours had often heard the engine being tested. 'It sounded like a giant chaffcutter,' said Savage. (The second time a Pearse engine had been likened to this particularly rowdy piece of machinery.) There were also one or two instances when the local council received complaints about the noise. Savage once saw Pearse put the plane through a static test. The airframe was anchored to the ground out behind the house, and with its engine running the plane's front wheels rose a foot above the ground.

Richard Savage was an amateur radio enthusiast, and Pearse at this stage, in the mid-1930s, himself developed a passing interest in radio. Most radio owners in these days constructed high aerials to pick up as many stations as possible, and Pearse was not to be outdone. Peter Turner, who lived over the road, remembers him building 'a huge aerial strung between tall manuka poles. It looked like an overgrown hammock. It even had a yardarm on it, and the whole thing looked extremely risky. One night there was a storm — and everyone's blew down except his!'

'Once a week,' according to Ian McBride, 'the old chap went round to the garage with a little tin for some petrol. Just enough to test his plane engine. When he wound it up it used to sound like an old Model T Ford.' On rare occasions he also gave his powercycle a run, but it was by now distinctly unroadworthy and his pushbike was safer.

Peter Turner, Ian McBride, John Reid, Ray Calvert, and Ray Falkingham were schoolboys at the time and often used to spy on Pearse from a distance when he was testing his aero engine. Turner remembers that they didn't dare cross the road to Pearse's side of the street and that all they could see from the other side of Wildberry Street was the top of the propeller rising above the height of the tin fence and Pearse's hand reaching up occasionally to give the prop a spin. 'The motor would cough a few times, chuff away for a while, then die out.' Because of the din it made, Pearse was apparently reluctant to let it run too long.

Once, when the inventor had gone off on his bike and the coast seemed clear, Ian and Peter sneaked across the road and through the gate, then crawled through the long grass to the fence. But all they could see through occasional holes in the tin was a securely locked garage. The gate on the path leading round the other side of the house to his backdoor was also locked. There was no chance of seeing any-thing more of the mystery plane, so the two lads scurried off before 'the old fellow' came home and caught them trespassing.

Occasionally, Pearse asked Mrs Bassan for some mint. He seemed to like the fragrance. She also gave him a bottle of 'Bidomac' tonic once, as a pick-me-up. And though his brusque style intimidated youngsters it was obvious to Mrs Bassan that he liked them. It was just that he did not want children around because they might meddle with his machin-ery and damage things or get hurt. To Mrs Bassan he confided that he would like to test his plane out on Woolston Park, but he never got around to doing this. Mr Bassan was once allowed to see Pearse's draw-ings and specifications for the plane. 'A brilliant man,' he told his fami-ly afterwards.

Apart from Savage and Bassan, the only other person to have seen what Richard Pearse was working on was Howard Galt. Howard was a nephew, one of the two children of Pearse's sister Maggie. The Galts had seen almost nothing of Richard since he came to Christchurch; however, when Howard Galt became interested in flying himself and joined the RNZAF, he visited his uncle every six months while on leave. The first of these visits was in 1937, when Howard Galt was 29 and his uncle was 60.

It would be fair to say that in his few meetings with Richard Pearse, Galt got closer to this intensely withdrawn man than any other person in later years. Pearse trusted his nephew to be discreet, and valued his experience as an airman. Moreover, Galt had an understanding of what his uncle was trying to do. For once in his life, Pearse had the friendship of a kindred spirit, and Howard Galt later recalled:

Having this common interest, we became friendly. He asked me if I would test-fly the machine when he had finally completed it, which from my observation would be some months in the future. His aircraft was quite revolutionary in design and for that reason he didn't welcome anyone who might wish to copy his ideas. I never saw the engine being tested but I believe he did have it turning as neighbours complained of the shattering noise. The engine was a double-acting one, on the same principle as used in steam engines. The idea was, of course, to reduce weight. Each cylinder was doing the work of two. The engine was pivoted so that on pulling a lever the motor complete with airscrew faced upwards to lift the craft straight up off the ground. And when sufficient height had been attained the lever would be pushed forward and the plane would then become a conventional aircraft in flight. The same method was to be used in landing, so that the aircraft could take off and land in his own backyard. As to Uncle Dick himself, he was a quiet person, minding his own business. He kept to himself. Very independent. All his time was given to the designing and building of the aircraft, to the detriment of his own personal appearance. His hair was unkempt and he cared little about wearing apparel, going about in old clothes. His home was a shambles for he had no interest in housekeeping, giving all his thoughts and time to the aircraft. His interests being so far removed from those of his brothers and sisters, and by nature being anything but gregarious — in fact something of a recluse — he had little in common with other members of the family. In the brief time I had contact with Uncle Dick I liked him. But one could not get close to him, as it were. He was a shy man who became increasingly uncommunicative, taciturn and unsociable in later life. In his younger years he was fairly religious but in later years he became, I think due to his scientific study, somewhat of an atheist. Apparently he once gave a public lecture in Christchurch on the theory of evolution.

Richard Pearse's mother, Sarah, died at Landue on 11 August 1937 at the age of 87. She had survived Digory by five years. As Florence had married a Matamata farmer, David Higgins, in 1935, Sarah was cared for in her last two years by her youngest child, Ruth. The Trewarlet estate now passed from Sarah, to Warne, who farmed it on behalf of the family.

In June 1939 Pearse applied to the Social Security Department for the old age benefit. He was now aged 62. His request was declined 'on

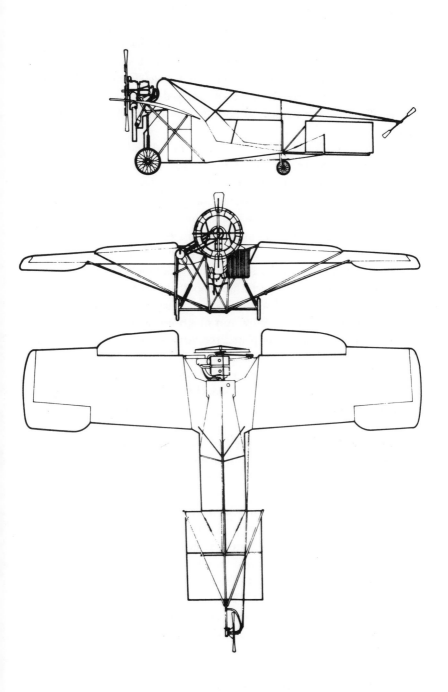

Modern general-arrangement drawings of Pearse's Utility Plane, now housed in MOTAT, *Auckland.* (E.R. Gibson)

account of income in excess of amount allowed, namely £52'. On 15 November of the same year he went to the Public Hospital to see if they would fix his teeth, which were giving him trouble. The hospital dentist informed him that his teeth were badly decayed and that they should all be taken out. Pearse refused, so nothing was done and he went home again.

The Second World War had by now started and he worked away even more earnestly at his aeroplane. He also tightened up further on security by screening off all peep-holes in his boundary fences with scrim and sacking. It had apparently occurred to him that his plane might have some use in wartime as a submarine spotter.

Howard Galt called on his uncle late in 1944 after finishing a tour of duty in the Pacific with No. 2 (General Reconnaissance) Squadron. It was on this occasion that Pearse asked him if he would test-fly the plane when it was finished. Galt, who was about to join No. 40 (Transport) Squadron, equipped with Dakotas, did not fancy trying his luck in such a contraption so did not show too much enthusiasm. Though the engine was mounted on the plane, the airframe was not at that stage fabric-covered and the wings were not fitted. This was the last time that Pearse and his nephew were in touch. After the war, Howard Galt settled down in Wellington where he bought a bookshop, and did not see his uncle again.

But much earlier than this Pearse had decided, although his plane was not completely built, that he must safeguard the principles behind its construction and operation. So in 1943 he opened negotiations with the New Zealand Patent Office.

Between November 1943 and September 1949 he wrote 24 letters to the Patent Office in Wellington, and between January 1944 and March 1950, nineteen letters to the Patent Office in Canberra. These letters are penned in bold, round, boyish handwriting and, except for four of them, are limited to a page in length. They are all written from 68 Wildberry Street and signed 'R.W. Pearse'. They are mostly concerned with matters of procedure and reveal, at times, an understandable impatience with the whole process. One can well imagine the ageing inventor muttering to himself about red tape and bumbling bureaucrats. The Patent Office officials must, for their part, have been sorely tried by his persistence, by the rough state of his specifications, and by his marked preference for compound-complex sentences.

Nevertheless, his letters to the New Zealand and Australian patent offices are extremely interesting for they are the only surviving letters by him apart from the two newspaper letters. They reveal something of his thinking processes and a great deal about his dedication.

Pearse's exchanges with the Wellington Patent Office began on 5 November 1943 when he forwarded to them an application and a £1 fee, together with a provisional specification describing the aeroplane-helicopter. 'In my specification I have given enough particulars for a complete patent and . . . I don't intend to give any more particulars as I am convinced there is enough to protect me, and so I intend to make the provisional specification do for both the provisional and the complete patent.' Pearse stated his intention of applying also for a patent in England and Australia. The specification he enclosed consisted of 57 handwritten foolscap pages detailing the construction and operation of both his aircraft and engine. The documents were duly filed at the Patent Office and given the official number 87637.

At about the same time he submitted his specification to the Inventions Board for appraisal. The function of this board during the war was to assess the military usefulness of new inventions. On 24 January 1944 the Patent Office told Pearse ' . . . the specification of your application has been referred to the Inventions Board and the board's technical officer who reports that: "This invention is of no value. Most of the ideas incorporated in either [the aircraft or engine] were disposed of as unsatisfactory in 1912 or 1913".'

Naturally, Pearse took umbrage at this abrupt dismissal of his aircraft: 'In reply to yours of the 24 inst. I have no comment to make on the military value of the private plane which took me eight years to build. As the brief assertion 'of no value' is capable of being construed into a general lack of novelty, which if allowed to go unchallenged might prejudice the breadth of my claims in the complete application which is to follow, I refer your examiner when looking into the prior aeroplane art, to my patent in NZ June 19th 1906 which was the first in the world to have hinged horizontal rudders at the wing tips, now called ailerons.' Then, to make it quite clear that he was not going to be put down so easily, Pearse declared that America might be added to the list of countries where his plane should be patented.

Shortly afterwards, he sent an application and provisional specification to the Australian Patent Office at Canberra. In his covering letter he wrote: 'I have the machine finished and want protection before offering it to the different governments of the Allies.' He also described his invention as a 'revolutionary type of aircraft'. His application was

8763/ Feb 2nd, 1944
68 Wildberry St. Woolston
Christchurch.

Dear sir

In reply to your's of the 24 inst. I have no comment to make on the military value of the private plane which took me 8 years to build. As the brief assertion "of no value" is capable of being construed into a general lack of novelty, which if allowed to go unchallenged might prejudice the breadth of my claims in the complete application which is to follow, I refer your examiner when looking into the prior aeroplane art, to my patent in N.Z. June 19th 1906 which was the first in the world to have hinged horizontal rudders at the wing tips now called ailerons. I mentioned Australia & England as two countries for which I would like to have — permits & I now include America. Please send with your next letter a complete application form. Yours ets. R. W. Pearse

Pearse's letter of 2 February 1944 to the Patent Office, Wellington.

filed on 3 March 1944. The text of the Australian provisional was sub-stantially the same as that of the New Zealand provisional.

In a preliminary examination of Pearse's application the Australian examiner objected to the application's covering two separate inventions, the aircraft and the engine. Pearse therefore decided to exclude the engine from the Australian provisional and from the complete specification he was preparing to file on both the Australian and New Zealand applications. 'The engine will remain a secret until the aircraft is marketed,' he confided to the Wellington office. His expressed intention to file fresh applications for the engine was never carried out.

On 6 June 1944 he forwarded to the Australian Patent Office an amended provisional specification from which all reference to the engine had been deleted. A rough draft of this specification salvaged with some other papers after his death also shows him removing all references to 'autogiro' — which he had originally used as an alternative term for the plane. To reduce his workload he asked the Australian Patent Office in another letter written the same day to treat this specification as his complete specification. A duplicate text and drawings were sent to the New Zealand Patent Office and filed there on 14 June 1944, the Australians receiving their specification a fortnight later. Pearse was in both cases well within the twelve-month priority period granted by 1939 legislation. By contrast he had had only nine months to work in, without extension of time, back in 1906–7.

Despite the fact that he had obtained permits to lodge applications in Britain and the USA, he intimated in July 1944 that he had 'postponed indefinitely, applications to Britain and America'.

As most of the New Zealand Patent Office examiners were away at the war, legislation had been passed permitting the Patent Office to accept complete specifications for grant of patents if corresponding specifications had been approved in certain overseas countries — including Australia. Pearse was fortunate in having filed an Australian application, and he kept the New Zealand Patent Office in touch with developments in Canberra.

The first report received from the Australian examiner at the end of 1945 was not encouraging, and dashed any hopes Pearse might have had that patenting his convertiplane would be an easy process. He wrote to the New Zealand Patent Office on 8 January 1946 describing Canberra's objections to his specification, particularly to the drawings: ' . . . it is unassembled and they won't acknowledge it as an aeroplane unless it is assembled; and the method of control for operating the tail unit or the wingtip units is not described and there is no indication of controlling means for the tilting engine assembly or for the variable pitch airscrew . . . I am now at work preparing drawings of the machine assembled . . . I will also have to alter the claims to make them apply to structure rather than the function of these structures.' Pearse concluded by saying he would send the Patent Office at Wellington copies of the redrafted specification and drawings, but expected that the job would take 'many weeks'.

In March 1946 he completed the tiresome task, revising specifications and drawings and filing the amended material with both offices. Further amendments were carried out to the description, claims and drawings of the Australian complete specification. Pearse's longest letter on the subject was five pages long and dated 14 October 1946. The specification was finally approved and accepted on 2 June 1947. Pearse described himself in the preamble as an 'inventor and owner of property'. The patent, no. 124430, was sealed on 24 September of that year.

But Pearse's troubles, 'my difficulties' as he modestly terms them, were not yet over. The Australian examiner had complained about the colour and quality of Pearse's ink, the style of his drawings, the size of his paper, the width of his margins, ambiguities in the text, and so on. Pearse was beginning to weary of the whole involved procedure and had no wish to go through it all yet another time. But there was some delay in sending him a printed copy of the Australian specification, so he had to set about doing the complete specification and drawings all over again. The duplicate was eventually sent to the Wellington Patent Office on 17 June 1948, just over a year after the Australian complete specification had been accepted. Except for slight changes in the wording of the preamble, and some reparagraphing, it was identical to the Australian version. The New Zealand complete specification, no. 87637, was duly sealed on 11 February 1949. The long labour was over. From conception to Letters Patent, Pearse's Utility Plane had been nigh on thirty years gestating.

Pearse's last letters to the Australian Patent Office dealt with renewal fees. The inventor, forgetting about the difference between New Zealand and Australian exchange rates, had overpaid the Australian office by five shillings. When he tried to recover this amount he found that it had been paid into the Australian Government's Consolidated Fund. The Canberra office gently suggested that Pearse consult a bank or post office next time he wished to send money overseas.

His last three letters to the New Zealand Patent Office also concern the renewal fees on the patent. By 1949 he was 72 years old and these last letters have a fatigued look about them, but he was still determined that no one should pirate his brainchild. To safeguard himself he paid the Wellington office renewal fees which ultimately kept the patent alive in New Zealand until 14 June 1960 — nearly seven years after his death.

18. The Utility Plane

When it comes to examining in detail what Pearse had accomplished with his Utility Plane, the task becomes even more complicated than sorting out the patenting process. There are indeed three different areas to examine when deciding what Pearse wished his plane to be: the provisional specification supplies the theory behind the plane; the complete specification elaborates and develops the theory; and the constructed plane shows its practical realisation, as far as was possible.

The specifications relating to Richard Pearse's convertiplane describe it as 'an aeroplane that can ascend and descend in very restricted areas'. The preamble to his Australian complete specification enlarges on Pearse's philosophy:

> This invention was designed in the first place to solve the problem of the private plane for the million, and in order to do this, it has been adapted to takeoff or land on any road or field. The vast network of roads that already exist must serve as takeoff and landing grounds. In order to make these available very low landing speeds are essential and the machine was specially designed for this purpose. In order to meet all these conditions, this new type of air-craft has been designed having all the advantages of helicopters in hovering or landing in very limited areas at very low speeds, or even taking off or landing vertically, while at the same time retaining all the advantages of the aeroplane while in flight. This hybrid air-craft which is a true aeroplane while in flight can be instantly turned into a helicopter for hovering or landing vertically, and it will then reap the advantages of the latter when landing vertically on rough ground or limited areas.

The machine which Pearse goes on to describe in his complete specification is a high-wing monoplane with seven distinctive features: a tilting engine; a variable-pitch 'windmill' propeller; wingtip control flaps; a multipurpose folding tail unit; a groundbrake; a sliding floor; and a capacity to fold up for storage. Pearse's explanation of some of these features, especially the engine, makes nightmare reading. It is not just that his theories are sometimes difficult to follow, but that much of his writing is repetitive on trivial issues and obscure on crucial ones.

There are several reasons for his text being a problem to the reader. The inventor was elderly and was trying to do without the services of a patent attorney. He was attempting to describe an aircraft whose construction and performance were in some respects near to being indescribable anyway. He was further handicapped in not having a technical vocabulary sufficiently advanced to make himself clear on all points. He was groping for words to describe aeronautical theories with little or no precedent, theories that would be complex enough even for a specialist engineer to write about. Bearing all this in mind, it is surprising that the specifications are as intelligible as they are. For an amateur, and in his circumstances, the effort was a valiant one.

It is clear from his correspondence with the Patent Office that it was not altogether his fault that the complete specification lacks balance in the information it provides. The examiner handling Pearse's Australian application objected that there was insufficient information on the means for tilting the engine, varying the propeller pitch, and operating the wingtip or tail control surfaces. So Pearse amended his specification to include detailed descriptions of these features. The result is an over-concentration on relatively unimportant control devices in the aircraft, particularly in relation to balancing the aircraft and tilting the engine.

Pearse's engine for the Utility Plane was the fourth complete aero-engine he made. It was also the largest and most complicated of them all, and in its conception even more ingenious than the others had been. Though the motor is not described in his complete specifications, it is described in the provisionals. We will therefore leave an examination of its construction until later. The engine's tilting capability, which is crucial to the performance of his aircraft, must first be studied.

According to the complete specification, the engine is to be mounted at its point of balance on an axle extending across the airframe. This axle is supported by two upright arms placed forward of the wing and the plane's centre of gravity. The engine may be tilted from its normally vertical position backwards through 90 degrees. When it is so pivoted, the motor lies on top of the airframe approximately level with the upper surfaces of the wings.

Pearse states that the aircraft's longitudinal balance is to be achieved by tilting the engine forwards or backwards, as well as by varying engine speed and the pitch of the propeller. Transition from vertical to horizontal thrust, or vice versa, would also be necessary during takeoff and landing, though he does not say as much and apparently takes this for granted. Nor is there instruction of any sort on takeoff or landing methods. With characteristic boldness he seems to accept without question the idea that an aeroplane-helicopter powered by a tilting engine is a practical proposition, despite the fact that there was no historical precedent for such an aircraft.

To tilt the engine, the pilot was to employ controls connected to a lever secured to the mounting axle for the engine. He describes three separate controls involving use of this lever: a foot pedal, a hand control consisting of a wire-and-chain attachment linking the lever to a lever for the groundbrake, and another hand control employing a small winch. These three methods of control show how the engine may be tilted back from the vertical to the horizontal but do not explain how the reverse operation is to take place. Evidently engine thrust was relied upon for forward tilting of the engine. Minor alterations in attitude were to be carried out by the groundbrake lever or foot controls. 'Rough balancing' was left to the hand winch. It would not be necessary to tilt the engine a full 90 degrees for horizontal rotation of the propeller. The engine could, for instance, be tilted 45 degrees and the tail of the aircraft lowered a corresponding amount.

Mounted directly on the engine crankshaft, so as to avoid any gearing, as for example in an autogiro, was what Pearse called a 'hybrid propeller-rotor'. This was, in the words of his specification, ' . . . a specially controllable pitch propeller which plays two roles: that of a propeller when revolving in a vertical plane and that of a rotor when rotating in a horizontal plane like a spinning top'.

The propeller-rotor is completely unorthodox in form. It consists of two opposed paddle blades with an inner circle of eight smaller blades spaced regularly apart and mounted windmill-fashion on two concentric metal rings. This was ' . . . for the purpose of getting a very large blade area in a compact form, so as to give lift efficiency by avoiding too high a pressure on each individual blade'. The total diameter of this propeller is much less than that of a conventional helicopter rotor, but Pearse wanted a blade diameter small enough to avoid losing downward thrust through interference by the wing surfaces. He hoped the extra blade area would make up for his rotor's deficiency in diameter. Additional efficiency for the propeller was claimed from the better distribution of pressure among the blades.

By means of an ingenious system of rods, levers and sliding sleeves the pitch of the blades could be controlled by the pilot from inside his cabin. The pilot could fix the pitch-control lever in any one of three ratchet positions in a selected range — maximum, intermediate and minimum. Maximum pitch was for the purpose of 'high speed' forward flight and minimum pitch for vertical descent. It was also intended to vary the propeller pitch for longitudinal balancing during horizontal or vertical descent.

There is little problem in following the inventor's description of the wingtip control surfaces and their mode of operation. Each wingtip unit consists of an L-shaped flap, the major portion of which tilts downwards while the smaller section — probably acting as a servo — tilts upwards. These flaps are similar to ailerons but tilt only in the direction described.

One function of these flaps was to maintain lateral balance during forward flight, when they were intended to deflect the associated wingtip upwards when operated. Another was to maintain lateral balance during vertical descent. In this circumstance either flap could be operated to reduce the surface area on that particular wing and enable it to sink more rapidly. Pearse points out that a reasonable rate of descent is necessary for this latter means of contol to be effective.

In theory, these wing flaps could all be pivoted to an angle of 90 degrees if necessary. A system of wires and bellcranks, in principle not unlike that recommended in the complete specification for Pearse's first aeroplane, permits the pilot to operate the wing control surfaces by using a T-shaped control column. If the control column were moved from side to side, the wingtip controls were worked; if it were moved back and forth, the rear elevator was worked; if the handle of the control stick were twisted, the rear rudder was worked. In addition to gripping the handle, the pilot could operate all three controls by using his feet to work a pedal lever mounted on the control column. Pearse believed that this would enable 'both hands and feet to be used separately or in conjunction for balance control'. He recommended that these controls be used to maintain in the descending aircraft a lateral inclination of something less than twenty degrees to counteract propeller torque. So, particularly while landing his plane, the pilot might expect to be very busy indeed.

The fourth interesting feature of Pearse's convertiplane as described in his complete specifications is the tail unit. This unit consists of tail-wheel, tailplane, elevator, fin and rudder, all of which are capable of controlled movement. The tailplane could be tilted up and held in any desired position by use of a lever and rack system. This system enabled the aeroplane to be stored more easily and it could also be used to counteract nose-heaviness during vertical descent. The elevator is hinged to the rear of the tailplane and controlled in its upward and downward movement by two wires linked to the control stick. It operates conventionally. The fin and rudder are mounted on the elevator, an unorthodox arrangement but one which would permit the tailplane to fold forward more easily.

The aeroplane-helicopter's next distinctive feature is its groundbrake. This is simply a skid which can be pivoted downwards from the aircraft by means of a bellcrank lever which is to be connected to the skid by a spring to absorb the shock, and which can be held securely in a rack at any angle the pilot wishes. With this groundbrake, to be situated a short distance aft of the front wheels, Pearse hoped to be able to pull the aircraft up in its own length. The groundbrake was also to be lowered during vertical touchdown to help cushion the landing.

To reduce risk to the pilot in the event of a crash landing, Pearse devised the sixth novel feature. This was a sliding floor to which the pilot's seat was attached. Under severe deceleration, clamps attaching the floor to the airframe would ' . . . allow the floor to slide forward with the correct amount of friction necessary to bring it to a state of rest gradually, and thus break the fall and eliminate shock . . . The efficiency of the contrivance depends on screwing the friction clamps to the right degree of tightness to give the correct amount of sliding friction, to bring the forward sliding floor to a state of rest gradually.' He goes on to justify this device by citing laws of inertia and rates of acceleration. He also explains how the pilot is ' . . . secured to the seat by several straps forming a kind of harness to spread the pressure over the whole body'.

The idea of a sliding seat seems to be a carryover from his first aeroplane. One refinement seemingly not allowed for in the convertiplane specification is that the pilot on his sliding platform would be abruptly halted — and possibly emasculated — by the permanently affixed control column.

The final unusual feature of Pearse's aircraft as described by the inventor is its storage capability. The tailplane can fold forward and the wings may be hinged so as to fold rearwards and upwards. Pearse believed his aircraft could thus be housed in the average car garage.

At the conclusion of his complete specifications he listed those features of the aircraft for which he wanted protection under a patent. His first claim is a general description of the machine's originality and usefully sums up the features we have just examined: 'A convertible aeroplane-helicopter having an engine carrying a controllable pitch propeller on its crankshaft, mounted for controlled tilting of this combination about a horizontal transverse axle, in combination with incidence-increasing wingtip control units, foldable tail piece, groundbrake and a sliding floor, all as parts of a combination.'

The other five claims are specifically directed to the wingtip controls, variable-pitch propeller, folding tailpiece, groundbrake, and sliding floor. The specification is then dated, signed by the applicant and, in the case of the Australian specification, witnessed. The witness was Mavis Emily Allan, wife of Pearse's Dampier Street tenant at that time.

'Unluckily,' David Peters remarks, 'from a legal point of view Pearse's six claims make the patent practically worthless. This is not so much a result of inexperienced drafting but rather the consequence of seeking to cover in the one patent inventions that fall into at least three separate and mutually exclusive groups. Since a patent, in the usual circumstances, can be issued only in respect of one invention, Pearse's one invention had to consist of a combination of these three groups . . . Infringement of any claim of the patent could be avoided by omission, in an otherwise identical aircraft, of such inconsequential features as the groundbrake or sliding floor.'

Thus the end result of Pearse's protracted toil was a patent which offered him almost no security at all. The only way for him to have safeguarded his ideas properly would have been to have patented each of them separately. As it turned out, both the Australian and New Zealand patents covering his Utility Plane were practically valueless.

While the two complete specifications are the chief source of information on Pearse's thinking, the provisional specifications add interestingly to the picture. The provisional specification relating to his New Zealand patent no. 87637 is handwritten and covers 34 pages of quarto paper.

The only ideas of any inventive importance which are mentioned in the provisional specification but not in the complete are anti-torque and lateral control rotors. In the former, a small rotor revolving in a vertical plane is provided at the rear of the aircraft to neutralise the reaction torque of the main propeller which is rotating in a horizontal plane during vertical descent. The blades of the tail rotor are variable in pitch and the pitch can in fact be reversed. Two small additional rotors, rotating in a horizontal plane, are provided at each wingtip for lateral control. The pitch of these rotor blades is also variable and reversible.

Apart from the rotors, Pearse's concept of the aircraft and its flight control systems in the provisional specification is virtually the same as for the complete specifications. Other differences are of a minor nature, sometimes amounting to additional information only. For example, the total length of the aircraft when folded is shown as not exceeding 15 feet (4.5 metres); the sliding floor is to move about 3 feet (1 metre) upon crash impact; the groundbrake is equipped with two skids rather than one; the fin and rudder of the tail unit are stated to be equivalent in area to the elevator and tailplane; and the wingtip flaps are said to be usable also for turning the aeroplane, operating much like steering air-brakes.

Some additional facts are given about the propeller-rotor. The rotor's diameter was to be 7 feet (2.1 metres) from tip to tip, while the diameter of the eight-bladed inner propeller was to be about 4 feet (1.2 metres). Pearse also refers to the gyroscopic effect which he expected the inner blades would produce when the rotor was revolving in a horizontal plane, and how this should assist both lateral and longitudinal balance when the plane was ascending or descending. The range of pitch adjustment on the blades is said to extend up to 45 degrees, this maximum being reserved for high-speed forward flight. Fine-pitch adjustment was for hovering and landing.

The location, mounting and use of the engine, as described in the provisional specification, appear to be the same as in the complete one. Pearse explains additionally that if hovering is contemplated, the aircraft should be loaded nose-heavy. Conversely, for normal forward flight it should be nose-light.

The engine itself is described only in the provisional specification. Pearse cut out all reference to his engine from the complete specification, as we have noted, with the intention of patenting it as a separate invention at a later date.

The engine designed for the Utility Plane is certainly most ingenious. In technical parlance it is of an inverted in-line configuration and is composed of two pairs of coaxial cylinders. The cylinders of each pair adjacent to the crankshaft are enclosed within the crankcase and are referred to by Pearse as inner or auxiliary cylinders; the others are called outer cylinders and are double-acting. This engine appears to be a logical development of his very first motor, the 'irrigation pipe' model. In essence it is a two-cylinder double-acting engine which uses an additional pair of cylinders and pistons in place of the conventional steam-engine type crosshead of the first engine.

The rods securing each pair of pistons pass through a 'stuffingbox' which separates the adjacent heads of the cylinders. This stuffingbox, another carryover from Pearse's first engine and its steam-engine influences, is to prevent gas leakage between the cylinders. It is composed of four spaced-apart pairs of diametrically divided bronze washers through which each piston rod slides. This metallic packing is described at considerable length in the specification, for efficient sealing between the two cylinders would be fundamental to efficient power delivery.

During normal operation the two double-acting cylinders are to take in and fire a petrol-air mixture on both sides of the piston on the four-stroke principle, making the pair of cylinders equivalent to a four-cylinder single-acting engine. In addition to this, the auxiliary cylinders could be used as single-acting four-stroke units to augment the power supplied by the double-acting cylinders. This would account for Pearse's description of the engine as being, in effect, equivalent to a six-cylinder engine. If this extra power were not required, the auxiliary cylinders could be used as superchargers to increase the density of the air reaching the double-acting cylinders, by compressing air either on one side of the piston or on both sides. Also, by altering the valve timing and linking the inlet and exhaust valves so that they worked together, the double-acting cylinders could be made to operate on the two-stroke principle. They could then be supercharged from the auxiliary cylinders by drawing air from one side or both sides of the auxiliary pistons.

Because of the amount of heat generated by the double-acting cylinders, Pearse specified that watercooling of these cylinders was essential, although optional for the auxiliary cylinders.

The only surviving illustrations of this engine consist of a simple sectional view of cylinders, pistons, crankcase and crankshaft, without any details of intake and exhaust ducting. There are also drawings of the form and arrangement of the divided washer sealants used between the outer and inner cylinders. The nature of these drawings suggests that they may have been intended for the engine patent for which he never applied.

Though the pedigree of his double-acting cylinders may be traced back to the steam engine, the principle does not seem to have found favour elsewhere in the field of petrol engines. Possibly the intricacy of the valve arrangements and the sealing of the piston rods against gas leakage were factors in its disfavour. It can only be assumed that Pearse persevered with the idea because of some success with his earlier efforts, and possibly because he was able to improve upon the sealing of the piston rods against gas leakage.

Supercharging by air pump has been tried out in diesel engines. Crankcase compression, too, is the accepted way for providing precompression of the charge in two-stroke engines. It is nevertheless uncommon with four-stroke petrol engines and certainly as far as aero engines are concerned. In this regard Pearse was breaking new ground.

The idea of using the engine either as a four-stroke or two-stroke engine seems to be quite novel. An early sketch of the engine, pasted to a document dated 1933, shows it as a four-stroke. But later drawings show porting for the inlet valves that would enable the incoming charge of gas to be directed down the cylinder wall to scavenge the cylinder of exhaust gases. Thus a two-stroke operation was feasible.

The engine could have worked in the way Pearse intended, both as a four-stroke or two-stroke engine, and in both the normally aspirated and supercharged conditions. In either configuration, though, it would have suffered from some degree of inefficiency because of its unorthodox and complicated design. Without more information than Pearse gives us in his specifications it is impossible to calculate the engine's power output but its power-weight ratio is likely to have been quite favourable. In a letter of 6 June 1944 to the Australian Patent Office Pearse indeed states: 'counted in cubic inches capacity this motor gives 1 h.p. for less than $1/2$ lb weight . . . '

In passing it must be said that his provisional patent specifications reveal some quaint notions which he did well to exclude from the final text. One of these concerns his plane's potential as a submarine-killer: 'A machine of this type can hover above a submarine and descend vertically with sufficient speed to keep control laterally, and by continually letting small weights or smoke bombs fall, the pilot can ascertain when he is vertical over the submarine by the splash or smoke, and when close enough to make a direct hit certain, the depth charge can be released.'

Pearse also believed, a little hopefully, that his sliding seat arrangement would ' . . . give the pilot and passengers a chance to survive up to a speed of 100 miles an hour'. Another idea which he toyed with in his rough draft of the provisional specification was that his aeroplane would be able to take off ' . . . under all conditions such as fog or darkness'.

The prototype Utility Plane which he eventually constructed in his Woolston garage differs in only minor respects from the patent specifications. As might be expected, since he had built most of his aircraft before he began work on the patent, the plane is closer to his first drafts for his patent than to his last. The most important features present in the aircraft but not in the specifications are leading-edge flaps on the wings, and a drive-belt arrangement linking the engine to one of the landing wheels.

The aircraft is constructed mainly of steel tubing and wood. It has an overall length of 8.32 metres and a wing span of 10.54 metres. Its height to the top of its wing is 1.9 metres and to the tip of its rotor is 3.14 metres. The length of the aircraft when its tail unit is folded forward for storage is 5.63 metres. This is about a metre longer than his provisional specification suggested, but still short enough to fit into the average garage.

The wing construction is similar to that found in conventional aircraft of that time. Two spars which carry spruce ribs closely spaced and securely attached by metal fittings are the basis of the braced wing structure. The wing fabric is light calico which has been stretched over the wing frame and secured by hand stitching. This 'stringing' has been done halfway between each pair of ribs. The whole covering has then been treated with a coat of silver dope or paint to tighten the fabric. The upper surface of the wings has a regular curvature which is continuous from the leading edge to the trailing edge and the wings are of an aerofoil section common in some aeroplanes built between the two world wars. They have an anhedral angle or downward inclination of three degrees and an approximately twelve degree angle of incidence.

The wings are each supported by means of two crossed struts attached to the lower fuselage rail or longeron by means of quick-release pins. These struts are of wood and extend to the outer portion of the wing, where more quick-release pins are used to facilitate assembly and dismantling. At the point where the struts cross they are hinged together by a single quarter-inch bolt. This gives some rigidity to the bracing and allows the struts to be folded together and kept as a pair. They are painted red and smoothly finished. The flimsy appearance of these struts does not give one much confidence in the Utility Plane's capacity to hold together, especially when landing, but it is possible that flying wires were intended to be used to help support some of the wingload. The wingroots are also secured by means of quick-release pins, and two people could conveniently remove and replace the wings. Control cables and bracing wire are fitted with quick-release dog clips to enable them to be removed or attached quickly and easily.

Ailerons similar to those described in the specifications are hinged to the rear spar of each wing. The servo portion of each aileron is longer and narrower than Pearse's own drawings suggest. As specified, this long balance section extends right to the leading edge of the wing, and forms the actual wingtip.

Inboard, at the front of each wing, is a large hinged panel not described by Pearse in his specifications. These droop-flaps would be deposed more or less under the propeller downdraught when the propeller was being used for direct lift and were perhaps intended to assist lateral control while the plane was hovering. If they were used in forward flight it would require some force to hold these control surfaces in a neutral position. However, Pearse has allowed, as a pre-flight operation, for the panels to be pinned rigidly in line with the chord of the wing if so desired, to render them ineffectual.

The ailerons are operated by a T-shaped control column inside the cockpit. Control wires fitted to the base of the column pass to the mid-aileron position via guides on the struts and terminate at a short king-post below each aileron. The control operation is instinctive. Thus if the control column is moved to the left the aircraft banks to the left. The upgoing forces are not catered for, however. If there were ever balance cables attached, there is now no sign of them. The elevator is raised or lowered by moving the control column backwards or forwards. The elevator control wires are four in number, two passing over the tailplane and two underneath it, this duplication of cables evidently providing for greater safety. The rudder is worked by foot pedals. It is not clear how the leading edge droop-flats were to be operated, as the control cables are missing, or were never fitted.

The tail section is large and ungainly in appearance. Its front is hinged to the rear of the fuselage, the hinges consisting of lengths of tubing which have been slid over a metal frame member at the back of the fuselage and brazed securely into position. The tail section may be folded forward by means of a lever situated in the floor of the cabin to the left of the pilot. The lower end of this lever projects below the cabin and is attached to a pushrod which runs under the fuselage to a kingpost underneath the tailplane. From here the load is transmitted to both right and left tailplanes to facilitate the pivoting process. Two large springs help carry the weight of the tailplane, which would otherwise tend to droop.

The groundbrake consists of two skids which are sprung to absorb landing impact, and is operated by a hand lever whose holding ratchet has several slots to allow for a range of height settings.

The cockpit is just large enough to seat the pilot and a passenger side by side. It contains a bewildering array of rudimentary controls: rods, switches, levers, pulleys, wires, chains, priming pumps, cables and so forth. Some of these are held in a rack within reach of the pilot when strapped into his complicated safety harness, although other controls are less acccessible. Visibility is limited. The pilot could see fairly well through the cabin's side windows, but his view forwards would be obstructed by the engine and its multitudinous controls. There is also no protection for the pilot from the front, the only direction in which the cabin is not enclosed. Therefore, propeller turbulence plus the natural elements would give the pilot a disagreeable time. There is enough space in the cabin for the seats to be able to slide forward about a metre (as the patent specifications suggest) to absorb any crash impact, but the seats appear to be fixed firmly in position. The cabin has a small door on both the pilot's and the passenger's sides. The cabin and the rest of the fuselage are covered in the same painted fabric as the wings.

The Utility Plane's engine is along the lines of the one described by Pearse in his provisional patent specifications. Ignition is by normal sparkplugs, and battery and buzzer coils reminiscent of Model T Ford days. A drip-feed system supplies fuel through surface carburettors. There is even a small fan blower to break up the fuel. The engine is lubricated by numerous oil drip appliances and is fitted with a radiator for water cooling. Judging from the amount of oil and grease still evident, the engine must have undergone a considerable amount of experimental running. Since Pearse's death no attempt has been made to run it, so no estimate of its horsepower is available. Though it could be operated as either a four-stroke or a two-stroke, he left the engine as a two-stroke so perhaps it acted best in that configuration.

An intriguing feature of the engine is the provision made for some twenty-four sparkplugs. It was once thought that Pearse might have used the extra plugs to bung up holes drilled in error, but it is now believed that he might have been attempting to complete combustion in the exhaust and inter-stage ducting. This may make Pearse not only a pioneer in the use of 'after-burners', but in anti-pollution technology as well! Strictly speaking, after-burners (also called 'reheat') are a modification of the jet engine exhaust or tail pipe section which permits additional fuel to be sprayed into the hot exhaust gases. The additional fuel combines with the unused oxygen in the exhaust gases and extra thrust is created. Pearse's convertiplane engine has not been dismantled sufficiently for it to be seen what his after-burners were really intended to do, but the above surmise seems reasonable.

The propeller-rotor is made of steel tubing, steel fence standards and sheet metal blades. The overall diameter of the rotor is two metres, only ten centimetres less than that recommended in the specifications. The diameter of the inner propeller is 1.29 m and there are eight of these smaller blades, as specified. The rotor and propeller blades can be angled to about twenty-five degrees. The pitch control can be regulated from the cockpit as described in the patent specifications except that there are six detent slots in the ratchet rather than three. The engine and propeller-rotor may be tilted through about ninety degrees, as recommended, for which Pearse provided both a hand lever and a winch system similar to that described in the patent. This hand crank operated a bicycle-chain drive connected rather inadequately to levers at the top and bottom of the engine.

There is a tail rotor, as described in the provisional specification. It is 1.21 m in diameter and driven direct from the engine by means of a universally jointed 12-mm steel rod. This rod has a flexible coupling at the front, another at the midway position by the tailplane hinge, and a third at the back where the drive is transmitted to the tail rotor. The universal joints are made from sections of waterpipe of differing diameters. The rotor is carried in a frame of light tubing and a most ingenious pitch-change mechanism is incorporated. The pitch is controlled from the cockpit by means of two cables which are taken through the fuselage and over guides to a system of levers at the rotor. The whole tail rotor unit is very flimsily constructed. There are no wingtip rotors as suggested in the provisional specification.

The aircraft is mounted on a tubular steel undercarriage with a two-metre wheelbase. The wheels themselves are 57 cm in diameter and fitted with Avon Extra Heavy tyres. The wheels and tyres are similar to those used on pre-war bicycles or light motorcycles. The tailwheel, which is steered by the rudder controls, seems to be off the front of a 'butcher-boy' delivery cycle.

A final interesting feature of the constructed Utility Plane is its starting gear. Because of the unusual format of the main propeller, swinging the engine by hand would be most difficult, so Pearse incorporated a starting system to help out. The front end of the crankshaft is connected to a pulley at the top of the undercarriage. From this pulley a large leather belt passes over two further pulleys — one of which can be tensioned from the cockpit — to be operated by the right-hand main landing wheel. This belt could be used to rotate the engine if the aircraft were pushed or towed. When the engine had started up, the tensioning pulley could be used to discontinue operating the belt. The device would also enable the plane to taxi along a road under its own power until the pilot wished to take to the air once more.

As a whole, Pearse's Utility Plane seems an extremely risky proposition from the pilot's point of view. The engine and undercarriage are strongly constructed but the rest of the aircraft is not nearly robust enough to withstand the stresses of actual flight. But considering his working methods and the fact that the whole contraption, probably excepting the engine cylinders, pistons and sparkplugs, is put together from odds and ends, it is surprising that the plane is not more rickety than it is. As it stands, it looks more like a mock-up than a practical flying machine. Or an Emmett cartoon sprung to life. Or something out of *Chitty Chitty Bang Bang*. Small wonder that Howard Galt, the Canterbury Aero Club instructors and even Pearse himself hesitated to put the 'hybrid-aeroplane' to the test.

When Henry Hughes Ltd, Pearse's former patent agents, were asked by the Christchurch Public Trust Office in 1954 to comment on the merit of Pearse's invention the reply was given: 'We do not think that a plane so constructed could fly as the stresses of converting the plane in flight would be so strong that the machine would break up unless it was made so heavy as to make it difficult to get off the ground. . . We quite appreciate that the inventor's idea is more in the way of a "dream" and is totally removed from considerations of aerodynamics etc. therefore it is not always prudent to criticise a dream which might come true.'

It is easy to criticise Pearse's Utility Plane, apart from its indifferent construction. Its engine probably lacks the power to get the machine into the air, though no one has ever tried out the idea. This is partly owing to doubts about the engine tilting mechanism, which is crucial to the aircraft's success as a convertiplane.

As Dennis Kemp, an Auckland aeronautical engineer with a long-standing interest in Pearse, puts it: 'The vibrations of the engine and the prop, plus any torque about the tilting axis due to the offset thrust line, would soon wreak dire destruction on the tilt control system and probably everything and anyone in the general area.'

Even if soundly built the plane would probably not be suitable for hovering as it would be unstable and need some forward motion to maintain lateral and longitudinal balance. The controls would need to be power-operated as the forces at work, should the plane achieve flight, would be beyond person-power alone. Features such as the groundbrake and sliding floor seem inadequate for such an aircraft anyhow.

In fact the Utility Plane, in its fine blend of the visionary and the antiquated, shows a splendid disregard for the state of aviation technology as it stood in the late 1930s and early 1940s. Kemp observes:

> In the period between his first flying attempts and his design of the MOTAT aircraft, Pearse had obviously failed to keep up with the rapidly advancing state of the art. No isolated man could. Because of this his attempt to put all these untried ideas into one machine seems naive. Also he tried to build this machine with the sort of engineering expertise which might have sufficed in pioneering days, but was no longer adequate. I think he overreached himself in attempting to design a 'do-everything' type of aircraft, particularly at a time when aviation had developed to a degree of sophistication which made it virtually impossible for one man to compete with established design teams. It was a valiant attempt by one man to 'one-up' the aviation industry. A David and Goliath story, but with a sadder ending. I guess that if the Wright brothers were restored to life and set to work in their bicycle shop, they could easily tarnish their reputations by producing something that would seem ridiculous judged by the standard of current engineering practice. This is more or less what Pearse has done with the MOTAT aircraft. None the less, the aircraft shows some ideas and some constructional details which indicate the ingenuity and resourcefulness of the man.

To begin with, no matter what reservations one might have about the final product, it was an incredible one-man effort to have designed and built such an aircraft. Pearse, after all, was an old-age pensioner for most of the process, and was working with hopelessly inadequate resources. As such he showed he had lost none of the persistence and mechanical guile which had got him into the air with his first aeroplane in earlier days. The whole operation revealed once more the courage and independent spirit without which he would never have attempted to build 'flying machines' in the first place.

Moreover, the whole philosophy behind the construction of his People's Plane is an appealing one. Pearse was more than just an able practical engineer: he was a thinker with a keen eye to the future. It may be, as the Inventions Board assessor decided, that most of the ideas in the plane had been propounded and rejected many years earlier. But perhaps not always for what would now be considered sound reasons. Dennis Kemp concludes:

> The fact that tilting engines and dropped leading edges are now considered practical possibilities shows that the state of the art has developed to the extent that ideas formerly impractical are now feasible. The ideas are not any better than they ever were but the implementation of these ideas is now possible. Basically his notions about vectored thrust or tilting engines, and dropped leading edges and the use of tail rotors, were sound. If not original in the sense that others elsewhere may have thought of them, they were nonetheless almost certainly developed independently by Pearse, and this testifies to his ingenuity. The ideas were all untried at the time Pearse started thinking of them.

Indeed, some were still untried by the time he had built his plane. The Utility Plane may have been a dream plane. But, to some extent at least, that dream was prophetic.

19. Last gamble

By about the end of 1945 Pearse had done as much to the aircraft as he could. He occasionally ran the machine forward a little so the prop was clear of the garage and gave the motor a run. But for the most part his aeroplane stayed out of sight. The garage doors were not only locked securely but wedged shut with wooden props. The war was over and he had filed his patent applications, so one would have thought that there was not quite the same need for secrecy. However, he still gave no encouragement to would-be spectators, especially small boys.

His principal concern was now for his three properties. They all required attention from time to time. Fences had to be fixed, spouting repaired, broken windows replaced, drains unblocked and — very occasionally — buildings painted. As he grew older, Pearse was less and less able to do these maintenance jobs, and his bungalows became increasingly shabby. Neither the Breezes Road nor the Dampier Street homes had proper lawns or any cultivation of flowers or shrubs. Tenants would occasionally plant vegetables, but otherwise the sections were in a state of nature.

Pearse's own needs were so simple and his possessions so few that he hardly needed the whole of 68 Wildberry Street to himself, so he let portions of his house there to two sets of tenants. A married couple, John and Dorothy Collins, rented two rooms plus the kitchen. A Mr Field rented a second bedroom, a portion of the hall and the entrance porch, which had been converted into a kitchen. Pearse, living in the remaining bedroom, had a scullery plus the use of the other half of the hall. They all shared the same bathroom, washhouse and outdoor lavatory.

In November 1947, in his seventieth year, Pearse had a dispute with Field over the amount of rent being charged. Field appealed to the Department of Labour under the terms of the Fair Rent Act and an independent valuation was made of the Wildberry Street property through Pearse's solicitors. The valuer's report came out in favour of Field: 'The

Pearse's farm at Louden's Gully, Milton, in 1971. Cottage to the right and barn-workshop to the left. It is thought Pearse tried to fly his plane from the field at right behind the cottage.

Close-up of Pearse's cottage in 1971, then serving as a shearing shed on Jim Barra's farm. Corrugated-iron sheds at either end were additions. Andrew Hood stands at front.

Pearse in a Trentham Camp platoon photograph, 1917, shortly before embarking for England. This is the last known photograph to be taken of Pearse.

A view of 68 Wildberry Street, the second of the three homes Pearse built in Christchurch. In the garage to the right he constructed his Utility Plane.

Pearse's powercycle, built circa 1912–13, as it was when located on a Tai Tapu farm by Geoge Bolt in 1959.

Pearse's first Christchurch house, substantially altered from Pearse's original construction, at 164 Breezes Road, Wainoni.

Pearse's third and last house, now stuccoed, at the corner of Dampier and Wildberry Streets, Woolston.

The Utility Plane in its shed at Wildberry Street. Pearse's last tenant took this shot hastily, circa 1947, when the inventor wasn't looking.

Pearse's Utility Plane as delivered to Auckland Airport in 1959.

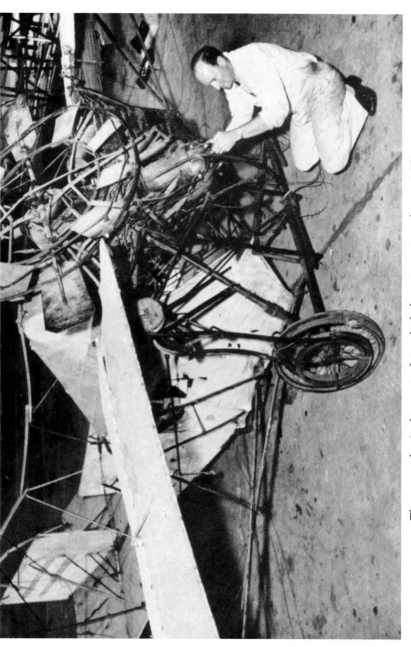

The convertiplane's tilting engine being checked over in an airport hangar, 1959.

Richard Pearse once asked his nephew, Howard Galt, if he would test fly his Utility Plane for him. Here Galt poses in front of the machine at MOTAT, 25 years later in 1971. On his left are Pearse's two youngest sisters, Ruth Gilpin and Florence Higgins.

Sunnyside Hospital, where Richard Pearse spent the last two years of his life. Another famous patient at about the same time was Janet Frame, one of New Zealand's foremost fiction authors.

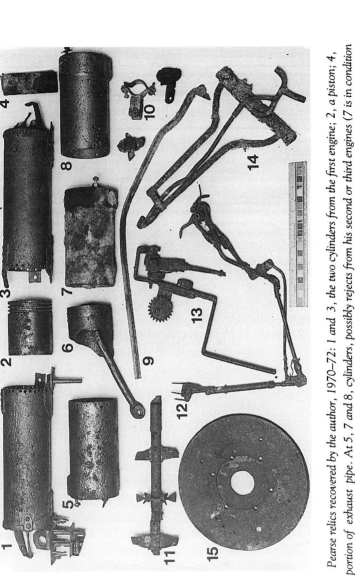

Pearse relics recovered by the author, 1970–72: 1 and 3, the two cylinders from the first engine; 2, a piston; 4, portion of exhaust pipe. At 5, 7 and 8, cylinders, possibly rejects from his second or third engines (7 is in condition as excavated). At 6, broken piston with connecting rod, from the second engine. At 9, piece of angle iron; 10, metal clips used for connecting bamboo rods on wing frame. At 11, worm from topdresser. At 12 and 13, portions of potato-planter. At 14, unidentified — possibly part of copper fuel pipe for farm machine. At 15, belt pulley made from two agricultural discs. (Items 1–10 from Opihi dump; 11–15 from Milton farm.)

conveniences offered Mr Field as a tenant are practically nil, as there is no hot water provided, no proper sink and no provision for a bathroom.'

The improvised kitchen-cum-entrance porch was the chief bother. Pearse seems to have put together houses in much the same way that he constructed aeroplanes — out of the first bits and pieces that came to hand. Field, among other things, had to put up with a ' . . . rough bench with hole cut to hold a hand basin which has a hole in the bottom in which is a bit of rubber hose which drains into a hand bucket; a safe built out of fruit boxes; two cupboards built out of fruit boxes'. The valuer concluded that 9s 1d a week for rent would be quite enough in the circumstances.

Field, having made his point, quit. Pearse made no attempt to update the facilities nor to secure another tenant. The Collinses stayed on.

Every Saturday Pearse used to collect his rents. To do this he usually got into a dark suit, donned a dark felt hat, rolled a coat up on his handlebars and cycled along to Dampier Street. Though it was only two blocks away, he would never have considered going without his bicycle. After a brief word or two to George Allan, who had rented the house there from 1941, he would then cycle the five and a half kilometres to Breezes Road where the John McLellans rented his other house. From these, after another chat and a cup of tea, he cycled his way back to Woolston.

In his last year or two he became too unsteady on his bicycle to ride it any more. He then used to wheel it instead. The Polkinghornes, who lived over the road from the McLellans, used to see the old gentleman approaching wearily from afar, usually along Wainoni Road. Mrs McLellan, a warmhearted Scotswoman, always treated him with kindness. Best of all, she listened to him patiently when he talked. She heard him speak often of his aeroplanes and other sidelines but never knew whether to take him seriously or not. Few ever did.

Bill Polkinghorne owned a Self Help store on the corner of Ferry Road and Hart Street from 1947 to 1949. It was only 800 m from Pearse at Wildberry Street and here the aviator used to buy his basic fare: flour, salt, cheese, plain biscuits, and a slice or two of bacon. Polkinghorne remembers him still: 'Mr Pearse was lanky, loose-limbed, with sunken cheeks and a weathered look. Very casually dressed. Somewhat unkempt. His clothes were well worn but not dirty. When he spoke, it was with assurance. You listened.'

Pearse got his milk and bread from a dairy further down Ferry Road near Radley Bridge. Mrs E.M. Turner, who lived across the road from Pearse in Wildberry Street, remembers him shopping there. He used to crank his way round on his old square-framed bicycle, carrying a fairly insanitary billy which the shopkeeper usually washed for him before putting in any fresh milk. As soon as Pearse entered the dairy other customers used to step aside and let him be served first.

Local people were beginning to feel sorry for him. He was now frailer than before and very neglected-looking. Because of his increasing deafness he was harder to talk to than ever, and he used to ramble on a lot about his planes. Most of what he said was beyond the comprehension of local listeners, who either did not understand the technicalities or thought he was demented.

In his last years at Wildberry Street, he again had as neighbours Joe and Alice Birchall, who had returned to the Woolston district after some years' absence. They moved into a house next to the Savages, and two doors away from Pearse.

'He was looking after himself better than when he was at Dampier Street,' says Mrs Birchall, 'but he had no visitors at all. I didn't see anyone on his property, ever, except a nephew. I suppose it was his own fault. He kept very much to himself. He only spoke when spoken to. But he was a real gentleman, Mr Pearse. An educated man, always very polite. Often when you went past his place you heard classical music coming from his radio. Only the very best. He was a very clever man, we all knew that.'

According to John Collins, Pearse lived very austerely. He habitually wore old pre-war clothes with leather leggings. He cooked his meals and heated his water with a large blowlamp which he ignited, to save matches, with 'an electric sparking wire'. Though offered meals by Dorothy Collins, he would rarely accept them. 'I don't want charity from anyone,' he'd say, as usual. Pearse once took his tenants to task for buying newspapers when they could go to the library and read them for nothing. On another occasion he bought a vast quantity of different sorts of paint from a store that was selling it off at a low price. He mixed it all together in a large container and applied it to his house. Eventually, the rain washed it all off.

Pearse told Collins he had had his convertiplane's engine cylinders cast by P & D Duncan, a Christchurch engineering firm, but had done everything else himself, including stitching on the fabric. The old fellow spent a lot of time pottering about in his garage but would not let anyone near the plane. He would talk about it though: 'Nobody has ever designed a plane like I have here,' he once exclaimed. 'The Americans haven't got anything like this. It's just right for getting down into jungle clearings. Just imagine if you were in New Guinea . . . '

He also spoke of his first aircraft, talked of crashing on to a gorse hedge, and at this stage he was claiming that he had flown before the Wrights. He seemed convinced that the Wrights had stolen ideas from him. In his last days at Wildberry Street, Collins recalls, Pearse could be heard in his room pounding the table with his fist and muttering to himself: 'You bloody fool, Pearse! Why did you let them put it over you?' Whether he was referring to the Wright brothers or the aviation companies is not now clear.

At the beginning of 1949 came another indication of how shaky he was becoming. On 6 February he fell and struck his head on a rock. Again he was taken to the Christchurch Public Hospital, where he was kept under observation for four days. The medical file reads 'Laceration of right frontal temporal region. No fracture. Concussion.'

It had taken him more than five years, from 5 November 1943 to 11 February 1949, to have his complete specification for patent 87637 accepted. During this time he had had to put a great deal of effort into rewriting those portions of the specification which were unacceptable to the Patent Office. All this hard work and anxiety had netted him nothing so far, neither financial reward nor acclaim. To keep his patent and its Australian equivalent alive cost money. Unless he could benefit from these patents the whole operation had been a dead loss.

Pearse now set out to try to interest the world's leading aircraft companies. This was his last sad gamble. He tried four different aviation concerns and all turned him down. The replies he received were found among his few papers at the end. They all date from between May and July 1950.

The De Havilland Aircraft Company informed him on 26 May: 'We have studied the contents of your letter carefully, but would inform you that at the present moment it is of no interest to us.'

The United Aircraft Corporation on behalf of its Pratt & Whitney Aircraft Division told him on 6 July it would not take his ideas seriously unless he could cover them by a United States patent.

The Bristol Aeroplane Company thanked him on 10 July but regretted to inform him: 'We are unable to interest ourselves in your proposed design of aircraft.'

Finally, on 12 July, Vickers-Armstrong wrote to him saying: 'We have now had an opportunity of considering your invention, but regret that we have come to the conclusion that it is not likely to be of interest to us.'

These refusals must have been a cruel setback. Thirty years' dreaming and twenty years' hard work had gone for nought. To have achieved some recognition for his Utility Plane would have compensated to some extent for his disappointment over the first aircraft. He had battled for half a century with the problems of powered flight, and it had got him nowhere.

His morale gone, Richard Pearse declined steadily in his last year at Wildberry Street. He became more introspective, curt and antisocial. His appearance grew rougher. He took less and less care of himself. He became more obsessed than ever with the idea that people were trying to rob him of his ideas and his aeroplane. Apart from collecting his rents and shopping for necessities he made little contact with anyone. Disillusion and failure had finally got the better of him.

His final months at Woolston were spent as a recluse. On 4 September 1950 Dr J.T.S. Buchan visited him. Pearse complained of indigestion and 'seemed garrulous and wandering'. After this the Collins couple sharing the house with him became increasingly worried about his condition, both physical and mental. Late in June 1951 Pearse complained to Dorothy Collins that she had been stealing his things, and his behaviour became noisy and threatening. He told her he was going to England to fight a company which had stolen his aeroplane invention. He also believed men were trying to gas him, and announced that he would fight them with his axe.

Dr Buchan was called in again. He found Pearse in a wandering and dishevelled state. Pearse told the doctor that people were watching him and trying to steal the keys to his house. He also stated that someone was attempting to gas him. Apropos of nothing in particular Pearse told the doctor that during the First World War when he was passing through the Canal, a person threw an orange to the ship and he caught it.

Dr Buchan concluded that Pearse needed institutional care. A second medical opinion was required by law so Dr J.R. Gilmour was called in. Gilmour visited him at Wildberry Street and found him pottering around outside in his stockinged feet. The room he lived in was extremely untidy, and he was rambling badly. His memory was defective and he failed to recall minor facts during ordinary conversation. Some of his talk about his inventions seemed to the doctor to be pure fabrication. He spoke of an engine of his which dated from the Boer War and claimed to be the first inventor of a flying machine.

One aspect of his poor memory which helps explain the 'attempts on his life' was that he sometimes left the gas taps on and gas seeped through into others parts of the house. He also wandered about the street at night and threatened complete strangers whom he imagined to be trying to break into his house to steal his money and inventions. Neighbours complained of his shouting and yelling. Pearse told the doctor that a nurse came to look after him, which was untrue; he wondered why the doctor did not know his relations at Temuka.

Dr Gilmour, like his colleague, decided that Pearse should be made to go into hospital for care and attention, and attributed his conditon to senility. When such a step is recommended a confirmatory police opinion is necessary by law so Sergeant R.J. Hart was called out from the Christchurch Central Police Station. Sergeant Hart spoke to Pearse and likewise found his mind to be wandering. The police report reads in part: ' He rambles on from one subject to another. One moment it is about the Catholics, then the French Revolution, then his inventions. None of his statements are coherent and it is impossible to get any sense out of him. He is not capable of looking afer himself. Mrs Collins says she is afraid he will do some person an injury as he has been making threats of that nature during the past week.'

At first Pearse was very unwilling to leave his home, but consented when it was explained that his aeroplane and inventions would be looked after. He had some sort of seizure while his report was being compiled and was taken to the Christchurch Public Hospital. He was not admitted there, however, as the doctor examining him suggested that he be taken to Sunnyside Psychiatric Hospital, some five kilometres away. There at 2.30 pm on Saturday 30 June 1951, Richard Pearse entered the institution which was to be his home until he died.

Once the Medical Superintendent and the Public Trust had between them confirmed that Pearse's Australian and New Zealand patents for the Utility Plane were up to date, the old gentleman from Wildberry Street seemed much more at ease.

But his trustees now began to receive complaints from the tenants of his other two properties. The Wainoni house needed repairs to the woodwork and a new coat of paint. The Dampier Street house needed considerable attention, especially to the spouting and drainage. The property inspector's conclusion when he viewed these houses was that:

'The maintenance has been neglected, and the repairs carried out have been done by the patient in an improvised and haphazard manner.'

A letter was sent to Dr Hunter explaining that Richard Pearse's three properties, his Wildberry Street residence included, were in a dilapidated state and required thorough renovation, and that Pearse had enough funds to meet the cost if he so wished. Pearse, when approached, was agreeable to repairs being made but wished to have details of the proposed work and to see a Public Trust Officer on the subject. An officer was sent to the hospital and explained the details to him. At the start of the discussion Pearse seemed to understand the nature of the enquiries, but towards the end he lost the drift of things and the interview had to be terminated.

A doctor observed about this time that though Pearse was 'mildy confused', he was 'very emphatic in his statements about his affairs and gave a good deal of circumstantial detail but it is not always possible to be sure what can be believed and what is fantasy'. Obviously, the patient had again been talking about his 'inventions'.

With all three houses again habitable and the tenants placated Pearse quietly resumed his hospital routines. At intervals he was visited by Warne Pearse from Timaru, but Warne was himself 70 years old and the 160-km journey could not be made very often. Apart from a young nephew in Christchurch, Tony Pearse, there were no other relations closer than Florence, Ruth and Howard Galt in the North Island. Jack, Maggie and Reg had died; Annie and Tom — himself near death — were in Australia.

Apparently, Warne told no one else in the family, not even his own children, what had become of Richard, electing to bear the burden of it himself.

By the time Richard had been at Sunnyside for a year his weight had increased by 6 kg and his physical condition was as good as could be expected for his age — except for trouble with his circulation. He ate and slept adequately, seemed quite content, and was able to do part-time work in the dormitory. At times, though, he would become restless and confused, and experience 'periodic delusions'.

In August 1952 his health took a turn for the worse and Warne was sent the following note: 'Regret to inform you that Mr Pearse is confined to bed and has senile gangrene of his left big toe. Although there is no immediate danger to life his physical condition is likely to deteriorate fairly rapidly.'

Though the gangrene spread no further and his toe healed, Pearse's general condition did worsen. He became very unsteady on his feet and twice hurt himself through tripping over. Once he was punched in the eye by another patient. His confusion increased at night time and he was given a room of his own. A doctor reported early in 1953 that Pearse did not always comprehend what was said to him, and sometimes on being questioned would reply, 'I don't understand pidgin English!'

His last few months were spent mostly in bed. Though he gradually lost weight he took part in occupational therapy classes and slept well, but his arterial condition worsened, the circulation to his feet and hands grew feebler, and his heart weakened.

On 29 July 1953 he suffered a heart attack. A telegram was sent to Warne by the Superintendent: 'Condition of Richard William Pearse causing anxiety advise visit.' Pearse knew how ill he was and told a doctor that he was dying. At 5.15 pm on the same day, before any relations could reach him, he passed away.

This was just 25 months after Richard Pearse was first admitted to Sunnyside, and he had reached the age of 75 years and 8 months. The causes of death were listed as coronary thrombosis, arteriosclerosis, cerebral arteriosclerosis, multiple emboli in both arms and right leg, and senility.

Two days later a simple funeral service was held at the Bromley Crematorium Chapel. It was presided over by the Rev. H.I. Hopkins, formerly vicar of Temuka, who had known Warne Pearse very well. The last remains of Richard William Pearse were then cremated. At the suggestion of Warne a memorial rose tree was planted over the ashes: appropriately, it was a 'Peace' rose. It is there still.

20. Recognition

There is no doubt that Richard Pearse was an inventor of a most extraordinary and versatile sort. Apart from his aeroplanes and aero-engines Pearse at various stages constructed a needle-threader, a string-pull helicopter toy, a lathe, a forge, a reciprocal-drive bamboo bicycle, a power-cycle, a recording machine, a 'magic-viewer', a harp, a power generator, a potato-planter, a topdresser, a motorised discer, two sorts of music box, three houses, and possibly other items we do not know about.

He had a restless, probing, questing mind. Any sort of mechanical problem fascinated him, but he often seemed to be more interested in grappling with the problem than in solving it. His potato-planter and motorised discs are examples of this.

His perennial difficulty was materials. Almost everything he made was improvised out of junk, mostly wire, tin, angle-iron, metal tubing and cast-off pieces of farm machinery. So he must nearly always have been disappointed by the finished result. Nothing worked as well as he hoped and all his handiwork has a jungly, Heath Robinson look about it. For most of his early years he could not afford to spend much money on his hobbies and later on, when he could afford to, his habits had become so frugal that he would not.

Unexpectedly, the aeroplane art is considerably in the debt of people like Pearse. Miller and Sawers in their aviation history calculate that a quarter of all aircraft inventions have come from inventors with no institutional backing. Most of the other inventions have been the product of universities and government-financed research institutes. Aeroplane manufacturers themselves have contributed very few original ideas.

Richard Pearse was basically a rule-of-thumb man, an inspired workshop potterer. With no technical training at all he worked largely by hit-or-miss methods and by intuition, reading what he could lay hands on in the way of scientific manuals. The only common ground between the New Zealander and the Wright brothers was a farsighted vision of air mastery, some experience of typhoid fever, and an interest in bicy-cles. Pearse's style was in all other respects quite dissimilar.

This was especially the case with his work habits. The Wrights kept a meticulous record, with dates, of every stage in their flight experi-ments. Pearse did not have this systematic approach. He was essentially amateurish. As far as can be determined, with his first plane he left no immediate impressions of what he was doing, not even idle jottings. Even with his last plane he did not seem to keep any private record at all of the planning and building process. With both planes, a handful of official communications plus circumstantial evidence is all the investi-gator has to go on. This is why the toughest task of all in Pearse research is dating his work.

Another perplexing aspect of his make-up is this: he was, especially in regard to his two aeroplanes, something of a visionary. At Waitohi he was trying to build an aeroplane and fly it before there were even motorcars in the district. At Milton he was generating power and motorising farm machinery well before anyone else thought of it. Even today, nothing quite comparable to his Woolston 'people's plane' con-cept has eventuated. Yet, despite his evident mechanical mindedness, other branches of technology seemed to have made no impact on him at all. Though he could have afforded to do so he at no stage owned a tractor, motorcar, washing machine, record player or telephone, though he did own a radio set. And after leaving Waitohi, where his family had at least been able to keep an eye on him, Pearse treated himself to a standard of living which was anything but visionary. In fact his preoccu-pation with a variety of hobbies at the expense of his own welfare led to that sorry self-neglect of his last years at Woolston.

Pearse's secretive methods, though understandable, were ultimately half his problem. What must have soured him from early on were the constant jibes of the what's-that-crank-up-to-now variety, plus the apparent failure of his first aircraft. Especially when he was working on his aeroplanes he learned that it was wisest to keep to himself. By nature reticent and introspective, he became more and more uncommu-nicative as his work developed. If he had been less proud it would have been easier for him, but he would neither ask for help nor accept it if it were offered. So he got none. The same with publicity.

Richard Pearse, as even his press letters show, was an unassuming fellow. He did not dispute the Wright brothers' claim to have made the first acceptable powered flight. All he wished to take credit for was being the first to use a pneumatic-tyred tricycle undercarriage, a steerable nosewheel, ailerons, and direct transmission from engine to propeller. There are other assertions which he might justifiably have made but did not, and these possibilities will be examined later. First of all, however, let us look at his own claims.

Pearse was not in fact the first to think of a tricycle undercarriage for an aeroplane. William Henson's design for an *Aerial Steam Carriage*, published in 1843, shows such an undercarriage, but Henson's machine was never built and the model based on the design could not have flown. When Felix Du Temple went down a ramp in 1874 in the world's first powered takeoff, his aeroplane was fitted with a tricycle undercarriage of three small wheels, the single one to the rear. In the next year Thomas Moy used a tricycle undercarriage on his model *Aerial Steamer* tested at the Crystal Palace. However, the wheels were hard-tyred and the front one was not steerable. Victor Tatin in 1879 tested a three-wheeled model monoplane which flew fifteen metres while tethered to a central pole. The Phillips multiplane of 1893 ran on three small wheels but with the single one at the rear. So Pearse's tricycle undercarriage had been anticipated by at least five other inventors, though he does not seem to have realised this; however, only three of these had the single wheel to the front and these were models, not full-sized aircraft.

In Pearse's case the originality of his first aeroplane's undercarriage lay in the use of pneumatic tyres and a steerable nosewheel on a full scale aircraft. We now take this sort of undercarriage for granted, but many of the early planes, including those of the Wright brothers, rested on skids. Others made use of guiderails, catapult launchers, runners or floats. Relatively few used wheels, and those that did most commonly adopted the four-wheel 'pram' undercarriage.

The next aviator after Pearse to use pneumatic tyres was a Rumanian doctor of law living in Paris, Trajan Vuia. His small monoplane with a four-wheeled undercarriage made some eleven powered takeoffs between March 1906 and March 1907. Santos-Dumont, whom Pearse mentioned with approval in his letters, made flights in September and October 1906 — the first successful powered flights in Europe — his plane resting on two air-filled tyres plus a tailskid. It was not until 1908 that Glenn Curtiss, mounting his *June Bug* on a tricycle undercarriage of three 50-cm pneumatic tyres, did anything comparable to Pearse. The *June Bug* won for Curtiss the *Scientific American* magazine's prize for the first official public flight, in the United States, of more than a kilometre.

Pearse's style of undercarriage did not really come into vogue until the 1950s. It is now common in planes of many sizes from Douglas DC-8s to Piper Cherokees. Here, Pearse was 50 years ahead of fashion.

When he claimed to have invented ailerons he was referring to his wingtip 'vanes' or 'rudders'. These, he believed, were the best means available for balancing aircraft and he claimed that history had proved him right.

Up to Pearse's time, the most effective system devised for maintaining lateral control on gliders and aeroplanes was wing-warping. This technique was hit upon by the German glider pioneer Otto Lilienthal, after observing carefully the flight of birds and noting that they twisted the tips of their wings to maintain lateral balance. He tested the idea on a glider he built in 1895, the year before he was killed. The Wright brothers, who did not know of Lilienthal's experiments with warping, devised a similar system of control in 1899.

Up till January 1906 the researches of the Wright brothers on lateral control had been kept secret, apart from Chanute's Paris lecture. Pearse could not have known anything of their wing-warping methods till after he had perfected his own system, but it is clear from his newspaper letters that he subsequently understood very clearly what the Wrights were trying to do. According to Warne Pearse he even corresponded with them, but no trace of this interchange survives either here or in the USA. He preferred his own control system, which he had arrived at independently, as asserted: 'So I can claim to have given the world "ailerons"; which were invented by me in 1904 and patented in 1906 on June 19'.

Unfortunately, this claim cannot be upheld. The term aileron was, in 1915, when Pearse raised the issue in his Milton letter, fairly loosely used to describe almost any sort of winglet employed for flight control. Now, however, careful distinctions are made between ailerons, flaps, spoilers, elevons and airbrakes. Ailerons are, strictly speaking, movable surfaces to control the rolling movements of an aeroplane, generally set in or by the trailing edges of wings, near the tips. They are capable of being moved either above or below the surface of the wing. Pearse's 'wing-vanes' which had only a one-way action may best be described as steering airbrakes.

Whether sited above the wing as in the text of the provisional and complete patent specifications or below the wing as in the drawing accompanying the substitute complete specification, Pearse's airbrakes would have the effect (when operated independently) of retarding the wing concerned and slewing the plane around, thus changing its heading. But they could not control roll, as orthodox ailerons do. Placed below the wing they would be less effective but less dangerous and would function more like flaps, increasing lift as well as drag. No one can be certain now in which position, above or below the wing, Pearse finally intended his airbrakes to be placed. Nor can it be decided whether the discrepancy between texts and diagram is accidental or deliberate.

Movable control surfaces attached to or set into aircraft wings are known to predate Pearse. M.P.W. Boulton patented ailerons in 1868, though he did not understand how they should best be worked. Richard Harte patented perfectly workable flap-type ailerons in 1870. Neither Boulton nor Harte took their ideas beyond the theoretical stage, and they influenced no one. Charles Renard's ten-wing glider of 1873 incorporated steering airbrakes, as did Alphonse Pénaud's model ornithopter of 1874. Elevons were used on an airframe built and tested by M.A. Goupil in 1833. Otto Lilienthal devised both leading-edge flaps and steering airbrakes for his no. 12 glider in 1895.

Evidently, Pearse did not know of any of these anticipations of his own control surfaces, but the fact remains that he was indeed the first to fit airbrakes or any similar surfaces to a full-sized aeroplane. And as the design and location of his airbrakes in no way resembles the efforts of his nineteenth-century predecessors it may be assumed that he devised them quite independently. He argues on these lines in his letters and was proud of the fact that systems like his had completely superseded the more clumsy wing-warping methods of the Wrights.

Though Esnault-Pelterie used elevons on a glider in 1904, and Samuel Cody used them on a kite-glider in 1905, the first after Pearse to employ wing-vanes as a means of flight control in full-sized aircraft were Blériot and Santos-Dumont in 1906, Curtiss and Farman in 1908 and Levavasseur in 1909.

It has to be said, however, that though Pearse, between his two patent specifications for the first plane, seems to have discovered all the basics for acceptable flight control, neither of the specifications on its own demonstrates these control devices in workable form. In neither of the specifications are his vanes combined with elevator and vertical rudder in such a way as to produce an acceptable three-axis system giving his plane longitudinal, lateral and directional control. He seems to have been within an ace of achieving this, and his letters suggest that

he may actually have done so but his aeroplane was too large and un-
wieldy to fly at a sufficient speed for the controls to be worked effectively. And, as he himself said, he did not have the patience, eventually, to
design a smaller aircraft.

George Bolt also thought that part of Pearse's flight control problem
must have been in the sheer size of his 65-square metre wing: 'The construction of a large wing such as this in bamboo would be a difficult
thing and I would be inclined to think that part of Pearse's control
problem would be the distortion of this wing as it commenced to take
the load. Very small variations of angle on one side or the other would
give bad turning effects.' Therefore, Pearse was never able to gauge the
efficiency of his control surfaces and make the appropriate modifications.

But it is clear nevertheless that he was a pioneer experimenter in a
field of flight control which was in less than a decade to oust completely
the Wright brothers' wing-warping. Moreover, he seems to have worked
at his system in a technological vacuum, as it were, influenced by no
one. In a sense he was a victim of his own secretive practices. Referring
to his system of balancing the first plane he later wrote, 'I thought of it
long before I took out a patent.' He seems not to have bothered applying to patent his system until he learnt that other aviators were trying
to achieve lateral control without ailerons.

By then it was too late. The Wrights' system of flight control was
given priority over all other systems. Deterred either by the scope of the
Wright patents or possibly by the costs involved, Pearse did not bother
to patent his invention outside New Zealand. And because of his
remoteness, and that of the Wellington Patent Office, nobody knew
what he had done. He influenced nobody. The unfortunate conse-
quences of this were that an invention which with minor modifiations
could have been made operable and which Pearse felt could have earned him a small fortune, earned him not a penny. The rewards and the
fame went elsewhere. Small wonder that he died a frustrated hermit.

So much for undercarriage and ailerons. The final claim Pearse made in
his press letters was expressed as follows: 'I was the first to simplify the
aeroplane by placing the propeller direct on the crankshaft of the engine, and by this idea I was able to do away with transmission gearing,
the clutch and the flywheel. The next man to do this was Santos-
Dumont. The Wrights followed Maxim and Langley . . . and had two
large propellers revolving at a slow speed, and to do this they had to

employ gearing, clutch and a flywheel. Practically all aeroplanes now have a single propeller direct on the crankshaft of the engine.'

The concept of a tractor or front-mounted propeller may seem commonplace to present-day readers, but up to about 1909 most aircraft were powered by pusher propellers functioning at the back of the plane, and very few operated by direct transmission. Nevertheless, Pearse's claim needs some modification. It appears from diagrams and photographs that Felix Du Temple, who patented his remarkable monoplane in 1857, used a tractor propeller with direct transmission to its steam-powered engine. Likewise Clement Ader in his *Eole* of 1890 and *Avion III* of 1897 seemed to use tractor propellers directly attached to steam-engine crankshafts. Others who used front propellers (twin tractor in each case) but with indirect transmission were Pénaud in 1877 and Victor Tatin in 1879. Pénaud's and Tatin's planes were models only, as already noted.

Pearse's nearest rivals, the Wright brothers, used with their *Wright Flyer I*, which flew four times on 17 December 1903, two geared-down pusher airscrews connected to the 12-hp motor by a cycle-chain transmission system encased in tubes.

The only European aviator working along Pearse's lines was Trajan Vuia. His 1906 machine, looking quaintly like a go-kart with bat's wings, had its propeller up front directly connected to the engine by a long crankshaft like Pearse's. Vuia's several ground-hops were not rated as flights, but his style of plane was to influence Blériot greatly, an achievement in its own right.

What, then, can be said about Pearse's claim regarding the propulsion of his aircraft? He was not the first to make use of a direct-drive airscrew but he was the first to do so with a full-sized aeroplane driven by a petrol engine. It should be said here that some aviators such as the Wrights, who had relatively efficient propellers, deliberately geared them down to 400–450 rpm in order to produce optimum thrust. Pearse's airscrew resembled the more rudimentary direct-drive 'paddles' (favoured by European fliers) which rotated at engine speeds of over 1,000 rpm. The invention of variable-pitch and constant-pitch propellers eventually gave direct-drive airscrews maximum efficiency in all conditions.

If these were the only innovations Pearse wished to be credited with, he was probably unaware of further possibilities. There are other features of his first plane well deserving of mention. For instance, the fabric-over-frame propeller he recommends in his 1907 specification was so constructed that 'the pitch of the propeller's sails or blades may be adjusted to any desired degree to suit circumstances'. Two-pitch airscrews were not seen elsewhere until 1918, though a variable-pitch propeller was tested at Farnborough in 1917. Practical variable-pitch propellers were not developed until 1932.

The pitch of Pearse's airscrew could not be adjusted by remote control, as could the propeller and rotor blades on his Utility Plane, but the idea is nevertheless farsighted and at that time there seems to have been no other propeller capable of similar adjustment. Pearse was also one of the first to use metal-bladed propellers, wood being the most commonly used material for airscrews then. Metal propellers did not become fashionable until the 1920s.

The first engine which he constructed to power his plane is even more ingenious. If, as is possible, he built this engine 'during the Boer War', it must rank among the earliest petrol-driven motors ever used in an aeroplane. Langley successfully flew a quarter-sized model plane powered by a small petrol engine in August 1903, and this has generally been credited with being the first petrol-engined aeroplane to fly tentatively. If Pearse did make his first successful takeoff in March 1903, his two-cylinder engine would rank as the first petrol-driven motor to get a full-sized manned aircraft off the ground.

In any case it enjoys the distinction of being the first horizontally opposed petrol engine to be used in a plane, and the first such (and perhaps the only one) to operate on the double-acting principle. Horizontally opposed engines now have a considerable vogue in the light aircraft field.

The most surprising thing about this engine is that Pearse made it almost entirely out of junk, in a primitive farm workshop, with help given only in the fabrication of his sparkplugs. His motor was like no other internal combustion engine anywhere else and seemed to owe as much to the steam engine as to Carl Benz. It is significant that hardly any of the pioneer aviators apart from Pearse and the Wright brothers made their own engines. Most had them made by engineers or bought them from factories: including Langley, Santos-Dumont, Blériot, Vuia, Ferber, Cody and Voisin. Pearse had to make his own motor because there were none available in his district, not even car engines. Nothing but steam. What is more, his engine was reliable, reasonably efficient, and probably the lightest in the world — at that time — in terms of its power output.

Two aspects of his first aeroplane's wing are interesting though not of any novelty — its camber, and Pearse's apparent attempt (in the provisional patent specification) to give it some dihedral angle. Both camber and wing-dihedral may be traced back to Cayley in the early nineteenth century. Whether Pearse worked out the value of camber and dihedral independently or was indebted to others cannot now be ascertained.

A more original but less practical aspect of his wing design was its incidence control. From where he sat the pilot could use a lever to alter the setting of the wing, which was hinged above him to the apex of the undercarriage. Though d'Esterno had patented a comparable idea in 1864, its practical application seems to have been another Pearse 'first'.

Pearse placed his elevator at the trailing edge of the wing. Though Cayley's 1804 model glider had a tail elevator, and though it may be the accepted thing for aeroplanes nowadays to have their elevators at the rear (albeit some distance from the wing), in Pearse's time the preference was for front elevators. The Wrights, Farman, Delagrange, Voisin, McCurdy, Cody, Curtiss and others used elevators of this sort. Again, Pearse was closer to the modern configuration than most of his contemporaries. The nature of the tail rudder which he mentions in his provisional patent specification and in his letters, though not in his complete specification, can only be guessed at.

The vertical stabiliser, a long keel-piece attached fore and aft to the top of the wing, seems now to be of dubious value, and no one recalls Pearse using it himself. It is an interesting throwback to Henson, perhaps. The only aviator of Pearse's vintage who seems to have favoured a dorsal fin at any stage was Blériot in the third version of his *Blériot XII*.

Another ingenious method of stabilising the plane while in flight was the use of a sliding seat which could be moved forwards and backwards as well as from side to side in order to shift the plane's centre of gravity. Count d'Esterno had anticipated this idea 40 years before Pearse, but his glider never got beyond the planning stage. The 'body-shift' method of stabilisng an aircraft had its effect on Lilienthal, Chanute, Pilcher and other hang-glider exponents, but Pearse appears to have been the first to try to use the technique in a powered aircraft. He also hoped that in the event of a crash, his sliding-seat would absorb some of the shock of impact.

His achievements with his first plane amount to these, then. He appears to be the first aviator in the British Empire to make a powered takeoff in an aeroplane. It matters little, as far as this claim is concerned, whether he did so in 1903 or 1904. His nearest rival was

Horatio Phillips, whose tentative powered flight at Streatham in England did not take place until mid-1907. If Pearse's first publicly witnessed takeoff occurred on the afternoon of Tuesday 31 March 1903, as seems most likely, he can also be credited with the fifth powered takeoff anywhere in the world. The New Zealander on this point is not in competition with the Wright brothers, whose pioneer flights of 17 December 1903 remain uncontested in terms of duration and control.

The other major claim Pearse has to recognition concerns the plane he used and patented. This aircraft must now be rated ahead of Trajan Vuia's 1906 machine as the first full-sized conventionally shaped tractor monoplane in history.

The prophetic configuration of his monoplane had other features to commend it. It was the first full-sized powered aircraft to rest on a pneumatic-tyred tricycle undercarriage with steerable nosewheel; the first to use steering airbrakes; the first to employ a variable-incidence wing control; the first with a movable pilot's seat to absorb crash impact if necessary and to trim the aircraft. The original motor he used was the first horizontally opposed double-acting engine to be used in an aeroplane. The propeller he recommends in his patent is probably the first adjustable-pitch airscrew on record. Finally, his plane seems to be the first specifically designed to be easily dismantled and stored.

It is impossible to determine the extent to which Pearse may have been influenced by developments elsewhere in the world. If, through the *Scientific American*, he did know what the Wrights or Langley were doing, he borrowed nothing from those sources. Nor does he incorporate any of the ideas of Jatho, Kress, Chanute, Pilcher, Lilienthal, Ader, Maxim, Hargrave, or others who immediately preceded him. Indeed if you were to try to identify the ancestors of Pearse's aircraft you might have to go back to Cayley's 1799 glider design or Mozhaiski's 1884 steam monoplane for the low-aspect-ratio wing shape; to Henson's *Aerial Steam Carriage* design of 1843 for the vertical stabiliser and tricycle undercarriage; to d'Esterno's glider design of 1864 for the sliding seat and variable-incidence wing control; and to Du Temple in 1857 for a tractor direct-drive propeller.

The only one of these flight pioneers about whom one can be fairly certain Pearse would have known is Henson, whose aeroplane design was famous the world over, largely because of Marriott's stylish engravings. But Pearse seems to owe little to anyone: the clean-lined simplicity of his high-wing monoplane is in marked contrast to the cluttered-up configurations of most other aircraft at the turn of the century. It was part of Pearse's lifestyle to be beholden to no one, and this first plane, like his other inventions, is almost perversely original.

His accomplishment in creating such an aircraft is considerable by any standards but, taken in the context of his times, with his minimal primary school education, his isolation, his rudimentary materials and equipment, his lack of encouragement and the absence of any stimulating contact with other aviators, his achievement is remarkable. Given more helpful circumstances including the factory facilities, technical aid and government grants that aviators elsewhere were getting, Richard Pearse and his first plane might have been famous well before this.

His importance as an aeronautical inventor does not end with his first patent. Pearse built between 1906 and 1911 two other engines of a novel sort to power his plane: a four-cylinder single-acting horizontally opposed engine of about 25 hp and a sixteen-cylinder opposed engine of about 60 hp which may be the same as the sixteen-cylinder 'rotary' engine referred to by a Temuka observer. A feature of all Pearse's engines, according to both the inventor and various witnesses, was their reliability. They were noisy and rudimentary but they worked, and were extremely light for their power output. As Pearse proudly wrote: 'An ordinary motorcar or motor bicycle motor weighs about 20 lbs per hp and my first aeroplane motor of 24 hp weighed 5 lbs per hp.' Pearse's 60 hp engine — if we accept this rating — weighed only 4 lbs per hp, a better power-weight ratio than that achieved by any other American or European aero engine of that vintage apart from the seven-cylinder rotary Gnôme designed by the Séguin brothers. (This 165-lb [74 kg] motor weighed out at 3.5 lbs per hp and was used to power Paulhan's Voisin in June 1909.)

Another development associated with Pearse's first plane was a circular or oval-winged configuration he was working on at Waitohi in 1910–11 shortly before leaving for Milton. As there is insufficient corroborative evidence, no claim, not even of novelty, can be made on behalf of this 'flying saucer' model and Pearse seems not to have persevered long with the idea. Oval wingshapes had been designed earlier by Steiger, Lilienthal, Pilcher and Blériot. Annular-winged aircraft had also been built by the US Keystone Company.

Unfortunately, Pearse left his run too late with the Utility Plane. By the time he had put his 1919 concept into effect, events had overtaken him. Several ideas which in the early 1920s would have had considerable originality were, by the time his patent was applied for, merely quaint. Others were perhaps too farsighted to be intelligible. The aircraft is a repository for his ideas and flight philosophy rather than being, when it was built, an answer to any plane manufacturer's prayers. He was trying to do too many things with one aircraft. It was a gallant effort but Pearse did not have the technical means to convert his theories into a workable proposition. Therefore, his last plane, with which he aspired to recover all his lost ground, survives as little more than an intriguing mechanical curiosity.

Yet some features of the MOTAT Utility Plane are certainly interesting enough. To recapitulate briefly, its engine may be worked as a two-stroke or four-stroke, its main cylinders are double-acting, it is equipped with superchargers and primitive after-burners, and the engine plus propeller may be tilted from the horizontal to the near-vertical to vary the angle of thrust. The propeller-rotor is variable in pitch and of a crafty design. There is a tail rotor, also of variable pitch, to counteract torque. The several control surfaces are of an ingenious sort. The pilot's seat was especially contrived, in theory anyway, so that it would absorb the impact of a crash landing. There is a sprung groundbrake fitted to help cushion normal landings and bring the plane to a halt. The landing wheels can be linked by a belt drive to the engine, possibly to permit the machine to be used as a road vehicle if necessary and to allow the engine to be started by towing or pushing the plane. Finally, the tail unit is capable of being folded forward so that the machine may be housed in an ordinary car garage.

Though Pearse seems not to have realised it, several of these ideas were not new. The first convertiplane had been designed by Cayley as early as 1843. Pomés and de la Pauze had in 1871 suggested a helicopter with a large adjustable-pitch rotor to be driven by gunpowder, and in 1877 Dieuaide experimented with a small vertical rotor to counteract rotation of the fuselage. Pénaud incorporated a tailskid, to which Pearse's groundbrake is related, in his 1876 design for an amphibious monoplane. The first people-carrying helicopters had been successfully tested in 1907 by Paul Cornu and the Breguet brothers. Superchargers were in use from 1916, and variable-pitch propellers from 1932.

However, after-burners, leading-edge wing flaps and tilting engines were not seen until after the Second World War, and in these areas Pearse was certainly a pioneer experimenter. His ingenuity lay in combining all these features in one aeroplane design and in singlehandedly building a full scale version of it, virtually from castoffs and scraps.

Pearse's Utility Plane would nowadays be classed as a V/STOL air-craft, a term devised by the United States National Aeronautics and Space Administration to cover all types of vertical/short takeoff and landing aircraft.

Autogiros and helicopters are two members of this family of aircraft familiar since the 1930s. But over the last 40 years many other types of V/STOL planes, the majority of them jet propelled, have been developed. NASA has attempted to classify them all according to their methods of converting vertical flight to horizontal flight. There are four such methods: the first is to tilt the entire aircraft; the second is to tilt the rotor, propeller, jet, or other source of thrust; the third method is to deflect or bend the thrust itself by the use of flaps or nozzles, according to whether airscrews or jets are being used; the fourth is a dual-propulsion system with separate engines for vertical and horizontal flight.

The Utility Plane of Pearse's patent specifications clearly belongs to the second category, where the transition from vertical to horiztontal flight is carried out principally by tilting the propeller-rotor and engine. The completed Pearse aircraft has most in common with the second group, but marginally resembles the third category of V/STOLs. It has been suggested that the plane's leading-edge flaps, situated where they are (under the propeller downdraught) may have been designed to deflect or vector the thrust. This could assist the transition from vertical to horizontal flight as well as aiding lateral control when the plane was hovering — if these flaps were operated independently. But it is more likely that Pearse thought it would be necessary to drop the leading edges which were 'washed' by the propeller slipstream, just to get them out of the way.

The V/STOL is certainly the aircraft of the future, but only time will tell if it ever becomes the plane for the million, the mass-produced, inexpensive, conveniently operated all-purpose aircraft that Pearse hoped for. The whole notion behind his 'people's plane' is as much the product of a philosopher and egalitarian dreamer as of a practical engineer. Herein lies much of its appeal.

But the most arresting feature of the whole Utility Plane story is that Richard Pearse seems, with this astonishing aircraft, to have anticipated by many years one of the most important developments in aviation technology; and that in the now vital area of tilting engines and vectored thrust he may have been in the vanguard of experimentation — on present published evidence, at any rate.

But, as with his first aeroplane, he influenced no one. He was too isolated, too secretive and too slow to capitalise on his ideas. By the time he got around to showing his convertiplane patent to aviation companies in 1950, they were no doubt working on their own much more sophisticated V/STOL concepts and had no use for the New Zealander's invention. The Utility Plane was simply not a viable proposition. Thus it cannot be said that Pearse, with either of his aircraft, has affected the course of aviation history in any way.

This is of course regrettable, but considering his temperament, environment and circumstances, not surprising. Indeed the whole Pearse story, right through to its tragic conclusion, has an almost despairing inevitability about it.

21. Postscript: the years since

For all sorts of reasons, the publication of *The Riddle of Richard Pearse* in 1973, reprinted the following year, could not have been more timely.

The public's interest in early aviation had been nicely whetted by the 1965 box office triumph of Twentieth Century Fox's *Those Magnificent Men in Their Flying Machines*, about an air race from London to Paris in 1910. A feature of this film was its hilarious credit sequence showing a wide variety of early flight attempts. If Pearse's first mono-plane had been included it would have seemed a great deal less wacky-looking than the machines of his European contemporaries, and the old film clips showed there was nothing exceptional about flying into gorse hedges.

Auckland's Museum of Transport and Technology also played an important part in preparing the New Zealand public for a biography of Pearse. For some years its Pearse exhibit (featuring the Utility Plane and other Pearse items brought up from Christchurch by George Bolt) had been one of MOTAT's principal drawcards. The release of a Richard Pearse Medal on 19 September 1971 — Battle of Britain Day — and the publication of a Pearse pamphlet, booklet and articles in the MOTAT journal helped to keep the subject alive. Profits from these enterprises also assisted the financing of MOTAT's Pioneers of Aviation pavilion.

Some of the museum's Pearse material tended to be over-exuberant and I ran a long correspondence with the then director, Ron Richardson, urging him not to allow too much to be claimed for Pearse, especially not the claim that he 'flew before the Wright brothers' and did so in 1902.

The possibility that the Wright brothers had a rival was by now known in America. I had been corresponding for some time with a Pearse supporter in Michigan. Gordon Gapper, strategically placed as journal assistant city editor of the *Flint Journal*, was raised in Temuka. As a child he had heard rumours and anecdotes about the local legend.

On 12 September 1971 Gapper published in his paper a feature on Pearse's exploits entitled 'The Mad Farmer'. It was widely syndicated. *Chases' Calendar of Annual Events*, which has a large circulation in the USA, then decided to include a paragraph on Pearse in its 31 March entry — also the birthday, it seems, of two English poets, Andrew Marvell and Edward Fitzgerald.

In a more sombre sense, the publication of *The Riddle of Richard Pearse* was also providential. When I began my research there were still over a dozen elderly witnesses to Pearse's Waitohi flight experiments alive and able to be interviewed. By the time the book came out there were only four. Within another five years there were none. Getting any sort of definitive biography published had been, in a very literal sense, a race against the clock. Fortunately, I seem to have gathered in virtually all that there was to be known.

One of the most conscientious and persistent advocates of an earlier flight date for Richard Pearse was C.G. Rodliffe, whose writings and public observations soon aroused the ire of D.A. Patterson, general manager of NAC. Patterson believed that exaggerated claims on Pearse's behalf were making the aviator and all his advocates look ridiculous. He began to say so frequently and this helped to fuel interest in the very subject he was trying to dampen down. Patterson was a figure of authority in aviation circles and his critical views of the Pearse flight claims were given wide press coverage. I agreed with his denunciation of the excessive claims being made on Pearse's behalf, but several times felt the need to counter some of the arguments he used.

In particular, I objected to Doug Patterson's view that if Pearse really had been carrying out flight experiments in 1903 or earlier, the newspapers would have got on to the story then, and not waited until 1909. But Pearse wanted no such publicity. To the end of his days he was very secretive about his work. Though Pearse continued his experiments and inventing at Louden's Gully near Milton, when he shifted there in 1911, the local *Bruce Herald* published no account of his work. Nor did the Christchurch papers (and there were four of them for some of the time) report anything about the fifteen years' work on the Utility Plane that Pearse later built at Woolston. Many neighbours in this heavily populated suburb knew he was working on the aircraft. One even photographed it. Still, no approach from the press. If you are to believe only what you read in the newspapers, Pearse's Utility Plane did not happen either.

Ongoing debate of this sort ensured that *The Riddle of Richard Pearse* did not have to struggle to life in a vacuum. Then came the book reviews. I have always found it very quaint when writers and performing artists pretend that they ignore reviews of their work. Few of them do in fact ignore reviews, nor can they afford to. In the case of *The Riddle of Richard Pearse* I was anxious that the book be at least tolerably well received, not just for the sake of my own reputation, but for the sake of Pearse himself whom I had tried so hard to rescue from unjust oblivion.

I need not have worried. With only one exception, out of nearly thirty reviews received the reports were highly flattering. Though little attempt had been made to promote the biography overseas, beyond sending review copies to leading aviation journals in America, Britain and Australia, the response from abroad was most encouraging. Chris Wren, writing for the London publication *Air Enthusiasts International*, especially delighted me with a reference to Pearse as 'New Zealand's Barnes Wallis'. The book was also reviewed helpfully on the BBC and in the *Guardian*.

Most surprising of all, I received a letter from Norris McWhirter, editor of *The Guinness Book of Records:* 'I am lost in admiration for your splendid book on Richard Pearse — a tour de force of painstaking but doubtless at times thrilling research . . . For many years I have received rather weak signals about him and you have now certainly put him in scholarly perspective. Wishing you every success with the book which certainly ought to have been well and widely reviewed and which I shall unhesitatingly recommend loud and long whenever and wherever the opportunity arises'.

The single exception to the run of supportive reviews was the one I had been secretly dreading all along — the response to the book by C.H. Gibbs-Smith. Charles Gibbs-Smith, Keeper Emeritus of the Victoria and Albert Museum, Honorary Companion of the Royal Aeronautical Society (London), had published nine books on the origins of the aeroplane and of powered flight, and dedicated the last of them to the Wright brothers. As early as 1959 he had responded to the first rather reckless claim by Warne Pearse that his brother had flown before the Wrights: 'On present showing it smells to high heaven'. His reaction to an article on Pearse distributed worldwide in 1971 by the New Zealand Information Service was that it was 'a mixture of lies and fantasy'.

I had exchanged several letters with the eminent historian in the course of forming my own conclusions on Richard Pearse. The exacting criteria Gibbs-Smith insisted upon before anyone could talk of 'flight' were well known to me, as was his scorn for testimony gathered from well-intentioned eyewitnesses well after the event. I had consequently been ultra-cautious in making my own claims for Pearse. But in the one matter of concluding that there was enough datable circumstantial evidence to suggest a possible flight attempt on 31 March 1903 (though Pearse wrote in his letter of 1904) I had never been able to get Gibbs-Smith's concurrence. So I expected to be jumped on from a great height. And I was not disappointed.

The editor of the New Zealand *Aviation Digest* had commissioned Gibbs-Smith to review the Pearse biography and gleefully headlined the result: 'Ogilvie resorts to rather desperate tactic'. Gibbs-Smith was gallant enough about the book as a whole. 'Mr Ogilvie is as fine an advocate as any inventor could wish for, and I admire his acumen, tenacity and devotion to the cause of Richard Pearse . . . The book is an excellent account of the life of a man who was obviously a talented self-taught engineer . . . [but Mr Ogilvie's] duckling must, we regret, remain a duckling and not the swan he had hoped for'.

The 'desperate tactic' was my suggestion that Pearse himself might have made an error in his 1915 and 1928 press letters about when he started his flight experiments; or that he might have been misunderstood about what he was trying to say in those letters; and that there might have been inconsistencies in his statements.

Gibbs-Smith was adamant. 'If the machine was uncontrollable; if it spun round directly it left the ground; and if [Pearse] says he never flew; there is simply no possibility at all that it performed as the eyewitnesses declared . . . Mr Ogilvie simply cannot have it both ways. We must either believe the explicit statements of the inventor himself or we must believe the alleged eyewitnesses' accounts 50 or more years later.'

My dating method for some of the testimony was to use cut-off points. A witness might have left the district (for example) by a particular date and could not have seen Pearse's experiments later than that date. Gibbs-Smith responded: 'In view of Mr Ogilvie's "cut-off points", it would seem that the witnesses must have witnessed "something" . . . If there was something seen in March 1903 I suggest, from Pearse's own evidence, it must have been an experiment with a model, which could easily have been magnified in retrospect to involve a full-scale manned machine'. (Neither Pearse nor any witnesses refer to models being used in this way, however.)

Charles Gibbs-Smith at least conceded (as he had done in private correspondence with me) that Pearse was doing something in 1903 by way of flight experimentation. But that was as far as he would go. Luckily most of the witnesses, now dead, were spared the experience of seeing their recollections written off as exaggerated fantasies. I might say I began the research work with a high degree of scepticism about elderly witnesses, also. But so many of them (including Bolt's and Cederman's informants) had seen Pearse in the air and were quite positive about it; and whatever the location or period in Pearse's Waitohi career, they could make some attempt to date the occasion with reference to teachers at the school, births, marriages, deaths, crop and meteorological details or property transactions, that my scepticism waned. Most were remembering episodes from their teenage years and early twenties when they were at their most alert and receptive.

Have you ever heard First World War veterans speak of their experiences? Those splendid Gallipoli survivors (all in their nineties) who were responsible a decade ago for helping Christopher Pugsley and Maurice Shadbolt with their research on the tragic Dardanelles campaign seemed to have total recall. Some seventy years after the event, not just fifty, they could still remember with stunning clarity their horrifying ordeal at Gallipoli, along with quite minute details — things said, rifle numbers, names of scores of dead mates, smells, weather conditions, dates, emotions, mail received, and so on. We believed them. Military records substantiated most of what they remembered. So I feel we should take seriously most of the Pearse witnesses, especially since they were tracked down in all parts of the country, with little chance of collaboration. Some of them did not even like the taciturn inventor and had no cause to perjure themselves.

Anyhow, I took the liberty of challenging some aspects of Gibbs-Smith's arguments in the following issue of *Aviation Digest*. The editor, who had now got a rise out of both of us, joyfully bannered my remarks with a rhyming headline: 'Riddle me, Riddle me ree; Gibbs-Smith and Ogilvie'.

Douglas Patterson and another of New Zealand's aviation authorities, A.C. Elworthy of Timaru, took up where Gibbs-Smith left off and continued to attack the 'Pearse myth' and the 'Pearse cult' (Patterson's phrases) wherever they found expression. And they were given plenty of target practice. An outbreak of Pearse feature articles hit the provincial papers, some of them wildly off target and claiming not merely that Pearse's experiments *might* have predated the Wright brothers', but that they *did*. Both Patterson and Elworthy were kept busy with their rebuttals.

The clash of ideologies reached fever pitch in 1979 with the unveiling of the Richard Pearse Memorial at Waitohi. The Temuka Borough Council and Geraldine County Council had, in 1974, both toyed with the idea of a memorial. An eager committee of Waitohi residents, led by Jim Crombie, took over the plan, working hard with professional help to design and construct a full-sized replica of the 1906 patent version of Pearse's first aircraft, with some modifications by Geoff Rodliffe. It was built of permanent materials and mounted on a high pole set into a limestone base bearing a descriptive plaque. Ivan Johnson of Parr & Co, an engineering firm in Timaru, built the aircraft's framework, and the Waitohi folk finished it off. One ingenious aspect of the memorial's construction is that Pearse's plane, like a wind vane, always faces into the breeze.

During the lead up to the unveiling ceremony, which was to take place, significantly, on 31 March, there was a great deal of speculation as to what should be inscribed on the plaque. Tony Elworthy, a younger brother of Lord Elworthy, had been nibbling away at the Pearse 'mythology' for some time. Now, barely a month before the unveiling, he decided to give the whole issue a thorough gnawing in two large feature articles he offered to the *Timaru Herald* (21–22 February 1979).

Tony Elworthy was a grandson of Archbishop Churchill Julius, an amateur inventor who had helped his even more mechanical son, George, to invent the totalisator. Elworthy had been an apprentice with the Bristol Aeroplane Company in 1930 and learned to fly in 1931. For some years he had run his own automotive engineering business and engaged in a medley of enthusiasms which ranged from gas turbines, gentleman farming and photography to yachting and aviation history. He also enjoyed a good old verbal scrap. Elworthy's view on Pearse, argued in the two articles, was that he did not fly, no matter what the suggested date (closely following the line pioneered by Gibbs-Smith); and to add insult to injury, he contended that Pearse's engineering and construction work was so crude that his aircraft hardly deserved to fly anyway.

The hinterland erupted in pain and fury. Waitohi residents, who were toiling so hard to commemorate the work of their local hero, could have cheerfully throttled Tony Elworthy. He was denounced in the correspondence columns as a foolish, reckless, stupid, dogmatic neanderthal. His arguments were variously taken apart. I penned a detailed reply of my own to Elworthy's main contentions. Since I was visiting Timaru anyway, I decided to deliver my item in person to the editor of the *Timaru Herald*. 'There's someone here you might like to meet,' he said with a wink. 'Let me introduce Tony Elworthy.' After a moment of mutual bewilderment (never having met before), we chatted away amiably enough and Tony corresponded with me, on and off, for another five years. 'Like you, I'm just struggling to get the facts right,' he once wrote. The two of us were at least able to carry on some sort of dialogue. Though I several times challenged Douglas Patterson's views I received no response from him at all.

Although the Elworthy name was scarcely flavour of the month in Waitohi, the Richard Pearse Memorial Committee had decided to invite New Zealand's top aviator, Lord Elworthy, to unveil the memorial. Lord Elworthy, in view of all the fuss, declined. I was invited to do the job instead and gladly complied. At the function afterwards, attended by about 350 South Canterbury dignitaries, local residents, Pearse enthusiasts and aviation buffs, there were several speeches, and then — for me, anyway — an unexpected extra. Geoffrey Rodliffe and Graham Bell, who were attending from Auckland, announced their claim — to be published six months later — that Pearse definitely flew in 1902. I nearly fell out of my chair, and was quite unable to join in the hearty applause. Gibbs-Smith, who thought even 1903 excessive, would have had a double hernia. One could even feel a little sorry for the Pearse Memorial Committee, which had just finished engraving 1903 on the plaque at great expense.

Despite all the attendant ructions, the Pearse memorial is truly magnificent — awesome, even. Sited at the side of the road by the spot where Pearse crashed on top of his own gorse hedge after that first historic takeoff, it is visible some distance away. As you approach closely enough to hear the wind humming through its rigging, you get the uncanny impression that this extraordinary machine on top of its pillar is pulsing and vibrating with a life of its own — trying desperately to prove to onlookers that it is indeed capable of flight. Pearse's tormented spirit seems to hover there with it. I know of no memorial as evocative as this one: absolutely faithful to its setting, the inventor and his vision.

The most enthusiastic Pearse advocate by far was still Geoff Rodliffe. Geoff and I knew each other well, having corresponded for nearly a decade on the subject of Richard Pearse. Geoff, a Cornishman like Digory Pearse, had first heard of the New Zealand inventor while serving with the RAF during the Second World War, and took up the trail again after emigrating to this country 22 years later. An aeronautical engineer, he took a skilled interest in the design of Pearse's first aircraft and its various modifications, as well as in its three different aero engines. He was later assisted by Malcolm Fraser, Curator of Aviation at MOTAT and formerly works manager of the Shuttleworth collection of 60 vintage aircraft in Bedfordshire — some of which had played a role in *Those Magnificent Men in Their Flying Machines*. Together they built a replica of Pearse's first plane, a hypothetical reconstruction combining elements from Pearse's patent specifications with other aspects recollected by witnesses of his first experimental flights.

Yet, though I had the utmost admiration for Geoff Rodliffe's engineering knowledge, I was unable to agree with him over some of the conclusions he drew from the historical material. In placing the first public flight attempt down the Main Waitohi Road a full year earlier (31 March 1902) and giving full credence to Robert Gibson's 'terrace flight of 1903' (the witness was only nine at the time), he was using evidence which I still think is arguable, even though he was firmly supported by another member of the Royal Aeronautical Society (Auckland) and fellow Pearse researcher, Graham Bell, in saying so.

Geoff Rodliffe's *Richard Pearse, Pioneer Aviator*, a 32-page booklet, was published in 1979 in association with MOTAT, and reprinted with modifications in 1983. In stating unequivocally that 'Richard Pearse flew his aeroplane in 1902 and 1903', this publication led to a further round of disputation between the Pearse 'cultists' and 'anti-cultists'. In trying to chart a middle course between these contenders, I occasionally got fired on from both sides: for claiming too little on Pearse's account, and for claiming too much!

In many other ways Richard Pearse had been catching on as a national celebrity. The new entertainment medium, television, played an important part. Murray Reece, Owen Patterson and Anna Cotterill all interviewed Pearse witnesses between 1969 and 1976 for the Christchurch studio's 'Town and Around' programme.

On 11 December 1975 *Pearse*, a documentary drama produced by Peter Muxlow, went to air. Probably the most memorable television drama produced in New Zealand up to that date, it featured Martyn Sanderson in the title role, with a wig and moustache giving him an eerie resemblance to the inventor.

The script writer, Roger Simpson, had used a copy of my manuscript to glean background to the story and captured the atmosphere of turn-of-the-century Waitohi very effectively. Geoff Rodliffe's and Malcolm Fraser's version of Pearse's first plane was used in the action shots. Much

of the filming was done at Loburn in North Canterbury where the land-
scape, generously equipped with gorse hedges and old cottages, much
resembled that of early Waitohi.

Just prior to the filming of the final dramatic shot of Pearse aloft for
the first time, an extraordinary thing happened. I was there to see for
myself, but shall let Geoff Rodliffe describe the episode:

> The film producer required a shot of the machine being drawn into
> starting position by a horse, but the horse had other ideas, stamped
> heavily on the foot of the actor leading it and then bolted off across
> the paddock, fortunately straight into the wind (estimated at 10
> mph). We watched this Hollywood spectacle fully expecting a wing
> to drop and the whole machine to roll over. It was with amazement
> that we saw it take off quite normally, apart from the elevator which
> flapped up and down, and then climb gently as far as the tow rope
> would allow before stalling and nosediving to the ground. During
> this episode, which was watched by a number of spectators including
> four professional cameramen and five or six amateurs holding movie
> cameras, no one had the presence of mind to pull the trigger; thus
> the most spectacular event of the day went unrecorded.

So Pearse's plane could fly after all!

As a result of damage done to the port wing and undercarriage, any
attempt to get the machine aloft under its own power for its final scene
was now ruled out. So it was hauled through the air beneath a helicopter for that celebrated encounter with the gorse hedge — a touch
which Pearse, with his later interest in convertiplane design, would
surely have enjoyed.

A decade later another television producer, Michael McNicholas,
made a documentary called *Plane for the Million*. This showed, graphically, how Pearse's first aircraft anticipated many of the features of
microlight aeroplanes in our own era. I provided a file of illustrative
material — photographs, documents and drawings — for the historic
background. Some of the film's most spectacular and imaginative
footage was shot at Waitohi itself. It featured, fittingly enough, a great-
nephew of Richard Pearse himself, Evan Gardiner, soaring effortlessly
over his forebear's memorial, the two aircraft looking astonishingly similar.

Pearse was not only becoming a television celebrity, his name was
spreading in other ways. The ten-storey head office of the Ministry of

Transport, Land Transport Division, completed in Wellington in 1974, was named Pearse House. Its architects, Fearn & Fearn, placed a bronze plaque in the foyer remembering Pearse's exploits. In August 1981 MOTAT's replica of Pearse's first plane went on tour to America where it was put on display at the World Trade Centre in Los Angeles and was later taken to San Diego.

From May 1982 the Timaru Airport became known officially as the Richard Pearse Airport, and a plaque installed there three months earlier records the reason. A street in Temuka was named after Pearse, as well as a restaurant in Timaru. The Pleasant Point Railway Museum asked me for a loan of some of Pearse's engine parts with which to mount an exhibit on the inventor. The remaining items in my possession, which I had recovered from excavations at Waitohi and from Pearse's farm at Louden's Gully, I lent to the Timaru Early Settlers' Museum.

Since September 1977, when the South Canterbury Historical Association was offered by MOTAT a second replica of Pearse's first plane, the museum had been considering mounting a special Pearse display. The replica, purchased in 1978, was eventually assembled by John Lowther. The museum director, Philip Howe, displaying the machine and other Pearse artefacts in such a way that they now became the museum's focal point, organised a grand opening on 19 April 1990. I was invited to speak, and among the invited guests were the aviator's nephew and niece, Richard Pearse and Margaret Gardiner. Two of Warne Pearse's children, they had helped me considerably with family information during the original writing of the biography.

Continuing the tradition of dramatic happenings at Pearse openings in South Canterbury, a woman in the front row collapsed suddenly in the middle of my oration and had to be taken away, prostrate, in an ambulance. I was much relieved to be told later that she was still alive, had succumbed because of the warmth of the evening rather than the text of my talk, and often did that sort of thing at meetings.

A month later, on 16 May 1990, New Zealand Post in its 'The Achievers' heritage series, issued an 80 cent Richard Pearse stamp designed by Elspeth Williamson. Aptly enough, it was intended for airmail and fastpost use.

Not surprisingly, Pearse's psychological complexities, when added to the drama, trauma and pathos of his life, have offered many possibilities to the creative writer. In addition to Muxlow's television drama, a poetry sequence and two stage plays have resulted. The first of the plays,

Pearse, was written by John Leask, then a pharmacist in Timaru, and successfully staged by the South Canterbury Drama League in June 1981. The second, entitled *Jean and Richard: a Fantasy*, was one of the last works to be written by playwright and director Mervyn Thompson. Produced by Christchurch's Court Theatre, the play's text was published just before Thompson's death in 1992 in his collection *Passing Through and other plays*.

Mervyn Thompson, long a solitary and controversial figure in New Zealand writing, found it easy to identify with another man who had to make his way with little assistance or encouragement. As Thompson wrote in the play's preface: 'Pearse struggled alone, invented alone, flew alone and died alone. Instead of the cheers and fame he deserved he remained obscure and unsung, known to few — and then mainly as a mad man!' Jean Batten was another famous New Zealand aviator who never married, was driven by her obsession with flying and ended her life unhappy, lonely and alienated. In Thompson's play, both these characters meet in a mindscape where both their stories are played out in a series of contrasted scenes, the author contriving to produce (in the face of all contrary evidence) a happy ending.

I was invited to the launch of Thompson's play collection because of his use of *The Riddle of Richard Pearse* for factual background. Ravaged by cancer, confined to a wheelchair, unable to make a speech or even sign a book, Thompson's very presence there was an act of remarkable courage. In almost too many ways his literary life had paralleled, poignantly, the undervalued and frequently deprecated career of Richard Pearse the inventor.

One would think that, with all the exposure the Pearse story had by now experienced, a great deal more information about him might have drifted to the surface. But very little did. While this was unexpected, it was also a comfort. It suggested that most of the important leads had been followed up, with nothing crucial bypassed or overlooked.

Two letters were received in 1974 from a Kaukapakapa expert on the *Boy's Own Paper*, R.E. Bodle, which offered the suggestion that Richard Pearse might have got some of his early ideas for constructing his string-pull helicopter, hand-cranked 'talking machine' and lathe from the paper. The *Boy's Own Paper* was extremely popular with Victorian youngsters, giving them detailed instructions about how to construct all sorts of mechanical objects, including those mentioned above. I had described in my biography how Pearse's London cousin, Alfred Pearse, was also an inventor. Though I did not know of Alfred's interest in aviation, Bodle sent me a copy of a *Boy's Own Paper* article of 7 October 1905 where Alfred Pearse described how one could make and sail a 'balloon airship'. Whether Richard Pearse saw any of his cousin's material is not known and there is no evidence that his family subscribed to the paper.

Another response, from Michael Jasper, enclosed an article from the January 1974 *Popular Science* which described a 'vertical bicycle' invented by Trevor Harris of Costa Mesa, California. Harris seems to have hit upon the same principle that Pearse patented over seventy years earlier in his 1902 bicycle. 'There is a good deal of lost motion in the [rotating] pedal action of a standard bicycle,' said Harris, so he had devised a machine with an up-and-down pedal movement. Even his gearing system was much the same as that of Pearse's lapsed patent. But the American seems to have missed out on the integral tyre pumps of Pearse's even more ingenious model.

I was also contacted by a 1980 contributor to the Christchurch *Press*, David Swift. Swift wrote of an anonymous Ashburton woman who had in her possession a small (11 cm by 6 cm) lead model of a bicycle with pump action pedals. She had bid for it at a Geraldine auction in 1973 which included items from a Pearse family estate. A number impressed on the back of the model, 14507, happened to be the very number of Pearse's patent specification for his revolutionary new cycling machine. No more is known of its origin or early ownership, but it is very likely to have once belonged to the inventor himself.

Few came forward to add to what we already know about Pearse's flight experiments at Waitohi. However, four more who had seen Pearse at work or knew him volunteered information. Mrs Vina Coles of Opuha, second daughter of Mrs Louie Johnson (already a published witness), declared she had always been told by her family that she was born in the year Pearse made his first 'flight'. Her birth year was 1903. Clifford Crawford of Ashburton remembered visiting Pearse's workshop and seeing the inventor's damaged plane after it had hit a fence shortly before (Crawford maintained) the Big Snow of 11 July 1903. Crawford's sister, Mrs D.M. McLean, also of Ashburton, said she witnessed a flight attempt down Galbraith Road on Pearse's eastern farm boundary. (The Johnson and Crawford families farmed near Pearse). James Andrews of Temuka informed me that as a lad he used to hang around the shop of local blacksmith, Albert Finlay, where Pearse used to buy fuel for his aeroplane and fossick about among Albert's old spark plugs. All other anecdotes and reminiscences came from descendants of those who had already contributed and added nothing new to the evidence.

Two fresh insights into those final, disturbing days when Pearse was moved unwillingly to Sunnyside Hospital also came my way. Calling by his old home at 68 Wildberry Street in Woolston about five years ago I asked the most recent owner if he knew who had once lived there. No, he knew nothing of Pearse's ownership, but told me of the time he had climbed through a trapdoor into the house's roof soon after taking possession himself. There he discovered (and promptly burned) an old mattress, discarded clothing, empty food tins and some elderly looking crusts. I told him Pearse had probably taken refuge there, during his last weeks at Woolston, so 'Russian spies' would not get at his secrets.

The other matter was of a particularly disquieting nature. One evening a decade earlier I received a toll call from Wanganui. On the line was an excited gentleman (he did not give his name) who had been on the staff at Sunnyside when Pearse was committed in 1951. Did I know, he asked, that the doctors had gone through the old fellow's suitcase when he arrived and tossed out everything except his health and social security records? There had been funny drawings and all sorts of calculations on bits of paper!

It is also clear that much material was dumped and burnt when Pearse's portion of his home was cleared out after his death in 1953. His sister, Ruth Gilpin, commented in a 1971 *Auckland Star* interview with Brian Lockstone: 'I think the answer to when he flew was in some thirty pages of notes Pearse left behind him. These were burnt some years back . . . '. Whether Mrs Gilpin was referring to Wildberry Street, Sunnyside or some other occasion I do not know. These papers may have dealt only with Pearse's Utility Plane, but nobody knows for sure. I wince to think of how, in those ashes, may lie the answer to many of the ifs and buts about Pearse's first aircraft.

As things stand, the ifs and buts still bedevil us. There is no absolutely conclusive contemporary evidence to allow us to be certain of the dates of Pearse's early flight attempts. There is always going to be conflict about whether his experiments amounted to flying or hopping. There will be continuing debate about the validity of some of the eyewitness testimony. The anomalies in Pearse's two published letters and in the newspaper reports of 1909 will remain.

In the two decades which have sped by since *The Riddle of Richard Pearse* was first published I have continued to be haunted by the dead inventor and his work. Though I have written eight other books of history and biography, it is Pearse who has generated the greatest long-term interest. I am still receiving letters and telephone calls about him, requests from school pupils doing projects, enquiries about lending my Pearse artefacts, and invitations to address service clubs, history groups and conferences. The subject will not leave me (or my wife and family) alone. Consequently, I still keep abreast of the topic, file away all new materials and regularly force myself to re-examine the issues, re-think the arguments.

For some time now I have been irked by the fact that virtually all attention is focused on the single issue of whether or not Pearse 'flew before the Wright brothers'. As I have repeatedly argued, this largely profitless line of enquiry has distracted attention from other attainments which deserve far more attention: the far-sighted ideas embodied in both Pearse's Waitohi aircraft and his Christchurch Utility Plane; his extraordinary achievement in producing such inventions despite minimal training, primitive materials and workshop facilities, isolation from the rest of the aviation world, and a complete lack of backing or encouragement. Pearse's other inventions such as his ingenious double-acting petrol engines, patent bicycle and farm equipment also deserve greater credit.

Nevertheless, despite my frequent plea for a broader appreciation of Pearse's inventive talent, I am usually hauled back to the issue which still stirs people's imagination the most — Pearse's main selling point, in advertising terms — the significance of his first flight experiments.

So after twenty years of further contemplation, where do I stand today? Did Richard Pearse fly and did he beat the Wright brothers?

First, the flying part. Though the answer largely depends on how you define flight, my view still is that Pearse did not fly in any acceptable sense if you include control and duration in your definition. Pearse said in his two letters that he did not 'fly', and it is futile trying to contradict the inventor himself. (Geoff Rodliffe's claim for a 'terrace flight' is, in my opinion, not sufficiently corroborated, nor can it be dated with any certainty.)

But this does not mean that Pearse did not become airborne in long hops, tentative flights or powered takeoffs. (This was itself a rare and difficult feat in those times.) There are far too many independent eyewitness accounts of Pearse leaving the ground, on a variety of occasions, for them to be ignored or written off as hallucinations or spectator inventions. (Twenty-one such witnesses are listed in the Bibliography, and this number does not include those who had died before investigations began in the 1950s.) In particular, there is his first public takeoff down the Main Waitohi Road, the minimum estimate for which was about forty-five metres, and which had several observers.

It is not merely latter day testimony which supports this view. Pearse himself, in his 1928 letter, said his aircraft would spin round broadside on 'directly it left the ground'. The *Otago Witness* report of 1 December 1909 refers to the late modification of Pearse's plane, which the reporter saw on Pearse's Waitohi farm, making 'a short jump'. The *Temuka Leader* report of 14 December 1909 comments on Pearse's experiments saying he had 'been off the ground several times . . . and in his latest effort he flew about 25 yards'. Referring to the public takeoff mentioned above, no doubt, Pearse told Woolston neighbours L.L. Preston and John Collins during the 1930s and 40s that he had once crashed on top of a hedge during an early flight attempt.

Charles Gibbs-Smith, always sceptical about Pearse, nevertheless had no compunction about including in his definitive *Aviation, an historical survey from its origins to the end of World War II* the following powered takeoffs: Du Temple (1874, a few metres following a down-ramp takeoff); Mozhaiski (1884, 20–30 metres after a down-ramp takeoff); Ader (1890, 50 metres or so); Maxim (1894, a second or two); Langley (8 October 1903, a vertical plunge from a launching catapult); Jatho (November 1903, 60 metres); Vuia (1906, 24 metres); Ellehammer (1906, 42 metres); Santos Dumont (1906, 7 metres); and so forth. Surely Richard Pearse qualifies for a listing in such company.

Now for the dating, an even more contentious topic. An analysis of witness testimony is significant, I believe, even if not absolutely conclusive. There are 4 advocates for a first flight attempt in 1902, 19 for 1903, and 3 for 1904. About a dozen observers placed Pearse's experiments in the general period 1903–6 without dating evidence. The year 1903 is therefore a conspicuous winner, with several flight attempts witnessed between March and May in addition to the Main Waitohi Road takeoff. Moreover, in two-thirds of the reports in favour of 1903, witnesses' evidence can be dated circumstantially.

If you wish to play it safely, take the press reports of 1909. Even this relatively late date allows Pearse to be judged the first in Australasia or the Southern Hemisphere to achieve a powered takeoff in a heavier-than-air machine. His tentative flights of October and November 1909 would also place him well among the frontrunners in the British Empire, where (apart from Horatio Phillips' 'hop flight' at Streatham in 1907) no one else was to leave the ground in their own aircraft until

1909 either. James McCurdy's true flight in Canada on 23 February 1909 was the first in the Empire; with J.T.C. Moore-Brabazon following in April-May and a powered hop by R.V. Roe in May. Pearse would be next in line, if 1909 is your choice. This alone is a feat not to be scorned.

If February or March 1904 (the date mentioned by Pearse in his letters, when he set out to 'solve the problem of aerial navigation') is your preference, Pearse then lies seventh in the world in the sequence of powered takeoffs cited by Gibbs-Smith. If 31 March 1903 is your choice, Pearse lies fifth in the world, after Sir Hiram Maxim. If, after studying his case, you prefer Geoff Rodliffe's 31 March 1902, Pearse still lies fifth. This, once more, is honour enough, even if he did not beat the Wright brothers, or anyone else, to 'fly'.

The best I can do with the information available is to conclude that Richard Pearse was probably working on his first aircraft and conducting flight experiments from 1903–4 (I would be more guarded about 1902); that it is likely that the first publicly witnessed powered takeoff took place on 31 March 1903 (despite his own reference to the year 1904); and that he had certainly achieved a number of tentative flights by the end of 1909. But, in the end, readers will have to make up their own minds.

I refuse to be more categorical than this about the dating. There is just not enough firm, incontestable evidence. Perhaps that evidence will yet turn up — a dated letter, photograph or diary entry, or a previously undiscovered newspaper report — and resolve all the uncertainty. Until then, though I wish I could report otherwise, the riddle persists.

Appendix I

Text of Pearse's letter to the Evening Star, *Dunedin, 10 May 1915.*

WHO INVENTED THE AEROPLANE?

Sir, — In your science up to date articles by James Collier is one enti-tled 'The Evolution of the Aeroplane'. When Dunlop discovered the air tyre he made the bicycle practicable, and this led up to the motor bicy-cle and car fitted with the light, high speed oil engine. As the motor bicycle and car led up to the development of the light motor, it was only a matter of making these types of engines still lighter in order to make a flight possible. It will thus be seen that Dunlop's invention revo-lutionised speed. The honour of inventing the aeroplane cannot be assigned wholly to one man; like most other inventions, it is the pro-duct of many minds. After all, there is nothing that succeeds like suc-cess, and for this reason pre-eminence will undoubtedly be given to the Wright brothers, of America, when the history of the aeroplane is writ-ten, as they were the first to actually make successful flights with a motor-driven aeroplane. At most America can only claim to have origi-nated the aeroplane. The honour of perfecting it and placing it on its present footing belongs to France.

As the Wright brothers' patent rights have been upheld both in America and France, and also by the British Government, who lately paid the Wrights £10,000, it will be of interest at this point to examine their patent. This patent related to balancing an aeroplane, and, briefly stated, was as follows: The tips of the wings are made flexible, and are capable of being warped, so that in the event of side-tipping, more angle can be given to either wing tip, and the machine can by this means be prevented from turning over. To prevent forward or backward tipping they used the usual horizontal rudder, which acted like the tail of a bird, and for steering a vertical rudder was used. By means of a han-dle which connected with both of the wings at the tips by wires, the operator was able at will to give either wing more angle at the flexible part, and thus preserve the balance. Now, when any particular wing is given more angle at the tip to prevent the machine from turning over sideways, there will be a drag on that wing, tending to turn the machine round, and in order to counteract this the Wrights had an automatic connection between the vertical rudder and the tips of the wings, so that the same handle that warped the wings also gave the vertical rudder the angle necesssary to keep the machine on a straight course.

The Wrights were successful in their suits against the Curtiss Company in America, and also against the French companies, and this will mean that they can demand royalties. It was held that although wing-warping alone may not be new, yet when done in conjunction with the vertical rudder, which is essential to keep the machine on a straight course, it was then novel, and that without bringing the vertical rudder into action the machine would spin in the air, under which circumstances dynamic flight would be impossible, and for this reason the Wrights were entitled to protection.

It will thus be seen that the Wright brothers' right to levy royalties on other companies is based solely on balancing. As a matter of fact I patented a system of balancing almost identical with theirs, and just as effective, in New Zealand on June 19, 1906. My system of balancing was to place a small horizontal rudder at the tip of each wing, which could be manipulated by a handle, for the purpose of preventing the machine from turning over sideways. To prevent backward or forward tipping I used the usual horizontal rudder at the rear, while a vertical rudder was used for steering. In the specifications I recognised that when the rudders at the wing tips were actuated there would be a drag at the particular wing tip that was being operated upon, tending to turn the machine round; but I proposed to counteract this with the vertical rudder at the rear. The Wrights used wings with flexible tips, which could be warped to prevent the machine from turning over sideways, while I used rigid wings with small, movable horizontal rudders mounted at the tips for the same purpose.

The one system is as effective as the other, as is proved by the fact that there are about as many machines fitted with the one as with the other. The French have termed the small, horizontal rudders at the tips of the wings for balancing 'ailerons'.

All aeroplanes are fitted with either ailerons or flexible wing tips that can be warped. Like the Wrights, I recognised that there would be a drag at the wing tips tending to turn the machine round when they were warped or the ailerons were actuated, and like them, I proposed to remedy this with the steering rudder, only with this difference, that I did not employ an automatic connection between the two. In view of the fact that the French aeroplanes, which are now far ahead of the Wright machine, are not fitted with an automatic connnection, its utility is doubtful.

The Wrights' first patent in America only beat me by about three months, while their second patent was behind mine, as it was taken out in 1907. After Wrights' patent was published G.H. Curtiss tried to evade the patent rights of their system of control by using ailerons, but in the suits that followed it was held that the principle was the same, and that therefore it was an infringement. As Wrights' patent was not published at the time I took out mine, it cannot be said that I copied, and as the principle has been held to be the same it amounts to this: that it is a case of two persons living on opposite sides of the world arriving at the same conclusion; and, this being so, I can justly claim to having discovered it independently.

The question is who invented it first. I thought of it long before I took out a patent, and in all probability the Wrights would not rush off to the patent office the moment they had designed it, for they would try to make their machine as perfect as they could before protecting it. After Langley's failure in 1903 I was still of [the] opinion that aerial navigation was possible, and I started out to solve the problem about March, 1904. The Wrights started at about the same time. Langley was subsidised to the extent of £10,000 by the American Government, and after his failure aerial navigation was thought to be an impossibility; in fact, 'flying machines that wouldn't fly' was a standing joke with the newspapers. I worked at the problem for about five and a half years. I was working at the problem fully two years before any of the Frenchmen had made a start on it, and Santos Dumont's flight at Issy took place about six months after my machine was fully patented. This was the first public flight with an aeroplane, and took place in November, 1906, but the Wrights had made some flights in private in 1905. Like the Wrights, I had to develop the light motor for myself, as none were procurable at the time. None of the Frenchmen, on the other hand, made their motors; they simply ordered them at motor car factories. My machine was the first to be mounted on three air-tyred wheels for starting and landing, while Santos Dumont was second. Wrights followed Maxim and Langley in this respect, and had a special launching apparatus, which consisted of a rail and weight.

When it was pointed out to them they they had not solved the problem of starting, they replied that trains and trams had special starting places. I was the first to simplify the aeroplane by placing the propeller direct on the crank-shaft of the engine, and by this idea I was able to do away with transmission gearing, the clutch, and the fly-wheel. The next man to do this was Santos Dumont. The Wrights followed Maxim and Langley in this also, and had two large propellers revolving at a slow speed, and to do this they had to employ gearing, a clutch, and a fly-wheel. Practically all aeroplanes now have a single propeller direct on the crank-shaft of the engine. The engines of motor cycles and cars, which weigh about 20 lb per horse-power were, before the advent of the aeroplane, thought to be marvels as far as lightness is concerned. The bulk of my time was spent in developing the light motor and in testing air propellers. The last engine I built was a 60 horse-power motor, weighing 250 lbs, which is slightly over 4 lb per horse-power. I only built one aeroplane, which was designed before anyone had made a flight, and after some trials with my last motor mounted on it, I found that in order to do the thing properly I would have to make such extensive alterations that it practically amounted to building a new machine. Neither the Wrights nor anyone else was successful with the first machine; they all had to build one or more experimental aeroplanes.

At this time, as aerial navigation was already an accomplished fact, I decided to give up the struggle, as it was useless to continue against men who had factories at their backs. These experiments took place when I was living near Temuka.

As an explanation for inflicting a letter of this length on you, I may say that my object is to show that New Zealand brains anticipated the essential features of the aeroplane. If I have claimed anything unduly, I want to know it, as I am open to correction. All my experimenting in aerial navigation was pioneer work, and when a history of the pioneers is being written I hold that I am within my rights in asserting my claims. — I am, etc.

R.W. PEARSE

Appendix II

Text of Pearse's letter to the Star, *Christchurch, 15 September 1928.*

WHO INVENTED THE AEROPLANE?

Dear Sir, — The article in your paper entitled 'Pioneers of Aviation' does not do justice to New Zealand brains as to the amount of pioneer work New Zealand inventors did and originated, and so I am writing this in the interests of history. I started my experiments on aerial navigation about February, 1904, with a monoplane which I designed and constructed, and by 1906 I had it sufficiently perfected to patent it in New Zealand, the actual date of the patent being June 19, 1906. This machine was a monoplane mounted on three air-tyred wheels for starting and landing, with a horizontal rudder behind for balancing fore and aft, a vertical rudder for steering, and also two small horizontal rudders at the wing tips (ailerons) to prevent side tipping. The propeller was in front, and was mounted direct on the engine crankshaft, thereby rendering clutches and gearing unnecessary. The Wrights, who were at this time working in secret, used flexible wings, which could be warped at the tips for side balancing, and this was the only novelty in their machine of any real value. The Wrights' patent rights were upheld in England, America, France and Germany, and it was this one feature which enabled them to control the aeroplane business in these countries, as it was held that dynamic flight could not be made sufficiently safe without wing warping or its equivalent (ailerons) and that the Wrights were entitled to protection for their master patent. After seeing the principle of the Wrights' system of balancing by wing warping, G.H. Curtis [*sic*], for the first time in 1908, used ailerons and sought to evade the Wrights' patent rights, but in the suit that followed it was held to be an infringement, as the principle was the same. So I can claim to have given the world 'ailerons' which were invented by me in 1904 and patented in 1906, on June 19. The Wrights' first patent was also in

218

1906, followed by a more complete patent in 1907. As wing-warping gave the Wrights a monopoly of the aeroplane business in America, England, France and Germany, so ailerons would have given me a monopoly in New Zealand if I had kept the patent covered, but I let it lapse in 1910 because I did not know the Great War was coming, and I did not see much prospect of selling aeroplanes in New Zealand. So I came to the conclusion that to keep it covered would be only throwing good money after bad. It is the Great War that made the aeroplane, and had I kept my patent covered I had the New Zealand Government in my power, as they had to import aeroplanes for the purpose of training pilots, and all these planes would have been declared infringements, if I had not let my patent lapse! Even up to the present no one has succeeded in making an aeroplane sufficiently safe to be practical without wing-warping or ailerons, and ailerons have superseded wing-warping. The Wrights did not completely solve the problem of flight, because they had to use a special catapult launching apparatus to start their plane, and when it was pointed out to them they replied that trams and trains had special starting places. I was the first to think of mounting an aeroplane on three air-tyred wheels for starting and landing in 1904, and patented it on June 19, 1906. Santos Dumont was second, in the first public aeroplane flight at Issy in November, 1906, the machine being fitted with wheels. The Wrights and myself were the first to produce motors sufficiently light to make flight possible, and we both designed and built our own motors, as they could not be bought at the time, while the French aeroplane men, like Santos Dumont and Blériot, who came in the field later, were able to buy their motors. An ordinary motor-car or motor-bicycle motor weighs about 20 lb per h.p., and my first aeroplane motor of 24 h.p. weighed 5 lb per h.p. As this motor was not powerful enough, I built a 60 horse-power motor that weighed 4 lb per horse-power. The Wrights' motor was 32 h.p. and weighed 5 lb per horse-power. My aeroplane was of enormous size, having 700 square feet of wing area, and it was extremely light, being made mainly of bamboo, and weighed, with [a] man on board, under 700 lb, so each square foot of wing area had to support 1 lb. At the trials it would start to rise off the ground when a speed of twenty miles an hour was attained. This speed was not sufficient to work the rudders, so, on account of its huge size and low speed, it was uncontrollable, and would spin round broadside on directly it left the ground. So I never flew with my first experimental 'plane, but no one else did with their first for that matter. But with my 60 horse-power motor, which proved very reliable, I had successful aerial navigation within my grasp, if I had had the patience to design a small plane that would be manageable. But I decided to give up the struggle, as it was useless to try to compete with men who had factories at their backs.

It is impossible to assign any invention wholly to one man, as all inventions are the product of many minds, and the most we can do is to give the man who had done the most some pre-eminence. As the Wrights were the first to make a successful flight in a motor-driven aeroplane, they will be given pre-eminence when the history of the aeroplane is written. — I am , etc.

R.W. PEARSE

Appendix III

Text and drawings of Pearse's complete patent specification No. 21476, for his first aircraft. The text is a transcript but the drawings are a reproduction of the originals filed in the New Zealand Patent Office by the Henry Hughes Patent and Trade-Marks Office in Wellington.

COMPLETE SPECIFICATION

'AN IMPROVED AERIAL OR FLYING MACHINE.'

I, Richard William Pearse, of Upper Waitohi, Temuka, in the Colony of New Zealand, Farmer, do hereby declare the nature of my invention for 'An Improved aerial or flying machine' and in what manner the same is to be performed, to be particularly described and ascertained in and by the following statement:—

This invention relates to an improved construction of aerial or flying machine of the aeroplane type, which has been designed in order to provide for the more effective handling and directing of the machine.

The invention consists in a special construction of frame for the sail or sheet of the machine, by which construction the machine may be put together and taken apart with ease and quickness, in order to provide for its transport from place to place, and by which, also, it may be freely adjusted upon the wheeled car, which supports it while on the ground. Other improvements relate to the use of rudders or hinged vanes by means of which the machine may be guided while afloat in the air, to the use of a central keel piece extending along its top for assisting in the maintenance of its equilibrium, and also to a special construction of propellor [sic], by means of which the machine is propelled.

In describing the invention, reference will be made to the accompanying drawings, in which, —

Figure 1 is an illustration of my invention, showing the framework

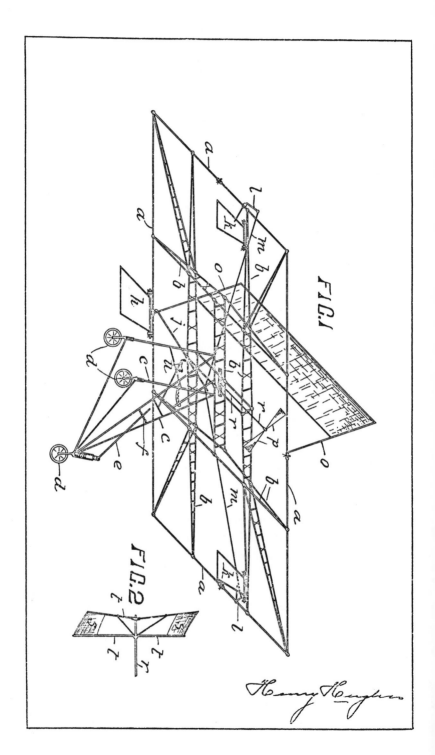

FIG.1

FIG.2

Henry Hughes

of aeroplane, with sail or cloth removed therefrom, and the frame tilted up to show the invention more to advantage, and with the truck swung out to show its contruction.

Figure 2 is an enlarged view of the propellor.

In carrying out the invention, the framework *a* is constructed of bamboo or other like material of rectangular shape and made of a number of trusses *b* that extend across the frame in both directions, as shown in the drawings. These trusses *b* are connected together in such a manner that they will afford a rigid frame, but which will allow them being taken apart with little trouble for packing purposes. Each truss *b* is arched upwards towards the middle, so that when the sheet or sail is secured over the frame *a* it will assume a correspondingly rigid form that will cause it to somewhat resemble the form assumed by a bird's wings when soaring.

The car for supporting the frame *a*, consists of a light framework *c* running upon suitable wheels *d* preferably provided with pneumatic tyres, and arranged in tricycle fashion, i.e., with a single front steering wheel. A lever *e* is provided for operating such wheel, and a rack *f* is provided for holding the lever from movement. The car is provided with bearings at its top, in which the main framework *a* of the aeroplane is articulated in such a manner that it may be tipped forward or backward to any desired angle, and a handle is provided for so adjusting it.

Articulated upon the back edge of the main frame, and at its middle, is a rudder *h* composed of a light rectangular frame arranged in the same plane as the main frame. This rudder is employed for deflecting the course of the machine upward or downwards when flying, and it is controlled by an arm *j* connected to it in such a manner that, as the arm is moved longitudinally in either direction, the rudder will be raised or lowered on its hinges. A similarly shaped rudder *k* is hinged upon the top of the frame near each side edge thereof. These rudders are normally retained, by springs, in a flat condition upon the top surface of the main frame, so that when not in use, they will present no obstruction to the course of the machine. Each of the rudders is provided with a bell crank lever *l* on its hinged edge, which lever is connected to a flexible connection *m* that extends inwards, and is fastened at its other end to the arm *j*, for operating the rear rudder. These connections are made in such a way that, by turning the arm in either direction, one or other of the side rudders may be turned up so as to extend upwards across the plane of flight, and thus serve to cause the corresponding edge to drag, thereby deflecting the course of the machine, and allowing of it being diverted in either direction at the will of the operator. These side rudders also serve to assist in keeping the machine evenly balanced, as should one edge show a tendency to dip down, the rudder on that edge may be partially raised so as to cause such edge to be deflected upwards again.

To assist in maintaining the machine in equilibrium, a keel piece n is attached to the top of the frame and extends centrally from the front to the back thereof. This keel piece is made of a light rectangular frame hinged by the side members o to the main frame, so as to be capable of lying flat thereon, and is covered with suitable canvas or other cloth. This keel piece will present an obstructing face against the machine tipping to either side, while, should a cross wind be encountered, it may be lowered, so as to lie flat against the main sail of the machine.

A support (not shown in the drawings) is formed on the underside, at the centre of the main fame, upon which the oil engine employed for driving the propelling mechanism, is placed. This engine may be of any of the approved forms, but preferably of the two cylinder type.

The propelling mechanism consists of a propellor p mounted on a shaft r that is in direct gearing with the engine crank axle. The shaft extends upwards and forwards through the main frame, so as to carry the propellor near the front of the machine. The form of propellor that is preferred, consists of a pair of canvas sails s each one of which is stretched across between the ends of a pair of arms t extending from the shaft. The lower one of each of these pairs of arms is made fast to the shaft, while the other is made adjustable longitudinally on the shaft, so that its angle may be altered. Means are provided for moving the two movable arms, and for holding them at any desired angle. By these means the angles, and consequently, the pitch of the propellor sails or blades, may be adjusted to any desired degree to suit varying circumstances.

A seat u for the operator, is provided in such a position that he will be able to operate the guide wheel d of the car c, the arm j for operating the three rudders, the keel n, and control the engine. This seat is made in such a manner that it will be capable of sliding backwards or forwards, or of moving to either side, in order that the operator may shift his weight to control the equilibrium and operations of the machine.

In use, the machine is first caused to run along the ground on its car by the revolution of the propellor. When it has gained sufficient speed, the operator will throw his weight backwards so that the front of the machine will be tilted up, thereby causing the machine to rise from the ground, until it reaches the desired height, when it will be placed in equilibrium by shifting the operator's weight forward again. The propellor being kept going, will keep the machine moving in the air, its course and the actions being controlled by the several means already described. It may be caused to descend by adjusting the rear rudder, or by tilting it forward.

Having now particularly described and ascertained the nature of my said invention, and in what manner the same is to be performed, I declare that what I claim, is:—

1. In flying machines of the aeroplane type, a frame for the main sail or sheet, composed of a series of trusses extending at right angles across each other, and jointed together in such a manner as to be freely taken apart, each of such trusses being formed with a top edge bowed upwards towards its centres, substantially as specified.

2. In flying machines of the aeroplane type, the combination with a frame for the main sail or sheet, of a rudder hinged to the back edge of the frame, and of a rudder hinged upon the top face of the frame near each side edge, all of such rudders being capable of movement in a vertical plane with regard to the frame, and being connected to an arm by the movement of which any one rudder may be operated independently of the others, substantially as specified.

3. In flying machines of the class herein described a keel piece extending centrally along above the top of the main sail or sheet, and from the front to the back thereof, such keel piece being so connected to the main sail as to be capable of lying flat thereon, or of being turned upwards at right angles thereto, substantially as and for the purposes herein specified.

4. The general arrangement, construction, and combination of parts in my improved aerial or flying machine, substantially as herein described and explained, and for the several purposes set forth.

Dated this 15th day of July, 1907.
    Henry Hughes

COMMONWEALTH OF AUSTRALIA.

PATENT SPECIFICATION

124,430

Application Date: 3rd Mar., 1944. No. 13,283/44.

Applicant (Actual Inventor) ..	..	RICHARD WILLIAM PEARSE.
Application and Provisional Specification	..	Accepted, 14th November, 1944.
Complete Specification after Provisional		
Specification	..	Lodged, 27th June, 1944.
Complete Specification Open to Public		
Inspection—Section 38A ..	..	19th June, 1947.
Complete Specification	..	Accepted, 2nd June, 1947.
Acceptance Advertised (Sec. 50) ..	..	19th June, 1947.

Class 90.3

Drawings (2 sheets) attached.

COMPLETE SPECIFICATION.

"An aeroplane that can ascend and descend in very restricted areas."

I, RICHARD WILLIAM PEARSE, of 68 Wildberry St., Woolston, Christchurch, New Zealand, Inventor and owner of property, hereby declare this invention, and the manner in which it is to be performed, to be fully described and ascertained in and by the following statement. This invention was designed in the first place to solve the problem of the private plane for the million, and in order to do this, it has been adapted to take off or land on any road or field.

The vast network of roads that already exist must serve as take off and landing grounds. In order to make these available very low landing speeds are essential and the machine was specially designed for this purpose. In order to meet all these conditions, this new type of air-craft has been designed having all the advantages of helicopters in hovering or landing in very limited areas at very low speeds or even

taking off or landing vertically, while at the same time retaining all the advantages of the aeroplane while in flight. This hybrid air-craft which is a true aeroplane while in flight can be instantly turned into a helicopter for hovering or landing vertically, and it will then reap the advantages of the latter when landing vertically on rough ground or limited areas. This invention is an aeroplane with a specially controllable pitch propeller, which plays two roles: that of a propeller when revolving in a vertical plane, and that of a rotor when rotating in a horizontal plane like a spinning top.

The hybrid propeller-rotor is mounted direct on the engine crank-shaft without any gearing whatever, and this has been made possible by mounting the engine on a transverse horizontal axle running across the full width of the fuselage, and if the engine is correctly balanced on this axle,

1

2

the operator can at will make the propeller-rotor rotate in a vertical or a horizontal plane or at any intermediate angle. This indirect way of altering the plane of rotation of the propeller by using a tilting engine assembly mounted on a horizontal transverse axle instead of a fixed engine, is the essential feature of this aeroplane-helicopter, as it does away with the necessity of gearing and clutches, and gives a choice of any angle between a vertical and horizontal plane of rotation. This indirect way of altering the plane of rotation of the propeller is limited to pivoted engines with the propeller direct on the crankshaft so that when the engine is tilted the propeller is likewise tilted, but for very large machines if it is not practical to drive the propeller at high speed, it may be geared down by the sun and planet cog-wheel system as used on the old geared ordinary bicycle or front driving safety bicycle, but this would increase the reaction torque, and so would not be so suitable for the small convertible aeroplane-helicopter and the downward draft of a large rotor would press the wings downward and so would waste power. This type of air-craft has all the advantages of helicopters for hovering or landing vertically in restricted areas, plus the additional safety given by the wings if the motor fails, and also the much greater efficiency of the aeroplane when flying. The next most important essential of this private aeroplane-helicopter is to give safe landings without any forward motion, which is accomplished by adapting the wing tip units to function with the wind generated by the downward motion of descending at sufficient speed, only in this case the wind strikes more in a direct impact against the under surface instead of at an angle, so there is no break in lateral control provided the machine is allowed to lose height at sufficient speed to create sufficient wind for the wing tip units to function by surface area reduction, which is brought about by bringing the wing-tip unit that is too high to nearly a vertical plane to make it fall faster. The wing-tip units are not interconnected like ailerons, but are independent of each other, and only one moves at a time.

The drag at the wing-tip when one unit is brought to almost a vertical plane can be utilised to stop a spin or stall when landing at a low speed, and this is more powerful in this respect than the rudder.

To back air is the same in principle as to back water with an oar and in both cases assists the rudder to hold the machine on a straight course. This arrangement makes it possible to back-air, which will greatly reduce the stalling speed when landing. As difficult landings will be frequent with private planes that do not use aerodromes, I have designed a ground brake that will pull the machine up in its own length without nosing over, and a safety nose-crash device consisting of a sliding floor which is capable of sliding forward under the braking influence of friction clutches to make the pull up gradual, and thus break the fall as far as the passengers are concerned.

Fig. 1 shows the skeleton frame-work of the fuselage with the engine assembly in two positions; the motor, which is of the upside down type with the crank-case on top, is shown in the position for ordinary flying with the propeller in a vertical plane and acting as a tractor. In dotted lines the engine is shown tilted enough to make the propeller revolve in a horizontal plane, and thus playing the role of a rotor for hovering or landing vertically. When it is desired to make the propeller rotate in a horizontal plane it is not necessary to tilt the motor a full right-angle, as the tail end of the plane can be lowered to the extent of 45 degrees without harmful effects, so a less angle will suffice.

Fig. 2 mainly a perspective drawing shows the engine and propeller in the position for hovering or descending vertically, that is to say the propeller is revolving in a horizontal plane, thus playing the role of a rotor. The frame-work of each of the two wings is also shown with the wing-tip units attached.

Fig. 1 only shows the inner end of the right wing 33 with the bell-crank lever 30 and the steel tube shaft 32 that traverses the full length of the wing, and to the end of which is firmly attached the wing-tip unit for lateral balancing. The ground brake is illustrated in Fig. 1 but is omitted in Fig. 2 for clearness as it is already overcrowded The sliding floor is illustrated in Fig. 1 but is omitted in Fig. 2 for the same reason. The tail-piece is illustrated in Fig. 1 in its working position, and also when

3

4

folded for housing in dashed lines. The whole tail piece is shown elevated to an extreme angle in Fig. 2 which is used only in an emergency to stop a nose dive if the motor stops when hovering or descending vertically. In this case the front of the air-craft being much more heavily loaded than the rear per sq. foot, it will fall faster, but this can be checked by reducing the supporting surface by about 50 per cent in the tail-piece unit.

So the tail-piece will then encounter about half its usual wind resistance, and will consequently fall faster. This means that limited control fore and aft can be still maintained by the stabiliser, which by the elimination of the fin, and the consequent larger angle of movement, can still maintain stabilisation fore and aft without any forward motion of the air-craft when the motor stops.

This means that the stalibiser has been adapted to stabilise the machine fore and aft continuously without a break, with or without forward movement of the air-craft when the motor stops, on the same principle as the wing-tip units work namely: reduction and variation of their supporting surfaces so as to encounter more or less air resistance, which is generated when the machine is allowed to lose height at a sufficient rate. The power of the control in both cases depends on the area of the supporting surfaces, the amount of the variation of their surfaces, and the rate at which the machine loses height, as the strength of the wind thus generated will depend on the speed of descent. Both Fig. 1 and Fig. 2 illustrate how the rudder is pivoted on the elevator, thus forming a combination that will steer as well as balance the machine fore and aft.

Fig. 3 illustrates the propeller-rotor from a front view and shows besides the two outer blades 118, 119 the inner ring of 8 blades mounted windmill fashion on the two rings 106 and 107 for the purpose of getting very large blade area in a compact form, so as to give lift efficiency by avoiding too high a pressure on each individual blade.

Fig. 5 shows one complete outer blade and one of the inner ring blades 23 and two small sections of the inner rings 106 and 107 to show how they are mounted on the rings. It also shows the fitting N with its

swivelled connection with the rocking control lever 10 enabling the pilot to control the pitch of the blades by the steel wire ropes 11, 13, 14 which are extended to come within his reach. A pawl or catch 12 is mounted on the lever to engage the notched rack 24 for the purpose of holding the pitch control lever 10 in the desired position. The fitting N when it is slided forward on the crankshaft, gives the lowest pitch to the blades, and the position of the fitting N with its connection with its rocking control lever 10 when it is slided backward on the crankshaft to give the greatest pitch, is shown in dotted lines. In dotted lines the fitting N is shown butting up against the bearing of the crankshaft K which is the normal position for high speed, and the position of the pitch lever 10 with its pawl catch attached to its lower end, is also shown in dotted lines when set for high speed travelling.

The positions of the two bell-crank levers X, X with their two small connecting rods O, O which connect them with lugs 95, 95 of fitting N are shown in dotted lines when set for high speed. The two bell-crank levers X, X which are welded rigidly to the sleeves 92 of the two outer blades for the purpose of twisting the blades on their axles are shown in front of the main propeller rod 90 for low pitch and behind it for high pitch.

Fig. 6 gives details of the pitch control lever 10 which is enlarged and twisted round to the extent of a right angle in order to clearly show its details. The split clamp 103 has its two halves held together by two bolts and each half has a protrudng spike 99 to enable it to be attached to the pitch lever. This rocking pitch control lever 10 which is pivoted at its centre by the bolt 15 has at its upper end a second fitting 101 bolted to it, and between these two halves the split clamp 103 is pivoted by means of the protruding spikes 99. The lower bolt 17 is for attaching the pawl catch 12 to this control ever as shown in Fig. 5.

The split clamp 103 is clamped into the groove W of fitting N and this makes a swivelled connection between the fitting N and the rocking control lever 10 and at the same time allows this fitting to revolve with the propeller, which it must do, as it consists of two sleeves, one in front of the main propeller rod, and one behind it, and con-

5   6

nected with each other by two bars preferably by welding, and thus forming one fitting **N**.

This fitting has two lugs **95, 95** on which two connecting rods **O, O** are connected in front of the main propeller rod **90** and the rear sleeve contains the groove **W** into which the split clamp shown in Fig. 6, **103** is bolted. This fitting **N** is free to slide backward and forward on the crankshaft to an extent sufficient to twist the two outer propeller blades on their axles by the two small connecting rods **O, O**. The spring **18** attached to the upper end of control lever **10** is to ensure this control lever will move back under the tension, to high pitch the normal position when the pawl catch **12** is pulled out of engagement with the rack **24** by pulling its control wire **14**. So the upper control wire **11** is not absolutely essential, the spring **18** will pull back the lever when it is released by raising the catch **12** out of engagement with the rack **24**, it is only there for an emergency when the spring fails through stiffness of the moving parts, when it is necessary to pull the control wire **11**. Before the pitch control lever can be moved in any direction the catch **12** must be raised out of engagement, and not released until the lever has been moved to the required position, when it is locked on release of the catch.

The catch **12** has a spring **98** which keeps it engaged unless its control wire is pulled. To give the blades low pitch the catch **12** must be lifted and held out of engagement until by means of the wire **13** being pulled, the upper end of the control lever **10** moves the fitting **N** forward into low pitch as shown in Fig. 5. To shift back to normal high pitch, it is as a rule only necessary to pull the lower wire **14** which lifts the catch out of engagement, so that the spring **18** will pull back the upper end of the control lever **10** into normal high pitch position shown in dotted lines in Fig. 5.

If the spring is not strong enough it must be helped by pulling the wire **11**. The small circle **99** on the control lever **10** is an end view of one of the protruding spikes **99** of the split clamp **103** which is shown on a large scale in Fig. 6.

The notched rack **24** is attached to the front beam **19** of the engine and the face plate **20** indicates where the cylinders are bolted on, they are below the crank-case.

The main rod **90** of the propeller is welded to the crankshaft **K** of the engine so that it can never work loose and one blade is shown complete in Fig. 5 constructed on this plan. The outer propeller blade **118** is fixed rigidly on the steel tubing sleeve **92** and uses the main propeller rod **90** as an axle on which it pivots for the purpose of altering the pitch. At the outer end of the main propeller rod **90** the cap **96** is bolted on to secure the propeller blade which is detachable, from sliding off, and this fitting forms a support to which the outer ring **107** is bolted to. The inner ring **106** is bolted to a bearing support in order to allow the sleeve **92** freedom to pivot when the pitch is altered.

The bell-crank lever **V** is fixed rigidly to the sleeve **92** and is connected to the other bell-crank lever **125** on the inner ring blade **23** and a connecting rod connects these two bell-crank levers so that the outer blade is connected with the inner ring of 8 blades; and also to the other outer blade, the lower end of its sleeve **92** is shown in Fig. 5, and it is connected with the inner ring of blades in just the same way, so that all 10 blades are interconnected and move together, controlled by the pitch control lever **10**.

Fig. 4 is one of the inner ring blades detached and twisted round to the extent of a right angle so that it can be viewed edgewise to illustrate their shape. Fig. 4, **114** the bell-crank lever and **115** the bolt for coupling it by a connecting rod with the other blades. The other two bolts **116, 117** connect it to the two rings **106, 107**, and on these two stud bolts it pivots when the pitch is changed. Fig. 3, the connecting rods **110, 111** couple the bell-crank lever **V** of the outer blade, and shown in dotted lines because it is behind the propeller, to the bell-crank levers **125** and **126** and so connects the outer blade **118** with the inner ring of blades, while the connecting rods **112, 113** couple the bell-crank lever **U** of the outer blade **119** with the bell-crank levers **127, 128** and so connects the outer blade **119** with the inner ring of 8 blades, so that all can be made to pivot on their axles together by one lever. As all blades are pivoted at or near the circumference instead of at the hub, they are not subjected to crushing pressures like hub pivoted blades, and they do not require hydraulic power to operate them, the mechanical sys-

7

8

229

tem will change their pitch without any fatigue to the pilot. The 10 connecting rods form a circle and interconnect all 10 blades. The flat steel rods 108, 109 are fastened to
5 the main propeller rod by four stays 120, 121, 122, 123 and all these rods and stays are welded together to form a framework on which the two rings 106 and 107 can be fastened, and on which the inner ring
10 blades pivot. This arrangement gives large blade area with little parasitic air resistance for lift efficiency and is compact enough to cause very little downward pressure on the wings by the downward air
15 draft when revolving in a horizontal plane. Both Fig. 1 and Fig. 2 show the tail unit consisting of stabiliser 5, elevator 6, the rudder 7 mounted and pivoted on the elevator 6, by the rod 56 which is its axle. The axle
20 rod 56 is fixed to the centre of the elevator in case of a single rudder, but on both right and left sides if two rudders are used. The double lever 9 is fixed rigidly on the rudder and the double lever 40 on the forked steer-
25 ing rod to which the rear wheel is attached at its lower end for steering when on the ground. The right end of lever 9 is connected to the right end of lever 40 by the control wire 54. The left arm of lever 9
30 is connected to the left arm of lever 40 by the wire rope 55.

The main control lever H consists of a horizontal handle bar for hand steering and the rocking lever P for steering with
35 the feet, which is normally in a horizontal position and sufficiently above the floor to allow the control lever to being moved sideways to the right or left in order to actuate the wing tip units. The handle bar H for
40 the hands and the rocking pedal lever P for the feet are both joined together, and form one fitting, and it has a sleeve to enable it to be telescoped over the fitting E which forms its support and connects it
45 with the horizontal axle D which traverses the fuselage laterally and to the left outer end of which the double bell-crank lever J is welded. The two prongs of the fork of fitting E are bored, also the axle D and
50 this enables the two to be connected by the bolt 26 thus forming a universal joint for the main control lever H, which when moved laterally from side to side, it actuates the wing tip units and when moved backward
55 and forward it actuates the elevator. The pedal lever P is part of the main control

lever H to which it is welded, and it enables both hands and feet to be used separately or in conjunction for balance control, and the fitting H is preferably mounted in the centre of the fuselage, so the axle D is pierced in its middle part, as it traverses laterally the full width of the fuselage. The sleeve of control lever H enables it to pivot on fitting E, so the right and left ends of P
10 may be made to rock backward and forward for rudder control, and up and down for controlling the wing tip units. The right and left ends of lever P each have two control wires fastened to their ends so
15 that by rocking the ends backward and forward steering is effected by the wires 52 and 53 which are connected at the rear to the double lever 40 controlling the rear wheel, and it has already been explained how the double lever 40 is connected to the
20 double lever 9 which controls the rudder by the wires 54 and 55. The control wire 52 connects the right end of lever P with the left end of lever 40, and the control wire 53 connects the left end of lever P
25 with the right end of double lever 40 so the two rudder control wires 52 and 53 for steering cross each other as shown in Fig. 1 and Fig. 2. The position of the main control lever H is set for turning to the left whether on
30 the ground or in the air, and the right end of rocking lever P is shown thrown forward, and it has by means of the wire 52 pulled the left end of double lever 40 forward, which in turn has pulled the left end of the
35 rudder double lever 9 forward by the wire 55 and this is the right position for turning to the left on the ground or in the air. When turning to the right the left end of the rocking lever P is thrown forward and
40 the right end drawn back, so that the control wire 53 will draw the right end of the double lever 9 forward by wire 54, which is the correct position for turning to the right on the ground or in the air. The wing tip
45 units have springs 31 and 91 to overcome gravity, also stops 70 and 68 to limit their angle of movement in one direction, that is to say the stop 70 shown in Fig. 2 on the right wing to stop wing-tip unit 67 from having less angle of incidence to the air than the wing, but allows unlimited greater angles than the wing, even to the extent of a vertical plane.

The wing-tip unit 67 is shown with its
55 rear edge lower than that of the wing and

9
10

the front edge higher, so that it has a greater angle of incidence to the air than the wing, and will consequently lift the wing tip upward. There is nothing to limit the increase of the angle of the wing-tip units which may be nearly a vertical plane when varying their supporting surfaces for lateral balance when descending vertically without any forward motion of the machine, or for back-air control to stop a spin at very low landing speeds. The stops prevent the wing tip units from having less angle of incidence to the air than the wing, so that unlike ailerons they cannot work by pulling the wing tips downward. They work only by lifting the wing that is too low upward when flying in the ordinary way with forward motion, but their angle of incidence to the air may be increased from a horizontal plane as used for ordinary flying to a vertical plane as used in vertical descents without forward motion or in back-airing. The spring **31** Fig. 1 and Fig. 2 balances gravity and keeps the right wing-tip unit **67** pressed against the stop **70** unless it is actuated as shown in Fig. 2. The left wing is exactly the same as the right, but its wing-tip unit is not depressed like the right wing-tip unit, it is hard up against the stop **68** and for this reason obscures it. The steel tube shaft **32** shown in Fig. 1 is meant to have a wing-tip unit on its outer end, and as the wing is only shown in Fig. 2 it is there that the mounting of the unit is shown, but on the inner end of shaft **32** the bell-crank lever is shown attached with its control wire **50** connected to it, while the other end of this wire couples it to the left end of double pedal lever **P**, making the second control wire to be attached there. The first control wire as already explained has to do with steering the rear wheel and rudder when the right end of **P** is moved forward. The vertical wire **50** pulls down the bell-crank lever **30** when the main control lever **H** is pulled sideways to the left as the left end of lever **P** then moves downward and it actuates the right wing-tip unit through the bell-crank lever **30** and the shaft **32** which traverses the whole length of the wing. The right end of lever **P** is at the same time lifted and this slackens the second vertical control wire **51** the upper end of which is fastened to the bell-crank lever **61** shown in Fig. 2, but the left wing tip is not actuated unless the right end of

P is moved downward toward the floor, when the slack wire rope **51** will be tightened, and bell-crank lever **61** will be pulled downward, so that the left wing-tip unit will be actuated, and given a greater angle, and so will lift the wing tip up. Pulling the wire **51** downward actuates the left wing-tip unit **69** through the bell-crank lever **61** and its transmission shaft **75**, which is twisted round, so the wing-tip unit **69** of the left wing is given more angle incidence to the air and the wing is thus lifted up in ordinary flying with the machine moving forward.

I mention this advisedly because in the case of a vertical descent by allowing the machine to lose height at speed without forward motion, the reverse occurs if any wing-tip unit is brought to an angle approaching a vertical plane; as before mentioned it will fall faster due to the reduction in the wing-tip area, as it will encounter less air resistance from the wind generated by descent at speed, and so will fall faster the greater the angle it is given until it approaches a vertical plane. So although the wing-tip units have been adapted to control lateral balance without any forward motion of the machine in still air, the control lever for operating them must be pulled in the reverse direction to that used in ordinary flying with forward motion, in order to get the same result. This does not apply to the tail unit when balancing fore and aft without forward motion of the machine, as the rear edges of the stabiliser and elevator are raised in order to get surface area reduction, which is the reverse of that used in the wing-tip units, which have their area reduced by lowering their rear edge surfaces; so the operation of the control lever remains the same without forward motion as in ordinary flying as far as fore and aft balance is concerned. This system is only used for fore and aft balance in an emergency, as a motor failure in a vertical descent to prevent a nose dive until the machine can acquire sufficient speed to balance in the ordinary way. Engine power is used to balance fore and aft when hovering or descending vertically without forward motion, by manipulating the plane of rotation of the propeller-rotor so that the nose may be lifted up when it is revolving in a horizontal plane, which lift disappears as the plane of rotation approaches a ver-

11

12

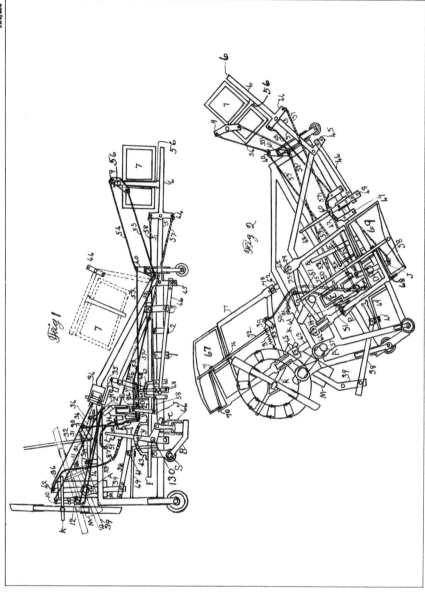

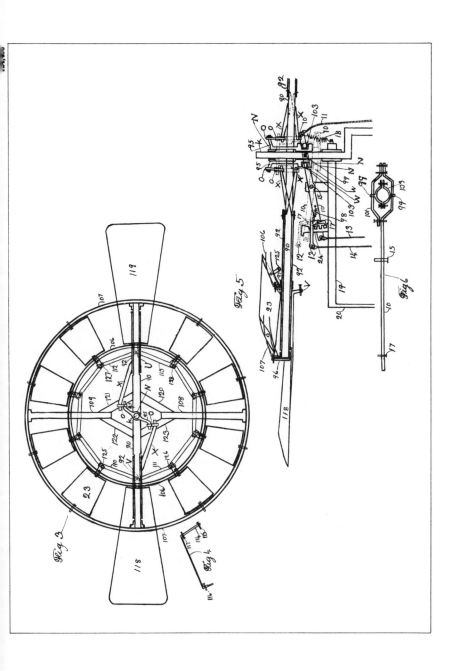

Fig 3

Fig 4

Fig 5

Fig 6

tical plane, and a horizontal thrust gradually takes its place. If the engine were placed at the centre of surface of the wings, the balance of the machine would remain unaffected whatever plane of rotation the motor was revolving in, but there would then be no means of balancing the machine fore and aft when hovering or descending vertically without forward motion.

So the motor is placed a little in front of the centre of surface of the wings, and this can be made to give very powerful control fore and aft when hovering or descending vertically without any forward motion of the machine when the ordinary elevator is useless. The motor is placed high up well above the centre of surface of the wings, and this tends to make the machine nose heavy when travelling forward, owing to the horizontal thrust of the propeller. When the propeller is revolving in a horizontal plane the nose of the plane is lifted up with a pressure proportional to the distance the engine is in front of the centre of surface of the wings, and the best all round distance can only be determined by experiment. This nose lift disappears in proportion as the plane of rotation approaches a vertical plane, when a horizontal thrust gradually takes its place, which on account of the high position of the propeller, has a slight tendency to press the nose down. Limited fore and aft control can also be got when descending vertically with the propeller in a horizontal plane permanently, by merely regulating the speed of the motor, thus varying the upward nose lift to suit the circumstances. An even better way is to vary the pitch of the propeller and so vary the upward nose lift, and if the propeller is reversible as well as variable in pitch, the propeller can be made to pull the nose down as well as lift it up. The wing-tip units will operate and control lateral balance in spite of stalling or spinning besides checking them, and their operation has already been described. The elevator 6 is connected to the main control lever **H** by the wires 57 and 58 and they cross each other. The double lever **J** is welded to the outer end of the axle **D** of the main control lever **H** and so it rocks backward and forward with it and actuates the elevator 6. The wire rope 57 connects the lower end of double bell-crank lever 44 with the upper end of the double bell-crank

lever **J** which is as mentioned before welded to the outer end of axle **D** of the control lever **H**, and the wire rope 58 connects the lower end of bell-crank lever **J** with the upper end of double bell-crank lever 44 so the two wires cross. When the upper end of double bell-crank lever **J** is rocked forward by the control lever **H**, its connecting wire 57 pulls the lower end of bell-crank lever 44 forward, so the rear edge of the elevator is depressed, and it is given more angle which will raise the rear of the plane, and if the lower end of lever **J** is moved forward by the pilot pulling the control lever **H** backward, the wire 58 will raise the rear edge of the elevator, as its rear end is connected with the upper end of bell-crank lever 44 which is attached to the elevator. In Fig. 1 the three control wires 11, 13, 14 for controlling the variation of the propeller's blades are shown to give their positions. Their front ends connect with different parts of the pitch control lever 10 shown in miniature in its assembled position with its catch 12 pivoted by a bolt to its lower end, to show the position of the parts. The three pitch control wires 11, 13, 14 all have their rear ends attached to the hook **Z** in order to be within reach of the pilot's seat **R**. Their operation has already been described, and the parts illustrated on a large scale in Fig. 5 and Fig. 6.

Fig. 1 shows three ways of controlling the angle of rotation of the propeller-rotor, and Fig. 2 one way the pedal control for the foot, and the position of the motor **M** in Fig. 2 illustrates the positions of the parts when the propeller-rotor is rotating in a horizontal plane. The pedal connecting rod 38 is connected at its front end to the lever 39 of the engine assembly, the clamp 41 guides its rear end and attaches it to the rail 49 and its pedal at the rear end comes within reach of the pilot's foot, and the pedal has been pushed forward in order to tilt the motor **M**, and make the propeller revolve in a horizontal plane. In Fig. 1 the motor **M** is shown in the position for ordinary flying with its propeller rotating in a vertical plane, and acting as a tractor. In this case the connecting rod 38 has been drawn backward along the rail 49. In Fig. 1 the motor **M** is also shown tilted to its full extent for hovering, or vertical descent without forward motion, and shows the

13

14

propeller rotating in a horizontal plane, shown in dotted lines. The winch 34 Fig. 1 with a reel and handle is connected to the top of the tilting motor M at 42 by the wire rope 36 which enables the pilot to tilt the motor M without reducing its speed. The wire 87 with its front end attached to the motor at 42 has a chain attached to its rear end for connecting it to the lever L of the ground brake, which is provided with two hooks for the purpose, so the lever and rack of the ground brake can be utilised when clear of the ground for fine balancing by hand to assist the foot. Its connecting wire 87 is shown slack when out of action, the links of the chain enable it to be tightened for action which can only take place when clear of the ground. The winch handle can be held in any position by the leather loop strap 35 which when slipped over the handle will hold the motor at any desired angle as long as desired. The winch 34 is used for rough balancing without reduction of engine speed, it is too slow for fine balancing which is done by the hand and foot, either separately or in conjunction. As balancing in this way by the propeller only begins to be powerful with a tilt of 45 degrees, the variation of tilt should be confined to between 45 degrees and 90 degrees. The hand and foot method of varying the engine tilt is quick and suitable for fine balancing, but the method of engine speed reduction must be used in conjunction, owing to the propeller thrust resisting any backward or downward movement of the engine assembly. Balancing fore and aft by varying the pitch of the propeller, and the consequent upward lift of the nose, would be the easiest way, and there would be no need to vary the engine speed then. In Fig. 1 and Fig. 2 the lever 48 controls the stabiliser 5 by the connecting rod 46 and notched rack 47 which holds it in any desired position by the tooth catch 60 engaging the notches on the side of the rack 47.

In Fig. 1 the ground brake is shown consisting of a skid lever B, pivoted at its front end on its axle S, and its rear end comes in contact with the ground in order to pull up the machine when landing, and at the same time it takes a considerable amount of weight off the landing wheels and for this reason is provided with the shock absorbing spring 66.

The handle L raises or lowers this skid lever by means of the connecting rod C. The rack 43 is notched on its side and the catch Y engages these notches, and 130 is its axle on which it pivots. Its position is important as the nearer the brake is placed to the front, the greater its braking power and the more weight it will take off the landing wheels, but it must be placed sufficiently behind the landing wheels to hold the machine on a straight course, and prevent a broadside. However fiercely this ground brake is applied it will not cause the machine to nose over, its tendency is to check this. In Fig. 1 the forward sliding floor F is shown attached to the two lower steel tube beams of the fuselage by the split metal clamp 3 which also acts as a friction brake to the forward sliding floor if a nose crash takes place. In addition to split clamp 3 the clamps 1 and 2 are placed on the beam at spaced intervals to make the retarding friction progressively greater, so that as the floor slides forward it encounters more clamps, so that the friction becomes progressively greater and this allows violent nose crashes to be catered for as well as mild ones. The friction clamps are preferably of the split type held in contact with the beam by two bolts which should be screwed to the right degree of tightness to allow the floor to slide forward with the correct amount of friction necessary to bring it to a state of rest gradually, and thus break the fall and eliminate shock. The seat R is rigidly fixed to the floor F and the pilot secured to the seat by several straps forming a kind of harness to spread the pressure over the whole body.

The efficiency of the contrivance depends on screwing the friction clamps to the right degree of tightness to give the correct amount of sliding friction, to bring the forward sliding floor to a state of rest gradually, and this can be calculated from the laws of falling bodies under gravity which can be found in a text book on mechanics. With a three-foot floor slide the pilot and passengers would be in the same position as a car with brakes powerful enough to pull up in a space of three feet if travelling at the same speed. If this floor slide is increased to six feet the shock would be reduced to a quarter of that of a three feet floor slide, and with nine feet floor slide,

15

16

one-ninth that of three feet floor slide, according to the laws of momentum or inertia. The shock is proportional inversely to the square of the rate at which the speed is arrested. So if each clamp is screwed to a degree of tightness that it requires a pressure of 300 lbs. to slide it forward, the distance the floor will require for a slide space can be calculated by comparing the retarding braking force with the laws of falling bodies, and their rate of acceleration when falling under gravity, which is found in a text book on mechanics. A falling body will accelerate to a speed of 32 feet per second in a time of one second, and 64 feet per second in two seconds, and to destroy this speed a retarding force equal to the accelerating force is necessary. The body falls through a space of 16 feet in one second and 64 feet in two seconds, and this is the necessary data that will enable the calculation to be made. Fig. 2, to fold the wings the inner edges or ends at the rear **78** and **79** are disconnected from the rear studs **62, 62**, which attach the rear beams to the machine.

The front swivelled hinges **64** and **65** are left permanently to function as hinges, and being swivelled the wings can when folded be turned to a vertical plane to lessen the width of the machine if desired. When about to land the machine either with or without forward motion, the controllable ground brake is let down, and it will then take a lot of weight off the wheels as well as pull up the machine. The pitch of the propeller should be reduced to a very fine angle to give lift, and the propeller brought to a horizontal plane, and the motor speeded up to its capacity, so that the upward lift of the propeller in conjunction with the weight taken off the wheels by the ground brake will make very light landings possible. This applies to landing with forward speed, and landing vertically without forward motion. When landing vertically the pilot should descend on an uneven keel by side tilting the whole machine to the right to counteract the reaction turning torque of the propeller if it is mounted on a right-handed or clock-wise rotating motor, but if the motor is anti-clock in the rotation of its crankshaft, the reverse procedure applies, the whole machine must be kept side tilted to the left at the correct angle to neutralise the reaction turning torque,

which in this case tends to turn the machine to the right, while in the former case of the clockwise motor, the reaction turning torque tends to turn the machine to the left.

If the machine is side tilted half a right angle (45 deg) half of the propeller thrust will be pulling the nose of the machine to the side to which it is tilted. The reaction turning torque is very small with a direct connected high speed propeller, as proved by the fact that an aileron suffices for this in ordinary machines. This means that the propeller is made to neutralise its own reaction turning torque by giving it the correct angle of side tilt, which is brought about by tilting the whole machine sideways, and this angle will probably be under 20 degrees and so will cause little or no inconvenience.

Having now fully described and ascertained my said invention and the manner in which it is to be performed, I declare that what I claim is:—

1. A convertible aeroplane-helicopter having an engine carrying a controllable pitch propeller on its crankshaft, mounted for controlled tilting of this combination about a horizontal transverse axle, in combination with incidence increasing wing-tip control units, foldable tail-piece, ground brake and a sliding floor, all as parts of a combination.

2. A convertible aeroplane-helicopter according to Claim 1, in which the said wing-tip control units are balanced and not interconnected but moving independently and limited in direction by stops and in angle incidence by springs, substantially as herein described and as illustrated in Fig. **2**.

3. A convertible aeroplane-helicopter according to Claim 1, in which the said controllable pitch propeller consisting of two outer blades pivoted on the two outer ends of the propeller rod which forms their support and connects them to the crankshaft, and the two rings carrying the inner ring of pivoted blades which are interconnected with each other and the two outer blades, substantially as herein described and as illustrated in Fig. 3 and Fig. 5.

4. A convertible areoplane-helicopter according to Claim 1, in which the said foldable tail-piece is adapted to be folded forward by the combination consisting of the

17　　　　　　　　　　　　18

rudder pivoted on the elevator, substantially as herein described and as illustrated in Fig. 1 and Fig. 2.

5. A convertible aeroplane-helicopter according to Claim 1, in which the said ground brake is pivoted at its front end while its rear end carries a shock absorbing spring and a connecting rod which couples it to the control lever, substantially as herein described and as illustrated in Fig. 1.

6. A convertible aeroplane-helicopter according to Claim 1, in which the said sliding floor is adapted to absorb shock by sliding forward in case of a nose crash, retarded by friction clamps at spaced intervals on the lower beams which carry the floor, substantially as herein described and as illustrated in Fig. 1.

Dated this 21st day of December, A.D. 1946.

R. W. PEARSE,
Applicant,
Witness—Mavis Emily Allan.

19

20

Printed for the DEPARTMENT OF PATENTS, COMMONWEALTH OF AUSTRALIA, by THE ARGUS AND AUSTRALASIAN LTD., 365 Elizabeth Street, Melbourne.

Appendix V

Pearse's description of his 'Special Motor', designed to power the Utility Plane. This account of the engine appears in the convertiplane's provisional patent specification but was excluded from the complete specification on the ground that the engine should be patented separately. It never was. The drawing is a copy of one found among Pearse's papers at Wildberry Street after his death.

THE SPECIAL MOTOR

A special 4 stroke motor has been designed which gives one working stroke for every revolution of the crank-shaft instead of 2 revolutions of the ordinary type of motor.

This is accomplished by making the cylinders and pistons double-acting like those of a steam engine, so it is a pull and push motor as regards the working strokes. It is a true 4 stroke motor that gives double the working strokes of the usual single-acting motor and thereby doubles the power without increasing the weight to any great extent. It takes in and explodes mixture on both sides of the pistons.

A 4 cylinder motor of this type has the same number of cubic inches swept by the pistons as an 8 cylinder engine of the usual single-acting cylinder type, and not much more than half the friction as there are only half the number of moving pistons, which cause over 75 per cent of the friction and so the power is more than doubled in the double acting motor when the saving in friction is taken into consideration.

To make a successful double-acting petrol motor it is essential to have metallic packing for the piston-rod which is sufficiently self-aligning to be gas tight when the piston and cross-heads and guides have some slackness caused by wear and to require no attention once inserted except for renewal like piston rings. Any form of soft packing is out of the question, it wouldn't stand the heat. Instead of the cross-head and slide guides of the steam engine I use for this purpose a cylinder and piston of the single-acting type which not only simplifies lubrication as the open outer end of the cylinder is in communication with the crankcase, but it can be turned into a very powerful supercharger to boost the engine for takeoff or high flying, while the inner closed end of the cylinder is joined up with the gland that contains the metallic packing of the piston rod and must be gas tight. The lower end of this single acting cylinder which is in line with the double acting motor cylinder so as to act as a continuation of it, and must be very accurately aligned with it longitudinally just as the slide guides on which the crosshead slides, must be accurately aligned with the cylinder in the steam engine. The inner closed end of the auxiliary single-acting cylinder which is installed to function as a cross-head and slide guides for the double-acting motor cylinder is fitted with valves and spark plugs so that it can be used as a single-acting motor cylinder, in which case it will add 50 per cent to the power of the engine, or it may be shut off for cruising by lifting the exhaust valves when it will no longer take in mixture as the intake valves are automatic, and finally if its ignition current is cut off, it can be used as a second supercharger so that the auxiliary cylinder is now supercharging from both ends. When the main double-acting cylinders of the engine are supercharging from the outer end of the auxiliary cylinder only, they have a double charge, but when supercharged from both ends they have a treble charge which is suitable for extremely high flying. The intake pipe system and the exhaust pipe system are provided with cut-outs in the shape of two-way taps which can stop the exhaust outlet, and switch that part of the exhaust pipe into communication with the intake pipe system where it is forced into the cylinder that happens to be taking in mixture at the time. A mixture pumped into the intake pipe system is forced to feed the cylinders as there is a one way automatic check valve which prevents back flow from the intake pipe system into the carburettor and this valve adds to the safety of the machine by preventing back-firing into the carburettor as well. The supercharge from the crank-case is also prevented from back-flowing into the crank-case by one way automatic valves, and so is pumped into the cylinder through the intake pipe system. When the inner closed end of the auxiliary cylinder is to be changed from a motor cylinder to a supercharger the first thing to be done is to cut off its ignition current and then there will be no exhaust.

The exhaust valve is then lifted to prevent compression in the cylinder, and the exhaust outlet closed, and that part of the exhaust pipe sytem placed in communication with the intake pipe system by turning a two way tap cut out. Once in the intake pipe system there is no escape as automatic valves prevent back-flow so it is forced into the motor cylinders. The smallest version of this motor consists of two double-acting cylinders in line with two auxiliary cylinders aligned with them longitudinally like a continuation of them, to take the place of the cross-head and slide guides of the steam engine, and to act as boosters. The outer ends of the auxiliary cylinders are open and are joined to the gland or stuffing box that contains the piston rod packing by a gas tight joint. The crank is of the two throw type set at right angles to each other, in order that when one is stationary at the dead centre the other is moving at maximum speed and this enables the double-acting motor cylinders to be supercharged at the dead centre like a two cycle motor and the effect of this is that the supercharge is always in addition to what it has already taken in during the intake stroke. This supercharging at the dead centre was designed mainly to make it possible to turn this 4 stroke motor into a 2 stroke version, and the intake pipe system was designed with the same object in view which will be described later in the 2 stroke version of this motor. This two double-acting cylinder in line version is of the upside down type with vertical cylinders and the crank-case on top, the two double-acting motor cylinders at the bottom and the two auxiliary cylinders functioning primarily as slide guides and secondarily as boosters in the centre, and connecting the double-acting motor cylinders with the crank-case. This forms a very high, but narrow motor, but its want of compactness in length is due to the connecting rod being connected to a piston-rod which adds to the length of the engine, but the width of the engine is not greater than a single-acting motor. The double-acting pistons of the motor cylinders are each welded to their respective piston-rods for a good heat contact and strength, while the single-acting pistons which are fastened to the other end of the piston-rod which projects outside the piston-rod gland, alone are detachable from the piston-rod, which is necessary in order to take it to pieces. So each piston-rod has two pistons mounted on it, one at each end, the double-acting piston being a fixture while the single-acting piston is detachable and is connected with the crank-shaft by a connecting rod. Each piston-rod has two pistons working in tandem, so a single connecting rod will connect both to the crank-shaft and that connection is made to the top single-acting piston by a gudgeon pin, or if the top of the piston-rod projects sufficiently through the piston, direct to the piston-rod itself which is preferable as the shock of the explosions would not then be liable to work the piston loose.

The crank-case is partitioned off making a separate compression chamber for each cylinder, and each such chamber is provided with a suction intake valve and an outlet pipe provided with an automatic one way valve to prevent back-flow into the crank-case, and the outlet pipes connected to the intake pipe system, where it is pressed into the motor cylinders. The separate chamber of the crank-case thus acts much in the same way as the crank-case of a single cylinder 2 stroke motor does with the advantage that very little compression takes place just enough to push the mixture past the one-way check valves into the cylinder, and there is not much loss of power, and the air-tightness need not be so perfect in the crank-case and intake pipe system as when a fair amount of compression is used.

Metallic packing of the piston-rods consists of split washers prefer-ably of phosphor bronze with an inside diameter the same as the piston-rod and the two halves of these washers are pressed and kept in contact with the piston rods by means of steel springs. The two halves have a groove on their out-side diameter for the reception of springs which may be flat or of wire, in the latter case several springs can be inserted side by side. The split washers are mounted in pairs with their wear gaps at right angles to each other and they have pins and holes inserted lat-erally to hold them in that position, although the pin need not pass entirely through both just enough anchorage to hold the wear gaps at a right angle to each other. The wear gaps of about 1/16 of an inch are essential to allow the two halves of the washers to approach each other as they wear, and thus keep in firm contact with the piston-rod, and avoid slackness and consequent leakage. The washers are placed in pairs in separate chambers with their wear gaps at right angles to each other which prevents leakage past the gaps, and brings down the pressure in each succeeding chamber progressively, so that leakage is correspond-ingly reduced. From 3 or 4 chambers are used in each piston-rod gland to pack the piston-rod making 6 to 8 split washers in all as a pair is inserted in each chamber. The springs are half circles of steel wire or flat steel with their ends bent to nearly a right angle at about 1/8 of an inch from the ends in order to get anchorage and prevent the springs from slipping out sideways when they are inserted into the grooves.

There are shallow holes in each half washer at the bottom of the groove on the outside diameter of the washers to receive the bent ends of the springs in order to give them anchorage, and prevent them from slipping out side-ways. If the springs are a little less than semicircles the effect produced is to make two ends of two half washers butt up against each other and have one gap for wear instead of two which is an advantage. There is then only one gap to plug to stop leakage instead of two. The partitions between the pairs of washers forming the chambers are made of split washers, and should be fairly gas tight. There is a tube ring which telescopes over the outer diameter of each pair of washers its length is exactly the same as the thickness of the combined pair, and its function is to prevent the washers from being pinched and allow them sufficient slackness to function, when the outer screw-plug of the gland is screwed tight. The pairs of washers must be accurately fitted to their particular chambers to prevent leakage, and have sufficient slackness to enable them to function on the same principle as piston rings. Although placing the split washers in pairs with their wear gaps at right angles to each other stops gases from blowing directly past them, there is still a slow radial leakage in and out of the different chambers which has to follow a winding passage and is consequently very small. This can be met by slotting the two ends of the washers laterally, care being taken that they are in alignment with each other at the wear gap, and into the slot thus formed a flat steel plug of the correct thickness is inserted. This plug must be shorter than the combined length of the slots forming one long slot, to allow freedom of movement of the two halves of the washer to take up wear. The effectiveness of this plug in stopping radial leakage in and out of the chambers will depend upon the accuracy of the fit. Besides doubling the power with an equal number of cylinders the double-acting cylinder motor has another advantage there is no pressure of the piston against the cylinder walls so they are not worn oval and require very little lubricating oil just enough to make rings tight and prevent wear on them. Besides the compression rings the piston is provided with an extra wide wear ring on which it floats made preferably of phosphor bronze on which it floats and so does not touch the cylinder unless the bronze ring becomes badly worn in which case it can be renewed as cheaply as the compression rings, so the piston is everlasting. The vertical cylinders are not worn oval and so reboring is unnecessary. As there is no pressure between the piston and cylinder walls the piston can be made a very slack fit without slap taking place, and if this is done seizure caused by the expansion of a heated piston will never take place. The side pressure in the double-acting motor comes on the cross-head and slide guides, and so in my motor it is only the single-acting pistons and cylinders that are worn oval and these auxiliary cylinders will require reboring.

If the auxiliary cylinders are used mainly as superchargers rather than as motor cylinders, there will be no heat to burn up the lubricating oil and their lubrication will be just as easy as that of the cross-head and slide guides of a steam engine. If the lower ends of the auxiliary cylinders are only used as motor cylinders at takeoff on rough or soft ground and then turned into superchargers for high flying if necessary, their lubricating oil will not be burned, and so very little will do.

THE 2 STROKE VERSION;

The 4 stroke double-acting motor just described was so designed that it could within a few hours be converted into a 2 stroke version of the double-acting type. As every alternate stroke is a working stroke in the 4 stroke version, every stroke is a working stroke in the 2 stroke version, there are no idle strokes. I call it a two stroke version because the number of working strokes is doubled and it takes in mixture and gets rid of the exhaust while the pistons are at or near the dead-centre like 2 stroke motors but really it does not work in cycles there are no idle strokes all being working strokes. The two double-acting cylinders alone work as motor cylinders, and they are charged with mixture from both ends of the auxiliary cylinders which now play the part of chargers only. No alterations in the intake and exhaust pipe-systems is required as they were designed to be equally suitable for charging the two double-acting motor cylinders at and near the dead-centre as for supercharging from both ends of the auxiliary cylinder in the 4 stroke version, and when set for one is equally suitable for both. When working on the 2 stroke the spark is first switched off the spark plugs of the auxiliary cylinders so that there will then be no exhaust, the exhaust valve is then lifted and the exhaust outlet closed by a two-way tap cut out which at the same time places that part of the exhaust pipe in communication with the intake pipe system where it charges the motor cylinder when the piston is at or near the dead-centre. This is exactly the procedure before described to make the auxiliary cylinders supercharge from both ends.

It was partly with this object in view that I used a two-throw crankshaft set at a right angle to each other, so that when one piston was at or near the dead-centre the other was moving at maximum speed and then was equally suitable for charging or supercharging. The same valves are used for both versions, it is their timing that is altered, and the sample applies to ignition when changing from the 4 stroke to the 2 stroke as the cylinders then have a different rotation in taking in and exploding mixture. The two to one gear of the cam-shaft must be cut out and the camshaft brought up to the same speed as the crank-shaft. An extra set of push-rods is required for the two stroke to connect the valves to different cams, as the intake valves open and shut at the same time as the exhaust valves, and so both can be interconnected by a rod or by separate rods to the same cam, which will then actuate both together. The spark plugs must be connected to different connections of the distributor to suit the changed order in which the cylinders take in and explode mixture. For the low tension primary current an extra contact spring with platinum point is wanted to be mounted in place of the other one which is too slow in making contact for the 2 stroke version. The re-timing of the valves and ignition system is the only thing that takes any length of time in changing from one version to another. This motor on the 2 stroke version will give one explosion for every quarter revolution of the crankshaft, the same as an 8 cylinder motor of the usual single-acting type, and this from two double-acting cylinders. This motor can continue charging the cylinder when the piston is well past the dead-centre thus enabling a bigger charge to be forced in, it is set to charge each cylinder for a quarter of a revolution of the crank-shaft, which is half the time of the intake stroke of the 4 stroke motor. On account of using valves instead of ports the intake and exhaust are at the ends of the cylinders and so the intake mixture when it enters its valve chamber is conducted and directed through a passage tube pointing in the direction of the other end of the cylinder so that when it enters the cylinder it will have sufficient momentum to carry it to the other end, when it will stroke the piston, and so very little of it will have time to make the return journey which it will have to do in order to escape with the exhaust.

The short passage connecting the intake valve chamber with the cylinder plays the part of a hose in directing the intake mixture down the side of the cylinder, close to, or in contact with the wall, with the result that there is less swirl and less opportunity for mixing with the exhaust gases, than if the mixture was directed down the centre.

The exhaust valves are not placed in the intake valve chambers for fear of mixing, they are placed in the head of the cylinder well away from the intake valve chamber. There is an extra intake valve on both double-acting cylinders with a separate intake pipe system made specially for supercharging with rotary charges or turbines, or for scavenging the exhaust gases out when on the two stroke, with pure air, in order to get a purer mixture. Experiment alone can determine which

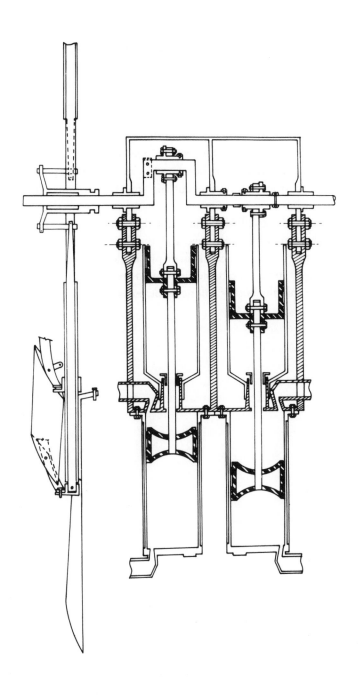

A modern copy of Pearse's drawing of his 'special motor', showing propeller-rotor attached. (E.R. Gibson)

will be most advantageous. As for the different spheres of the two versions, the 4 stroke is equal to a 6 cylinder with the two auxiliary cylinders functioning as motor cylinders, and so would probably be more powerful, but if given a sufficiently powerful super-charger the 2 stroke may beat the 4 stroke.

All brasses or bronzes are capable of sliding in and out when mounting or dismounting so that the pressure does not come direct on the thread of bolts, which are not then burred. Small bolts are only used to hold the parts together, and prevent the split halves from sliding out sideways.

The pins of the crank-shaft have their bronze bearings mounted in this way. These are of the split type and in order to slide the two halves in and out, the rim of the crank-shaft pin is filed off for a distance of half way round, and a detachable rim is used and bolted to this filed off gap to ensure that the bushes will not slide out sideways when in action.

Appendix VI

OTAGO WITNESS REPORT OF
1 DECEMBER 1909

The following description of Pearse's first aeroplane was located by Errol Martyn in the Dunedin Otago Witness of 1 December 1909 just as the first edition of this volume was going to press. The account, written by Sam H. Carter, was published in the interval between the two Temuka Leader descriptions. It contains explicit details, not found elsewhere, of the aircraft's configuration and engine performance. It also confirms the impression that Pearse had adopted a front elevator, and reveals that — also like the Wrights — he was now using a starting derrick.

Some of the material is at variance with information given in the patent specifications, in Pearse's own letters, and in other eyewitness accounts, but this is evidently a later version of his first plane than the one with which he carried out his first trials in 1903, and is different again from the partly hypothetical version described in the patent and the one he was seen experimenting with later in 1910. He appears to have been working on this particular machine since 1904.

A NEW ZEALAND AEROPLANE

In a wheatfield ten miles inland from Temuka stands an aeroplane starting derrick, made familiar by means of the illustrated papers and cinematograph pictures. This big tripod is the first sign to inform a visitor that New Zealand has at last a flying machine actually made and ready for trial. Nearby is the aeroplane itself, where it landed after a short jump which, though of a few yards only, is the first attempted flight of a heavier-than-air machine in the Dominion. The only building within some miles is the small but fully-equipped workshop in which the inventor, Mr Richard Pearse, toiled for five long years in putting together this intricate construction, with which he hopes to solve the problem of the mastery of the air. Mr Pearse has always been of an inventive turn of mind, as a visit to his workshop will show. Just lately the *Scientific American* printed an idea of his for an improved sparking plug for either high or low tension. It is remarkable that he has had no help, the whole thing — motor, radiator, propeller, chassis, frame, etc. — being entirely his own work. Time after time parts, having been made too light, gave way, and were reconstructed slightly heavier. The inventor took nothing for granted, but experimented with dogged perseverence upon every part until it was, though extremely light, suitable for its purpose. For instance, seven crankshafts were made and broken until one was found strong enough. Three types of engine were tried. Every detail of the aeroplane is the result of Mr Pearse's own ingenuity. He mentions that he had patented in New Zealand ailerons for maintaining lateral stability long before they were used in Europe.

The machine is of the monoplane type; area nearly 800 ft, weight complete with motor, 340 lb, span, 34 ft, aspect ratio, 1.2. The lateral control is by ailerons (balancing planes). The wing is oval-shaped, single-surfaced, with no camber. The elevator in front is within 3 ft of the main wing. At present no vertical rudder is to be seen. The frame is of steel tubing, with three wheels, the front one being steerable. It has pneumatic tyres. The motor is a 25 hp horizontal four-cylinder double opposed type, the valves, inlet and exhaust being placed over the cylinders, and connected (two to one) to the shafts by a bicycle chain. The weight is 112 lb. The engine and pilot's seat are below the main plane. The propeller is four bladed, keyed direct to the shaft, and there is no flywheel. The propeller is to be altered or remade, as with it the motor runs at only 800 revolutions, at which rate it gives eighty pounds fan thrust. In a week or two, after some alterations, the inventor expects to have another trial, when it is to be hoped we shall hear of a successful flight, though it must be remembered that Voisin Frères were a month in getting their first machine to leave the ground, and every inventor has found a lot of tuning up necessary before success was finally achieved. The machine is not at present open to public inspection.

Bibliography

I. Aviation History and Technology

Alexander, R.T. *High Adventure — from Balloons to Boeings in New Zealand*, NAC, 1968.

Etkin, B. *Dynamics in Flight*. Wiley. 1959.

Gibbs-Smith, C.H. *The Aeroplane: an historical survey*. HMSO, 1960.

Gibbs-Smith, C.H. *A Directory & Nomenclature of the First Aeroplanes 1809–1909*. HMSO, 1966.

Gibbs-Smith, C.H. *The Invention of the Aeroplane, 1809–1909*. HMSO, 1966.

Gibbs-Smith, C.H. *Aviation: an historical survey from its origins to the end of World War II*. HMSO, 1969.

Harvie, E.F. *Venture The Far Horizon: The Pioneer Long-Distance Flights in New Zealand*. Whitcombe & Tombs, 1966.

Kermode, A.C. *The Aeroplane Structure*. Pitman, 1964.

Lambermont, P. & Pirie, A. *Helicopters & Autogiros of the World*. Cassell, 1958.

Lewis, P. *British Aircraft 1804–1914*. Putnam, 1962.

Miller, R. & Sawers, D. *The Technical Development of Modern Aviation*. Routledge & Kegan Paul, 1968.

Munson, K. *Pioneer Aircraft, 1903–14*. Blandford Press, 1969.

Nayler, J.L. *Aviation: Its technical development*. Peter Owen/Vision Press, 1965.

Payne, L.G.S. *Air Dates*. Heinemann, 1957.

Penrose, Harald, *British Aviation: the Pioneer Years 1903–14*. Putnam, 1967.

Rolfe, D. & Dawydoff, A. *Aeroplanes of the World*. Kimber, 1969.

The Illustrated Encyclopaedia of Aviation and Space. AFE Press, 1971.

White, Leo. *Wingspread*. Unity Press, 1941.

Whitehouse, Arch. *The Early Birds*. Nelson, 1967.

II. Regional Background (published)

Andersen, J.C. *Jubilee History of South Canterbury*. Whitcombe & Tombs, 1916.

Encyclopaedia of New Zealand. Government Printer, 1968.

Gillespie, O.A. 'South Canterbury, A Record of Settlement'. *Timaru Herald*, 1971.

Milton Borough Council. *Milton Borough Centenary*. Evening Star Co. Ltd, 1966.

Morrison, J.P. *Christchurch and its Suburbs: The Evolution of a City*. Whitcombe & Tombs, 1946.

Ogilvie, G.B. *Moonshine Country: The Story of Waitohi, South Canterbury*. Caxton, 1971.

Sumpter, D.J. & Lewis, J.J. *Faith & Toil — The Story of Tokomairiro*. Whitcombe & Tombs, 1949.

Wilson, Helen. *My First Eighty Years*. Paul, 1950.

Wilson, Helen. *Moonshine*. Paul, 1956.

III. Regional Background (unpublished)

G.R. Macdonald, *Dictionary of Canterbury Biographies*, Canterbury Museum.

Lower Waitohi School Committee Minute Book 1886–1900.

Upper Waitohi School Committee Minute Book 1885–1906.

Waitohi Tennis Club Committee Minute Books.

Lower Waitohi Library Records.

IV. Pearse's Own Writings

Patent Office Files, Wellington and Canberra.
(Specifications and letters.)

Evening Star, Dunedin. 10 May 1915. (Letter.)

The Star, Christchurch, 15 September 1928. (Letter.)

V. Unpublished Manuscripts and Typescripts

Bolt, G.B. *Richard Pearse*, 1961.

Cornthwaite, B. *Richard Pearse*, 1970.

Darby, d'E.C. *Richard Pearse and the First Temuka Flight*, 1968.

Darby, d'E.C. *Report on Trip to Temuka*, 1971.

Gibbs-Smith, C.H. *The Flight Claims for Richard Pearse*, 1970.
Gibbs-Smith, C.H. *The Pearse Story*, 1971.
Holdsworth, Mrs S. *Richard Pearse*, 1971.
Johnston, J.W. *Richard Pearse's Aero Engines*, 1971.
Peters, D.N. *New Zealand Patent No. 21476: R.W. Pearse*, 1971.
Peters, D.N. *New Zealand Patent No. 14507: R.W. Pearse*, 1972.
Peters, D.N. *New Zealand Patent No. 87637: R.W. Pearse*, 1972.
Rodliffe, C.G. *Richard Pearse, Pioneer Aviator*, 1972.

VI. (1) Patent Office, Wellington

Patent No. 14507, Improvements in and connected with bicycles, Provisional Spec. 8 February 1902.

Patent No. 14507, Improvements in and connected with bicycles, Complete Spec. 8 November 1902.

Patent No. 21476, An Improved Aerial or Flying Machine, Provisional Spec. 19 July 1906.

Patent No. 21476, An Improved Aerial or Flying Machine, Complete Spec. 19 April 1907.

Patent No. 21476, An Improved Aerial or Flying Machine, Substitute Comp. Spec. 15 July 1907.

Patent No. 87637, An aeroplane that can ascend and descend in very restricted areas, Provisional Spec. 8 Nov. 1943.

Patent No. 87637, An aeroplane that can ascend and descend in very restricted areas, Complete Spec. 18 March 1944.

Correspondence relating to Patent No. 87637.

(2) Patent Office, Canberra

Patent No. 124430, An aeroplane that can ascend and descend in very restricted areas, Provisional Spec. 3 March 1944.

Patent No. 124430, An aeroplane that can ascend and descend in very restricted areas, Complete Spec. 21 December 1946.

Correspondence relating to Patent No. 124430.

VII. Files on Pearse

(1) Official
Alexander Turnbull Library, Wellington.
Bolt Papers, Walsh Memorial Aviation Library, MOTAT, Auckland.

Geraldine County Council.
Television New Zealand (formerly NZBC), Wellington.
South Canterbury Historical Society, Timaru.

(2) Private
T.P. Bradley, Timaru.
M.A. Cameron, Temuka.
Mrs H. Cederman, Auckland.
J.D. Coll, Tauranga.
J.H. Malcolm, Auckland.
G.B. Ogilvie, Christchurch.
R.W. Pearse, Waitohi. (Nephew of inventor.)
D.N. Peters, Christchurch.
C.G. Rodliffe, Auckland.

VIII. Waitohi Witnesses

The most vital eyewitness testimony (including affidavits, declarations, letters and interview material) was collected from the following 37 ex-residents of Waitohi. Their evidence relates either to Pearse's flight experiments or to the dating of them.

An asterisk identifies the 21 witnesses who believe they saw Pearse airborne on at least one occasion. Much of this testimony is to be found in the Bolt Papers at MOTAT's Walsh Memorial Aviation Library in Auckland. The Rodliffe references are to *Richard Pearse, Pioneer Aviator*, by C.G. Rodliffe (1979). The Bolt references are to the typescript *Richard Pearse* by G.B. Bolt (1961).

* Barker, Mrs W. Bolt p. 7.
  Baxter, Stewart. Author interview.
* Bedford, Mary. Basil Bedford affidavit 22 September 1967.
* Bedford, William. Basil Bedford affidavit 22 September 1967.
  Bourn, Ethel. Affidavit 27 March 1969.
* Brosnahan, Harry. Affidavit 20 July 1961.
  Campbell, James. Bolt p. 8.
* Casey, John. Casey to Rodliffe 22 August 1967.
* Coll, Joseph. Coll to Bolt 19 April 1960. Rodliffe pp. 21–22.
  Letters to author.
* Connell, Miss Cissie. Rodliffe p. 25. Author interview.
* Connell, Daniel. Bolt p. 7. Author interview.

* Connell, Jack. Affidavit 4 October 1961. Bolt p. 7.
* Crawford, Clifford. *Ashburton Guardian*, 4 September 1975.
  CHTV3 interview 1976. Rodliffe p. 23.
* Cunningham, Jack. Coll to author.
  Currie, Jean. Author interview. Rodliffe p. 25.
* Davis, C. Rodliffe p. 25.
* Edgeler, William. Rodliffe p. 25.
* Friel, Mrs Daniel. Affidavit 4 October 1961.
  Friel, Michael. Rodliffe p. 24.
* Gibson, Robert. Statement to MOTAT, April 1964.
  Rodliffe p. 22.
  Gilpin, Ruth. Affidavit 9 September 1967. Letters to author.
  Gregan, D.A. Gregan to Bolt 15 March 1960, 11 May 1960.
* Hart, Mrs James. Bolt p. 8.
  Hide, Tom. Affidavit 16 August 1961. Bolt. pp. 7-8. Rodliffe p. 23.
  Higgins, Florence. Affidavits 9 September 1967, 3 April 1969.
  Letters to author.
  Hullen, Peter. Bolt pp. 8-9.
  Hullen, Miss Wanaka. Rodliffe p. 25.
* Johnson, Mrs Louie. Affidavit 4 August 1961. Bolt. p. 7.
  McAteer, Nellie. Author interview.
* McLean, Mrs Daisy. *Ashburton Guardian*, 4 September 1975
  Rodliffe p. 23.
* Martin, Amos. CHTV3 interview 1969. Rodliffe pp. 22–23.
  Moore, William. Bolt to Cederman 5 August 1960.
* Pearse, Warne. Affidavit 6 August 1961. Bolt pp. 3–5.
  Smart, Bert. Author interview.
  Smith, Steve. Rodliffe p. 24.
* Stoakes, Harry. Stoakes to Bolt (undated). Rodliffe p. 25.
* Tozer, Arthur. Tozer to Bolt (undated). Rodliffe p. 28.

The following 22 witnesses also contributed information about Pearse's work during his Waitohi years: Frank Agnew, Jim Andrews, Frank Biggs, Annie Casey, James Campbell, James Chapman, Fred Cone, Dick Connell, Jim Connell, Maggie Esler, John Fraser, Frank Friel, Tom Hally, Mrs Charles Inwood, Michael McAteer, Hugh McCully, J.R. Parmenter, Alice Pettigrew, Alice Southby, Charles Verity, Tom Wade, Dick Williams. Notes from interviews or correspondence with most of these witnesses, recorded by George Bolt and Harold Cederman, are to found in the Bolt Papers at MOTAT.

IX. Newspapers

Bruce Herald, Milton.
Dominion, Wellington.
Evening Post, Wellington.
Evening Star. Dunedin.
Flint Journal, Michigan, USA.
New Zealand Herald, Auckland.
Otago Daily Times, Dunedin.
Otago Witness, Dunedin.
Temuka Leader.
The Press, Christchurch.
The Star, Christchurch.
Timaru Herald.
Weekly News, Auckland.

X. Periodicals and Pamphlets

Aviation Historical Society of New Zealand Journal
Flight (Great Britain).
Richard Pearse and his Aircraft, 1900–1914. MOTAT, Auckland.
Scientific American.

XI. Other References

Aerospace, Aviation Digest, Aviation in New Zealand (MOTAT), *Better Business, Digest of Digests, Journal of American Aviation Historical Society, Museum News* (MOTAT), *NAC Airline Review, New Science and Science Journal, New Zealand Travel News, People, The Inventor*.

XII. The Pearse Debate — Some Published Contributions

Avery, Max, 'World's second flight was in New Zealand'. *Press*, 4 July 1970.
Coleman, Terry, 'Flying Kiwi'. *Guardian*, 17 April 1977.
Drake, D.E., *Wings over South Canterbury: A Record of Aviation*. Herald Communications Ltd, Timaru, 1993.
Elworthy, A.C., 'Richard Pearse — he could not have flown'. *Timaru Herald*, 21 February 1979.
—— 'Writer replies to critics'. *Timaru Herald*, (?) March 1979.

—— 'Richard Pearse — engine and propeller'. *Timaru Herald*, 22 February 1979.

Finlayson, Ian, 'The Wizard of Waitohi'. *Auckland Star*, 4 August 1973.

Gapper, S. Gordon, 'The Mad Farmer'. *Flint Journal*, 12 September 1971.

Gibbs-Smith, C.H., 'First-flight feature — it's fantasy'. *Aviation Digest*, 30 June 1971.

—— 'Ogilvie resorts to rather desperate tactic'. *Aviation Digest*, 51, 1974.

Lockstone, Brian, 'That magnificent man and his flying machine'. *Auckland Star*, 9 October 1971.

McCausland, Ray, 'Pearse — a man who blazed a trail to the future'. *Ashburton Guardian*, 4 September 1975.

Ogilvie, Gordon, 'Riddle me, riddle me ree, Gibbs-Smith and Ogilvie'. *Aviation Digest*, 53, 1974.

—— 'Richard Pearse riddle remains unsolved'. *Timaru Herald*, (?) March 1979.

—— 'Recognition of Pearse achievement'. *Timaru Herald*, 2 April 1979.

—— 'That amazing young man on his cycling machine'. *Press*, 14 June 1980.

—— 'Richard Pearse of Waitohi — time for some stocktaking'. *New Zealand Wings*, August 1982.

—— 'Plane Talk' (letter). *Journal*, Aviation Historical Society of New Zealand, August 1990.

Patterson, D.A., 'Richard William Pearse: did he fly before the Wright brothers?' *Journal*, A.H.S.N.Z., December 1989.

Potter, Tony, 'Pearse may now officially be a genius'. *Star Weekender*, 6 February 1982.

Riley, Lyn, 'The Richard Pearse story, author sifts facts from fancy'. *Christchurch Star*, 17 November 1973.

Rodliffe, C.G., 'New claim for Pearse in air'. *Timaru Herald*, 2 April 1979.

—— *Richard Pearse: pioneer aviator*. Museum of Transport and Technology, Auckland, 1979.

—— *Wings over Waitohi — The Story of Richard Pearse*. Avon Press Ltd, Auckland, 1993.

Swift, David, 'Pearse's bicycle'. *Press*, 21 June 1980.

Thompson, Mervyn, *Jean and Richard: A Fantasy*, published in *Passing Through and other plays*. Hazard Press, Christchurch, 1992.

Index

Martin, A.A., 77–8
Matthews, James, 30
Maxim, Sir Hiram, 42, 43, 58,
126, 190, 193, 212–3, 216–7
Mee, T.P.D., 81
Melhuish, J.J., 26, 29
Melville, Robert, 108
Mercer, 'Bert', 136, 143
Military Service Board, 131
Miller, Oscar, 102
Milton, 115, 134, 136, 185, 199
Milton Athenaeum, 116
Milton district, 108
Moore, William, 64
Moore-Brabazon, J.T.C., 101, 212
MOTAT see Western Springs
Museum
Moy, Thomas, 186
Mozhaiski, Alexander 41, 58,
193, 212
Murray, Frederick, 21
music-box construction, 97–8,
184
Muxlow, Peter, 205

Nash, John, 139
National Airways Corporation
(NAC), 8, 199
Neave, John, 6
needle-threading invention, 31,
184
Newton, P.M., 39
New Zealand Information
Service, 200
NZ Official Gazette, 38

Ogilvie, Bertram, 42
Ollivier, Geoff, 35
Orr, James, 33, 36–7, 47, 48, 55,
57, 96

Orr, Tommy, 34, 36–7, 47, 48, 55,
57
Otago Daily Times, 124
Otago Infantry Regiment, 132
Otago Witness, 212, 247

Parmenter, James, 49, 113
Parr & Co, 102, 203
Parr, Roger, 102
Parrish, Mrs, 20
Patent Office (Australia), 7, 147,
155, 157–9, 161, 168, 179
Patent Office (New Zealand),
18–9, 38, 49, 81, 82–3, 100–1,
147, 155–9, 161, 189
Patterson, D.A., 199, 202–4
Patterson, Owen, 205
Paul, Albert, 107–9, 113
Paul, William, 30
Paulhan, Louis, 194
Pearse, Captain Alfred (cousin of
R.W.P.), 15–9, 208–9
Pearse, ancestry, 14–6
Pearse, Charlotte Anne (Mrs W.
Smart, sister of R.W.P.), 5, 24,
27, 34, 97, 182
Pearse, Digory Sargent (R.W.P.'s
father), 19, 20–4, 26, 28, 30,
34, 36, 59, 97, 106, 147
Pearse, Digory Warne (brother of
R.W.P.): arranges allowance for
R.W.P. in hospital, 2
disposal of R.W.P.'s estate, 3
interviewed by Press, 6–7
contacted by Bolt, 9
reminiscences printed, 11
urged to moderate statements,
12
born 1881, 24
recollections of R.W.P., 27

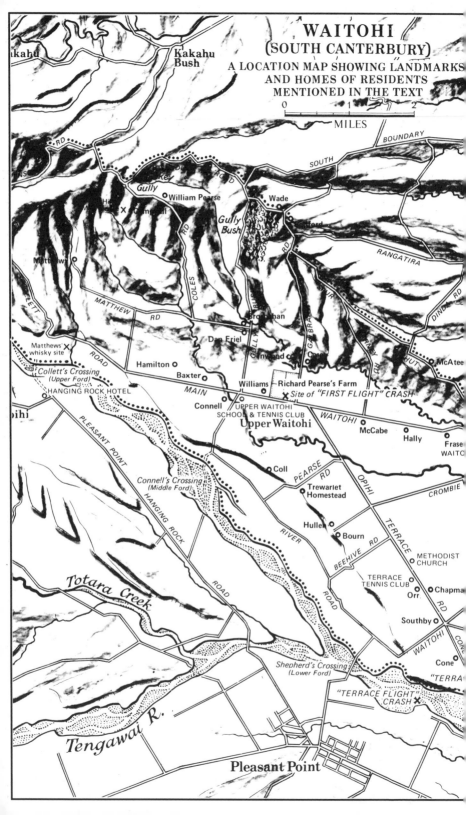